RANDOM ACTS OF AUTOMATION

How to Fight Back When Automation Threatens
Your Work, Your Life, and Everything You Do

CRAIG LE CLAIR

Post Hill
PRESS

A POST HILL PRESS BOOK
ISBN: 979-8-88845-704-7
ISBN (eBook): 979-8-88845-705-4

Cover design by Jim Villaflores

Much of the information in the book comes from in-person, telephone, and email interviews by the author with workers and representatives of the companies described in the book. Extensive use of human narratives from people of different ages, educational backgrounds, and demographics were used. As noted, some of these interviewees wanted to remain anonymous, and we have respected and noted that wish. Facts and quotes that don't have a cited source are from either public sources or these personal interviews.

This book, as well as any other Post Hill Press publications, may be purchased in bulk quantities at a special discounted rate. Contact orders@posthillpress.com for more information.

All people, locations, events, and situations are portrayed to the best of the author's memory. While all of the events described are true, many names and identifying details have been changed to protect the privacy of the people involved.

Post Hill Press
New York • Nashville
posthillpress.com

Published in the United States of America
1 2 3 4 5 6 7 8 9 10

CONTENTS

Introduction 7

PART I - THE DARK SIDE OF AUTOMATION

Chapter 1 We Need Humans in the Loop 23

Chapter 2 Automation: Where We Are Headed 43

Chapter 3 The Self-Service Time Bomb 56

PART II - THE WORKERS

Chapter 4 How Workers in the Middle Can Automation-Proof Themselves 79

Chapter 5 Robot Coworkers Will Benefit Human-Touch Workers 109

Chapter 6 A Digital Elite Class Takes Over 136

Chapter 7 Pioneers in the New Work-Life Movement ... 172

PART III - MENTAL HEALTH CHALLENGES AT WORK

Chapter 8 Trust 196

Chapter 9 Invasion 221

Chapter 10 Isolation 248

PART IV - CAN WE SAVE THE WORKPLACE?

Chapter 11 AI Leaves "Learn to Code" Behind 267

Chapter 12 Sorry, but You Have the Wrong Number ... 294

Chapter 13 Human-Centered Automation 306

Endnotes 321

About the Author 347

INTRODUCTION

WORKING FROM HOME ON A brisk New England day, I was lured outside by the noises of truck engines and grinding machines. Standing outside my front door, I watched the garbage men—or, excuse me, the sanitation engineers—at work. The newer garbage trucks were impressive. A futuristic-attached mechanical arm hoisted each trash can high in the air and dumped them into the truck's belly. The driver seemed a bit hesitant, unsure of the best place to grab the container. However, once the arm's jaws secured it, the up-and-down motion was swift if a bit jerky. But in the end, the hydraulic-controlled arm banged the truck's steel belly mouth, whose lid was already open.

It was all good. The job was now less injury-prone and faster, although the workers would lose some muscle tone. Walking down the driveway to retrieve my containers, I noticed a wheel on one of my cans was missing and nowhere to be found. The robot had eaten a wheel.

My job entails conducting research, so I learned through a few simple searches that there has been a lot of trash talking lately. For example, more than twenty-five thousand reports of cracked lids, broken bins, missing wheels, and other damage were filed with Solid Waste Management in Memphis from September 2020 through February 2022. I was intrigued and decided to contact Waste Management, Inc. to follow up. While they weren't specific, they admitted "lots" of cans were destroyed, especially by new drivers.[1] In fact, the waste management worker assigned to fix my can disclosed that he had spent thirty-four hours that week dealing with trash cans destroyed by robot arms. "When metal meets plastic, the plastic doesn't win," he noted.

Even as I was writing and speaking about automation trends at Forrester, the wheels in my head began to turn upon encountering such a disappointing truth. Could the current path of automation increasingly lead to unforeseen trouble?

I have been an industry analyst for more than fifteen years. Every day I speak to business leaders frantic to apply AI and overly confident tech vendors eager to help. This rush to automate is creating unintended consequences that affect all of us. My goal is to provide an unflinching, honest, balanced, and from-the-ground perspective on where automation will take us. I interview displaced workers tossed into the gig economy, workers who struggle with technology upgrades, and mothers concerned for their children's future.

And now is the time. The current AI push is different. GenAI and large language models are the most dramatic technical innovations in my professional lifetime, with the potential to alter the workplace in the way we have feared for decades. It is more dramatic than the power our phones have given us, more impactful than the information access that the internet provides, and more disruptive than any physical or robotic automation we have seen. I've spent my career helping businesses adopt or create the latest automation. Despite the job losses, we told ourselves that there would always be more things for working people to do. I did not think much about or try to help those workers, but now I am concerned about them. That's why I'm writing this book.

One Big Movement

The book's main theme is automation will trigger a seismic shift in the workforce that few anticipate. Millions of middle workers will slip into "gig" work or become human-touch workers while others leverage automation to become the digital elite. Millions of digital elites will fall to the middle or be forced to take human-touch positions. Traditional full-time employment will decline as many opt to become "work-life pioneers."

In essence, this glimpse into the future of automation reveals its potential trajectory and likely impact on the workforce. This book is a blueprint for workers to navigate this upheaval and understand their current position and potential paths. It is also a valuable guide for parents to help their kids with career decisions.

Politicians, pundits, and journalists focus on specific and often dramatic examples of AI and work but miss the bigger picture. This is all one trend: the factory workers at Amazon, the restaurant workers in a Jamaican restaurant, the sales workers replaced by chatbots, the middle managers pressed into new challenges, and the skilled laborers reduced to "gig" workers. No other book looks at all these labor shifts and puts them all in a common context. An important job of the next presidential administration will be to deal with the disruption caused by these labor shifts.

The Fact Is We All Need Help

The relentless AI advancement may feel like a personal threat looming over your well-paying job. You fear a future driving a delivery truck for Amazon, or worse, losing your work identity altogether. Your once-trusted professional training and credentials feel increasingly outdated amidst the brilliance of the latest GenAI release. At work, the watchful eyes of monitoring systems seem to scrutinize your every move, fueling a sense of unease and mistrust.

The barrage of information about AI solutions leaves you feeling lost, and you're not sure what education, training, or upskilling is right for you. Even your home becomes a battleground against cunning digital scams, further isolating you from colleagues and the familiar comfort of your community. The aggressive push toward self-service technology across every aspect of life leaves you stripped of your agency and individuality. In a world where everything is automated, who or what can you trust?

You may have these problems but don't know what to do about them. The pace of automation is altering the landscape of your workplace and life, leaving you feeling anxious, uncertain, and isolated. Our current race toward automation creates unintended consequences that disrupt our work life and mental state.

This book is a blueprint for workers impacted by automation across all segments, from front-line to professional roles who need help with career choices, daily work decisions, personal life behavior, and educational direction. It is your guide through these turbulent waters, offering a lifeline of understanding, practical advice, and hope. Each chapter presents automation-based concerns along with corresponding recommendations that workers and individuals can employ. Government-led policy will be too slow and ineffective and have unintended consequences. Instead, workers must confront the repercussions of automation head-on. To help, this book is divided into four parts.

Part 1: The Dark Side of Automation makes the case for the inherent randomness of advancing technologies through examples and analysis. It defines automation, traces its evolution, and unveils the unpredictability that lies at its core. An unflinching, balanced, and from-the-ground perspective highlights nine-billion-dollar AI real estate blunders, a robotic dog that terrorizes the homeless, machinists that can no longer operate their equipment, and back-office workers replaced with bots, all victims of the unintended consequences of advancing automation.

Part 2: The Workers examines the worker types used throughout the book: a growing human-touch front-line service segment, a digital elite segment, an uneasy middle, and emerging work-life pioneers. These segments are defined by their relationship to automation. It captures the practical on-the-ground realities and concludes with clear, concise recommendations designed to help them navigate this ever-shifting landscape.

Part 3: The Mind Under Siege examines the mental impact of automation on workers. Here, we delve into the anxieties sparked by invasive monitoring technologies, the insidious threats of AI-powered scams, and the unsettling reality of intelligent bots competing for jobs and even concert tickets.

Part 4: Reimagining Work: A Path to Optimism shifts the focus toward a brighter future, exploring novel approaches to skill development and rethinking our definition of progress. We embark on a journey of hope, seeking innovative solutions to thrive in an ever-evolving workplace.

What Are Random Acts of Automation?

Random acts lack a definite plan, purpose, or pattern. A random act of automation might produce a poor product more rapidly, hire the wrong candidate based on a biased algorithm, negatively impact an employee's mental health, or simulate a creepy experience using robotics. Societally, unintended automation consequences include the acceleration of wealth and skill-based gaps. I call these changes random because they were not predicted or planned. They affect us without the intervention of our conscious decision-making with no pattern or predictability.

For over a hundred years, many debates have surrounded the effects of automation on society, starting with Karl Marx's *Das Kapital* in 1867. For example, a well-known research area called Technology Determinism (TD) argues that automation directly affects social change. Some TD proponents also posit that most automation effects are far from random and instead are launched with specific goals in mind, such as suppressing workers. On the other hand, several views in the recent past argue that automation does not shape society but only human action will.

This book's argument lies somewhere midway on this spectrum, claiming that several automation technologies have unintended consequences, and as AI advances, this number will rise. In short, as we continue to roll out automation, we don't know how it will turn out for us. And, in all honesty, how could we? Humans' work patterns and mental states change with new use cases of technology.

Automation can now learn and evolve independently from its operating environment. In such a scenario, how can we be sure of the outcomes? Several years of firsthand observation at Forrester Research, examining how automation is implemented across tech, business, and government sectors, have informed this pragmatic, real-world perspective.

The Workers

To connect automation trends and worker advice, the book uses four distinct work groups. The framework is helpful for several reasons. Firstly, automation trends will affect each group differently. Physical automation, such as a new robot janitor, poses a greater disruption to human-touch workers than it does to digital elite workers, for instance. Secondly, the advice that a worker needs varies depending on their segment. Workers can better understand their current position, but more importantly see the potential paths available. Finally, the framework allows us to see how automation will shift workers from one segment to another.

The Digital Elite

The digital elites are the first group. Social scientists might see them as a subset of the historical Professional Managerial Class (PMC), a term coined in 1977 to describe a class of workers that leveraged education to separate from the working class. The digital elites share a similar playbook.

Digital elites encompass a growing pool of technologists, including tech industry executives, TED talkers, programmers, cybersecurity analysts, data scientists, and machine learning specialists. They actively design, build, and manage the technology we rely on. Their innate talent and education empower them to extract the full potential of this technology.

Furthermore, the digital elites include non-tech professionals—occupations like lawyers, marketing specialists, and business leaders with positions at the top of the work pyramid. Automation has reduced their work to words and numbers on a screen, and this screen can now be anywhere. Technological advancement propels their careers without writing a single line of code.

Consider Phil, the head of business development for a tech firm, a fancy name for sales. His firm develops "virtual agent" technology, which often translates into the clumsy chatbot experience we suffer through when we can't access human support. He describes himself as a regular guy, good at games like golf and tennis, but not a true tech entrepreneur or engineer, and admits he was a C student at the community college he attended. He struggles to understand technology but has strong "people" skills that earned him a spot to contribute to the next big thing.

We'll revisit Phil later. The crux of the issue is this: the digital elite's power is surging as our collective understanding of automation dwindles. This growing gap allows them to exert unprecedented influence. A prime example is OpenAI: a small, isolated group controls ChatGPT's output filters by embedding their ethical views without public oversight.

The Uneasy Middle Worker

In the technological spectrum, middle workers fall between human-touch workers and the digital elite. These jobs require a certain amount of education, several years of experience, and advanced skills. In the past, a middle worker could put in hard work and see it eventually pay off with higher wages and a better life. His or her children would have access to a better education and achieve more in turn. A nice suburban home was within reach, with a late-model car in the garage and a comfortable mid-sixties retirement ahead. Compared to when Ronald Reagan was president, these ambitions are far less achievable now.

Robert Jacobsen is a good example. He completed high school and volunteered to enroll in the navy in World War 2. His job title was "floor covering mechanic," a fancy union name. He put down tile and carpet. Jacobsen put down a hundred miles of it, mostly in New Jersey malls. All in, he spent over forty years on his knees. While some claim that anybody could have done the job, he would disagree. He would cite the tricks, extra measurement, adjustments made with your eyes, mistakes you learn to avoid, and so on, all of which took years to get right.

The only thing that bothered Jacobsen were his knees. Even with heavy-duty pads, they were not a pretty site—swollen, blueish, and streaked with dark veins. He rarely passed up a visit to the local "gin mill" on the way home and always had time for his version of "the luckiest man in the world" speech:

> Look at me. I did not come from much, but I make a good salary thanks to the union. I have a small lot on a lagoon at the Jersey Shore, that takes you through Barnegat Bay out to the Atlantic Ocean. I've got my own keg of beer at home, a nine-foot slate

pool table, and my German Shepard, Shafer. What else could a man want?

Life was indeed good for Jacobsen. But will it be good for today's high-school graduates? Can we even expect millennials with college degrees to do as well? The middle worker continues to suffer and can no longer attain the standard of living as Jacobsen. The French even have a name for it: *le grand déclassement.*

The Human-Touch Worker

Olek Sumoski came to this country from central Europe.[2] He graduated from high school and has held various security officer positions. Millions like Sumoski work at banks, office buildings, or shipping facilities and live a life of suffering with low wages and self-esteem that is even worse. To Sumoski, "A security officer is a thankless job. Sadly, you get mocked for it. People think you're a failed cop. It doesn't affect me much, since I never wanted to be a cop, anyway."

Human-touch jobs like Sumoski's offer employment opportunities to people with limited education and experience. The term is not perfect but captures the nature of services delivered. These jobs provide essential services that require significant human-to-human interaction. They became frontline heroes in difficult times like the pandemic. As we will see, they serve as community connectors and bridge relationships between the digital elite and middle workers.

Human-touch workers might toil as janitors or in a warehouse or wash cars they do not drive. They might be a third-world nanny pushing strollers with first-world babies, or a street vendor in Mexico City. They might opt to serve as a health services worker such as a nursing aide, orderly, or attendant; a store clerk; or the driver cruising down your street to deliver a package. They prepare food and beverages for us and wait on our tables. They clean the buildings and cut our lawns at homes and offices.

So, who are the people behind that practiced smile? For one, they tend to be poor white, black, and brown. Typically, they are high school graduates and earn low wages. For them, life is fragile. Many live in garages, huddle in small apartments, or live with parents into adulthood. Their work emphasizes human agility and requires a local presence in frontline locations like health care, retail, construction, agriculture, and manufacturing.

Work-Life Pioneers

When John Lennon was five years old, his teachers asked him what he wanted to be when he grew up. He wrote, "Happy." They supposedly told him he did not understand the assignment, and he supposedly told them they did not understand life.

Young John makes a relevant point today: we should set life goals in alignment with happiness and not an occupation. This shift in people's attitudes and behavior is evident. People today want to experience life more, work less, and find jobs in areas that align with their values. The tools now exist to allow them to reject traditional work patterns.

How Random Acts Is Different

Most discussions of AI and automation target the business or technical professional and therefore miss the mark for the average reader. The only way to understand where work is going is to speak to readers through people they know and stories they can relate to. To do this, I'm standing on the broad shoulders of Studs Terkel. He captured the state of work in America in the 1970s by entering the workplace and letting firemen, police, and teachers tell their stories. Little insight or analysis was provided, but the raw exposure of work life struck a chord.

Toward that goal and using the worker's voice, this book isn't about the fearmongering of AI stealing jobs or the technical jargon that leaves you confused. Sure, AI will displace some jobs, but more important and practical to understand are the disruptions and shifts that will reshape what work means for millions. The four defined worker segments provide a framework to do that. The key is for a worker to understand their current job and figure out where automation will take them and how to prepare.

Another distinction is the focus on the mental state of workers going forward. Humans are the only animals that know they will someday die and the only ones that drink alcohol. This is more than a coincidence. Most animals are lucky: they do not give the future a second thought. Their anxiety exists only in the present, an instinct that also makes the chipmunk dart into a nearby hole when sensing a bird of prey cruising the thermals above. Humans are cursed with existential worry, both in the present and about the future.

Driven by the promise of efficiency, businesses today rush to automate, often neglecting the mental state of their employees. This is not a criticism. They are paid to achieve fast results that target business objectives. In the equation that they are trying to solve, random acts such as isolation, lowered self-esteem, trust anxiety, fear of invasive monitoring, and stress from gaps in required skills are not yet variables.

Our current path toward all forms of self-service automation is one example. Too many companies focus their automation efforts on replacing people. As an employee, you'll see that this is one of the basic threats to your job. And as a customer, you will do a greater proportion of the work that employees used to do for you. At the current pace, automation will force all but the affluent to service themselves in most situations. Advances in physical automation—or if you want a simple word for them, robots—threaten humans with creepy experiences and psychological discomfort.

This book hopes to unify workers concerned about their jobs. The same forces impact factory workers in Detroit, service workers in the Midwest, software testers in Silicon Valley, call center workers overwhelmed by AI-driven chatbots, and waitresses facing increased workloads and stress. From the raw tales of real workers comes a clear and common understanding of the challenges and opportunities presented by automation, along with practical advice for navigating the evolving workplace. This book helps with career choices, daily work decisions, personal life behavior, and educational direction. This book tells us where we are headed, and, more importantly, what to do.

PART I

The Dark Side of Automation

Part 1 provides background in automation past and present to better understand projected workplace effects.

Chapter 1, Humans in the Loop, argues that the tech industry's approach to automation often leads to unreliable outcomes, supported by historical and contemporary examples. It emphasizes the need for human involvement and ethical considerations in technological advancement.

Chapter 2, Automation: Where We Are Headed, traces the history of automation from the Industrial Revolution to the present and beyond through three phases. Understanding where automation has been and where it will go is essential context to understand future workforce impacts.

Chapter 3, The Self-Service Time Bomb, highlights self-service automation as an example of automation that has gone too far. Today, we push automation on people prematurely and are too quick to eliminate humans. Overreliance on self-service automation can have negative human and social consequences.

Part 1 lays the groundwork for a deep dive into the four worker segments explored in Part 2. This understanding will be crucial in deciphering how automation will trigger shifts among these segments, the challenges workers will face, and the potential paths they must navigate.

CHAPTER 1

WE NEED HUMANS IN THE LOOP

THIS CHAPTER ADDRESSES TWO MAIN points: the tech industry's approach to innovation leads to unreliable outcomes, and advancing automation is inherently unpredictable. These conditions lead to random acts, which leads us to the chapter's main argument. We need to integrate humans into processes where the consequences of errors are high. In the cases presented here, it was irrational to trust the machine without placing a human in the loop. We need leaders who listen to technologists, relevant stakeholders, and affected communities. Automation must be approached with humility and caution.

There Is an Inherent Unreliability in the Tech Industry

On November 16, 2021, starting soon after 12:00 p.m. Eastern, thousands of companies witnessed their websites crashing, replaced by the Google "404-page error" message. For a few companies, outages lasted for days, and this was just one incident in a long year of technology-related disruptions. Companies are rapidly adopting public cloud infrastructures to run their businesses, and in doing so, have become prone to third-party vendors like Amazon, Microsoft, Google, and a host of others in entirely new ways.

Google Cloud apologized for the service outage and described the root cause as "a latent bug in a network configuration service." A similar perfect storm of disruption unfolded in July 2024 when a routine software update from cyber-security vendor CrowdStrike triggered widespread chaos. Like the Google example, the culprit was a routine software update. Airports grounded flights, hospitals halted surgeries, financial institutions froze, and essential services faltered. At Denver International Airport, large screens where arrivals and departures would usually be displayed were flashing error messages against an eerie background, called the "Blue screen of death", leaving passengers confused and anxious. Delta's CEO groused that CrowdStrike cost them 500 million in lost revenue. They generously compensated those affected by the worldwide disruption with a $10.00 gift card.

Ironically, CrowdStrike software was installed to counter global threats from online intruders and cyberattacks but instead managed to instantly wreck computer systems worldwide. This starkly revealed the vulnerability of the world's core infrastructure that so much automation depends on.

Software bugs are inevitable, but our hyperconnected digital infrastructure amplifies the potential consequences of these errors.

The tech industry's fast-paced, "move fast and break things" mentality exacerbates this issue. The common practice known as "vaporware" prematurely releases incomplete software with the promise of future improvements, to gain a competitive edge, for example. While this strategy might have been successful in the past, the growing dependence on AI and automation necessitates a more rigorous approach.

Think of it this way: a first release of any software is often like the first pancake off the griddle. Maybe the stove temperature wasn't right, or the frying pan's surface was sticky. The chef might be unsure of when to make the flip. The second batch of pancakes is always better, and this rule can be applied to software too. But this loose approach isn't acceptable for AI. Applications in health care, the military, and finance, for example, will not tolerate the usual software risk with AI in play.

Software is about to be released at a scale not seen before. If the tech industry gets its way, we can create automation without formal training. The rise of "low-code and no-code" platforms lets individuals with no prior coding experience, also known as "citizen developers," build applications. It is estimated that the worldwide market for low-code technologies will reach $26.9 billion in 2026.

With these tools, people who do not have adequate computer training can develop software applications. Generative AI (GenAI) will take this even further. If you can text into your phone, you can develop software. In essence, the next programming language will be human. To more cautious observers, this is the equivalent of giving your son the keys to the car before the first driving test.

Automation can now affect a greater number of people and systems. In the 404-page error scenario, Google did not make a configuration change to a few dozen servers. Instead, it used automation to attain this for thousands. It boils down to the following: the rapid digitization, increasing opaqueness, and extreme digital connectivity creates a concentration risk and presents a double-edged sword. While it amplifies our potential for greatness, it also magnifies the impact of our mistakes.

It becomes a serious threat when it uses algorithms based on probability to control critical systems, such as the software in our cars, or a plane's navigation system, or to determine who to hire or grant a loan to. Humans are being removed from important oversight positions, with less visibility into the machine's inner workings.

Automation software often stumbles forward without the extra human and safety reviews required for advancing technologies. A glance at Figure 1.1 illustrates this point. Overall, over a thousand automation-induced negative incidents have been reported. These included accidents caused by self-driving cars, illegal monitoring of workers, or incorrect outcomes from predictive analytics. It is interesting to note that GenAI, which has been used for less than a year, already claims the number two spot.

GenAI Is Climbing Up The Random Act Leader Board

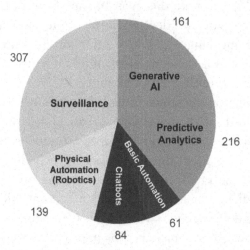

Based on over one thousand automation incidents to the AI Algorithmic and Automation Incidents And Controversies (AIAAIC) Repository

Figure 1-1: Negative incidents in automation are increasing.

AI Is a Gamble Where Not Even the House Knows the Odds

I would ask: do you like to gamble, and if so, are you good at it? You may answer the first question with a resounding *yes* but with a strong no to the second: I'm not too good at it. After all, it's just luck. The dealer pulls a high card and busts; a roll of the dice hits your number; you draw the right card to hit a flush in Texas Hold'em.

In layman's terms, you are essentially saying gamblers play the odds or probabilities, which amounts to luck. As such, how could anyone be good at it? And there lies the problem with AI. It, too, is based on probability. Historical data is employed by machine learning to establish relationships and make predictions based on the patterns. Large language models like ChatGPT predict the most probable next word to use. While static calculations are currently in use, it is gradually evolving to employ incoming data for improving and reconfiguring models without human intervention.

Think of it this way: no one is tracking what you watch on Netflix or what you buy at Amazon with a master spreadsheet. Algorithms automatically update your actions. Your category is sharpened through refreshed data for various commercial purposes; some you know about and some you don't. This power to learn and adjust forms the core of automation's disruptive potential and unreliability.

Significant literature has pertained to AI's unpredictability, and not just in recent times. The famous mathematician Norbert Wiener warned us more than fifty years ago, "If we use, to achieve our purposes, a mechanical agency with whose operation we cannot interfere with effectively, we had better quite sure that the purpose put into the machine is the purpose we really desire."

Brian Christian, in *The Alignment Problem: Machine Learning and Human Values*, brings Wiener's concerns up to date. He dives deep into why AI developer intentions sometimes lead to unintended outcomes. The dependence on probability is the root problem. Most businesses will soon be using statistical methods for management and will need to address the resulting uncertainties.

To illustrate the differing approaches to automation, consider an analogy between music and automation. Imagine a classical pianist who meticulously follows sheet music, precisely playing every predefined note. This approach represents yesterday's automation, where machines followed rigid instructions. In contrast, modern automation is how jazz musicians play. They improvise within a framework provided by a "lead sheet" that uses only a single melody line and one or two chord changes per measure. The lead sheet is like an executive summary of the song: it contains the minimum amount of information to express the musical idea.

In this way, the song is never played the same way twice. Jazz musicians make their "arrangement" (specific notes, timing, chord phrasing, and tempo). They improvise around the basic framework. This parallels how modern automation learns and adapts to changing situations.

Before the advent of AI, automation used the classical pianist approach. Every action or rule is explicitly programmed into the app. Automation specialists use the term "deterministic" to capture the simple notion that all actions for the software are predetermined and follow an unalterable sequence.

On the other hand, AI developers take the lead-sheet style. They create a model containing the important variables or data elements. The "algorithm" connects these variables statistically to achieve the desired outcome. When new data comes in, the variables are updated automatically, and the algorithm can take on different shapes and patterns to arrive at different conclusions. The prediction or decision is not predetermined but based on calculated probabilities. In other words, machine learning can improvise.

Our Tech Workforce Is Not Ready for The Probabilistic Age

The rapid expansion of technology has outstripped the development of discipline and training needed. In the past, when technology relied on deterministic tools—predictable, rule-based systems—this skills gap wasn't as critical. However, as seen in the music analogy above, we now depend on probability and complex algorithms. This requires an understanding of core principles that are just developing. We need to find ways to ensure key positions possess this evolving knowledge, and today they do not,

In fact, as we enter the probabilistic age, our tech titles deceive us. Let's illustrate this with Enterprise Architects. As an analyst that covers automation, I speak to them frequently. These senior technology positions design and oversee an organizations' technology infrastructure of computer servers, networks, and applications, that allows information to flow throughout an organization. It is that unseen foundation that much like your home's plumbing, is critical but taken for granted.

The title evokes images of licensed professionals ensuring structural integrity, but unlike your plumber, no certification or training is required to get that position. My wife is a registered architect and cringes when she hears that term. She had to learn fundamentals, like how to keep a building from collapsing, and prove it over a three- or four-day test to get her certification.

In essence, titles like "Enterprise Architect," "Data Scientist," and "Software Engineer," sound impressive, but don't embody the implied skillsets or certifications that those professions imply. Data scientists lack the scientific discipline needed to analyze complex data, for example to eliminate bias. Most software engineers receive no formal engineering training. In short, enterprise architects are not architects, data scientists are not scientists, and software engineers are not engineers. These professionals don't have the necessary knowledge or credentials to build reliable, ethical, and sustainable technological solutions. Yet they are responsible for doing so.

Keep a Human in The Loop Where Consequences Are Dire

The business world is pushing to optimize systems to achieve greater operational scale. This relentless pursuit of efficiency leads to more tightly wound closed loop or Level 4 patterns (discussed in the next chapter). Previously isolated automations now find themselves as nodes on integrated networks. Automation links our digital activities with sensor-equipped physical assets, further tightening global supply chains. AI Agents acting as digital coworkers exchange richer and faster-flowing information. AI's power will undoubtedly push systems even further in this direction.

While this interconnectedness promises efficiency, it comes with a hidden cost. The tighter the coupling of automation end points, the more susceptible it is to random, unanticipated events or disruptions. James Shore documented these dangers in "The Art of Agile Development" in the context of software development, but the principles apply more acutely to complex systems driven by AI's statistical models, where the potential for misdirection is even higher.

Warnings surrounding the unpredictability of AI's algorithms and their implications are not new. As early as 2016, Cathy O'Neil, in *Weapons of Math Destruction*, warned about the societal impact of algorithms. She showed how their use in fields like insurance, advertising, education, and policing, can lead to decisions that harm society. Algorithms can be opaque, unregulated, and difficult to contest.

To reduce random acts and enhance system safety, we need to loosen the coupling. The most effective way to achieve this is by introducing a human in the loop (HITL). The tech industry has used the term HITL terms for years in the context of designing machine learning algorithms. The "human" selects and prepares data to train the machine, and the algorithms are tested and revised through various human-driven tasks.

But now we need HITL raised to the application or process level. Human intervention allows for the identification and handling of unexpected situations that might otherwise cripple tightly coupled systems. Humans must be actively injected into the work stream to deal with AI's unpredictability. We are too quick to put automation in charge, which must be avoided in case of serious implications on people. Human checkpoints will help prevent a biased hiring decision, the arrest of innocent people, or poor decision-making in business. A HITL reduces pressure to build the perfect algorithm with perfect data.

Automation Can Get Us in Trouble Even Without AI

Hanna "John" Ayoub was relaxing at his New Jersey home one day, when he heard a hard knock at the door. He opened the door to police officers who put him in handcuffs and took him downtown. He was charged with stealing a truck he rented from Hertz, despite properly returning it. It was eventually determined that the computer system that tracked car inventories was the main culprit. It couldn't locate the vehicle and filed a stolen car report. Ayoub was jailed for three months before the criminal charges were dropped. Over two thousand customers have been arrested for car theft. Court documents claim customers spent 2,742 days in jail due to false arrests.

The entire conundrum can be traced back to Hertz's failure to have a human security officer review the report before the police were notified. Thus, if automation can result in serious consequences, they must employ a human default or checkpoint, particularly when underlying systems are unreliable. At the time of writing this book, 230 lawsuits against Hertz are in flight, and incredibly, the problem persists. Five Hertz customers filed 2022 lawsuits, while Hertz admitted that it still files at least 3,365 theft reports a year against customers.[3]

Even automation with no AI algorithms can be dangerous. Donnie Williams worked for Uber for several years. He is a process improvement expert with a resume full of arcane terms like "Kaizen," a leading method to eliminate waste in systems.[4] He commented on Uber's attitude toward automation, "Uber emphasized speed in all aspects of the business, whether getting a fair or resolving a customer issue. There was no opportunity for automation that was overlooked, and that included responding instantly to social media posts."

According to Williams, a third-party tool called "Sprinklr"[5] was installed to respond to Twitter comments at web speed. Unfortunately, a Twitter user who posed as an Uber customer set their Twitter display name to a racist slur. Uber's automated response system repeated the offensive language in their response, "We are so sorry, ********. Please send us your contact information so we can connect." The customer support team apologized for the offensive tweet, but the damage was already done.[6] This incident demonstrates the dangers underlying automated systems that emphasize speed over quality and do not have basic filters.

The examples above used basic automation and still got in trouble. What happens when AI gets in gear? Many projects today plan to use AI to shift decision-making from humans to software without considering the consequences. This "move fast and break things" approach, made famous by Mark Zuckerberg, and well documented in Jonathan Taplin's book of the same name, is not an acceptable approach for many decisions.

Machines should not be given full responsibility in cases where the consequences are severe.

Human Review Can Mitigate Bias in AI

Brandon Purcell is a leading analyst on "Responsible AI" at Forrester Research. He believes it is impossible to attain 100 percent elimination of bias in AI. Further, he believes that bias is so inherent in AI models that new executive positions with titles like Chief Ethics Officer will be required. Salesforce, Airbnb, and Fidelity already employ individuals for such roles.

Bias in AI algorithms is a well-researched area. Leading thinkers would argue that machine racism is systemic, institutionalized, and deeply embedded in society's technological apparatus. Moreover, the bias is not random but results from long-standing intentional racism that has infected our data and technology.

Ruha Benjamin's 2019 *Race After Technology* is one such study. It demonstrates how algorithms can mimic and perpetuate this institutional racism. Safiya Umoja Noble's *Algorithms of Oppression* (2018) exposed negative biases against women of color by analyzing search engine results. Virginia Eubanks' 2019 *Automating Inequality: How High-Tech Tools Profile, Police, and Punish the Poor* outlines the life-and-death implications of automated decision-making for welfare provision, supporting the homeless and child protection services.

Reading these books, you might conclude that racism is more ingrained in machines than most humans, although the designers did not intend to create a racist outcome. Most were unaware of the bias inherent in the data. For example, AI may prefer males for programming jobs based on forty years of data that shows longer work histories for men than women. Police-operated computers might falsely flag Black defendants as future criminals at twice the rate as white defendants, as they did in Broward County, Florida.[7] While we can't let AI designers off the hook, it is important to understand these results were unintended from their perspective. It is another example of misalignment or the gap between the intended and actual results.

Bias is embedded and pervasive and infiltrates in too many subtle and unintended ways. For example, most voice recognition systems are built by male programmers and trained on their voices. They don't hear females as well. Data discrimination like this runs deep, is hard to spot, and is not easily resolvable by merely tweaking an algorithm. However, the solution is straightforward: human review with the right tools and authority.

Leaders Must Champion Inclusive Stakeholder Engagement

Human beings' ability to manage automation has been challenged for some time. Einstein expressed concerns about this ability when writing for *The Nation* in 1932. He suggested the organizing power of man has not kept pace with his technical advances: "As it is, the achievements of the machine age in the hands of our generation are as dangerous as a razor in the hands of a three-year-old child."

This holds true even today, probably more so than before. There is a need to maintain a healthy skepticism about what AI can achieve today. Business and government decision-makers must involve a wide range of stakeholders, not just within their enterprises but also within their affected communities.

Advances in automation, whether using GenAI to repair a machine or a new closed-loop industrial pattern, will challenge our leaders to do so. Boeing's 737 Max disaster can provide further insights. Despite boasting one of the strongest safety cultures ever created, this company didn't integrate the guardrails needed to prevent an automation disaster. When AI advances and reaches the average company, imagine the future implications.

We all know the story by now. The brand-new 737 was behaving strangely. Lion Air pilots had about ten minutes to save the lives of 189 passengers. They skimmed through checklists and manuals calmly to control a plane that had a mind of its own. Despite their best efforts, Indonesian Lion Air Flight 610 plunged into the Java Sea in 2018, killing all 189 passengers and crew due to auto-pilot technology.[8] Another similar incident was the 2019 air crash in Ethiopia.[9]

In both these incidents, the "angle of attack" sensor insisted the nose of the plane was too high. This caused automation to take over: the now-famous Maneuvering Characteristics Augmentation System (MCAS), used to counter the larger size of the Max engines, forced the nose of the plane downward, sending the plane plummeting. Pilots found it challenging to override the MCAS automation.

This tragedy can be attributed to deficiencies in engineering and training.[10] If either was conducted properly, these horrific accidents could have been prevented. The plane could have had two sensors feeding the algorithm instead of one. Authorities could have mandated simulator training for the MCAS system for all pilots. Few aviation experts were aware of the MCAS system. What occurred was a human/machine struggle that we are certain to encounter more frequently. In this case, the pilots fought the machine and the machine won.

The 737 Max problem was a "black swan" event for Boeing—exceedingly rare. Few companies have contributed more to the technical advancement of the US than Boeing. They contributed to virtually every major engineering milestone, whether space exploration, unmanned military planes, or commercial airliners.

I recently spoke with a senior Boeing leader. His remarks emphasized the pride second- and third-generation engineers and factory workers held regarding the quality of their work, in an engineering and safety-first culture. He quipped, "Elon Musk's SpaceX can blow up a rocket on the launch pad and celebrate the event as innovation. Boeing doesn't blow things up."

However, following this incident, the media painted Boeing as a broken and compromised culture. Management was too focused on Wall Street and rushed production schedules. Outsourcing critical components weakened quality control, which resurfaced in 2023 after Alaska Airlines was forced to make an emergency landing after a door blew off in flight. They also ignored warnings from their engineers and misled regulators.

The drama at Boeing continued: the 737 Max faced renewed safety concerns in 2023 following a series of incidents. A new Southwest Airlines Max experienced a malfunction with its automated stabilizing system, leading to an emergency landing. Shortly after, an Alaska Airlines Max with was grounded due to a fire detection system issue. Most worryingly, a brand-new United Airlines Max suffered an engine failure at cruising altitude. These incidents prompted an FAA audit that uncovered widespread quality control problems within Boeing's manufacturing process. Further compounding the issue, a key supplier raised fresh concerns about their overall safety culture, despite supposed improvements implemented after the deadly crashes in 2018 and 2019.

These allegations are scary enough, but my takeaway raises a broader and more frightening concern. Boeing had one of the strongest safety and engineering cultures ever created, and yet, it wasn't enough in the face of management pressure to rush production schedules and reduce costs. Imagine what the world may witness as AI advances and permeates your average business. Most never needed to develop a safety or governance culture directed at advanced use of technology.

Automation will become more complex, opaque, and less predictable. Simultaneously, leadership needs to be more sensitive to a wider range of views to counter these effects. Complex automation projects will have hundreds if not thousands of voices. Most will claim everything is fine, but a few always say, "No, everything is not fine." We need to listen to the engineers who know the most, even with non-mainstream views.

Caution and Humility Are Key to Responsible Automation

In the above example, Boeing was so confident in the perfect execution of the system that they did not invest adequately in training pilots or incorporate the requisite redundant processes in critical systems. The debacle at Zillow is a better example. Remember when selling your house meant your realtor gave you a few "comps" and shuffled through binders? Fast forward a few years, and you're punching up a "Zestimate" provided by the real estate company Zillow. Instant gratification. Hundreds of AI-powered variables are right at your fingertips. Surely, this must be an upgrade.

Zillow thought so. Intoxicated by its data science prowess, they strutted into the housing market, wielding its AI algorithm like Excalibur, the mythical sword of King Arthur. To give them credit, they put real money behind that confidence. They began to buy and flip houses based on the information AI provided. And not just one or two but thousands. It was simple enough: people could offer their homes directly to Zillow. If the algorithm thought it was a good deal, Zillow would buy the property, do some touch up, and sell it. The company planned to scale the operation and be "flipping" thousands of homes a month by 2024.

So, what could potentially go wrong? It turns out, just about everything. The home-buying division lost hundreds of millions of dollars, despite buying in an appreciating housing market. Thousands lost their jobs. The data scientist team admitted they were unable to predict future home prices.

And here's the problem: machine learning may easily predict situations like when the coffee shop is busy or when traffic will slow you down. The history is clear and stable and correlations are high. The best time to try the Long Island Expressway is spot-on (the answer is *never* as this is a road locals refer to as the longest parking lot in the world).

I spoke to Scott Woodward, a real estate veteran and software entrepreneur. The Zillow Group acquired his company, ShowingTime. The Chicago-based startup developed software to virtually show homes, which made it a killer app during the pandemic. Woodward wasn't inside Zillow's Offer group or part of the data science team, but he shared this view, "Here's the thing with the Offer division. The real estate market is not straight up or straight down, and hence doesn't conform nicely to a predictive algorithm. Factors like view, sun orientation, and proximity to other neighborhoods are hard to model. Real estate is just a less stable environment, subject to swings in interest rates and buyer sentiment."

To make his point, he took his hand and with a slight tilt showed the occasional sideways movement, "Here's the second thing. The predicted price was accurate for that moment, but there was often a big time gap between then and when they could flip the house."

My point is not to criticize their data science but question the confidence of decision-makers at Zillow. They placed a huge bet on nascent technology. This business arrogance is precisely what frightens those that understand the power and limitations of AI.

One lesson from this book is that no one knows what will happen or when, so don't be fooled by the tech industry's confidence. Events such as COVID accelerated technology investment and deployment, even (or especially) when it wasn't ready. In fact, automation of all forms rose at a rapid rate. Humans were immediately painted as choke points in operations, points of disease and legal liabilities, and friction to smooth digital pathways. Rapid deployment of automation was seen as the perfect solution to replace them. This momentum to automate perfectly complemented the tech industry's "move fast and break things" attitude. In short: be prepared for random acts.

Responsible Automation Can Mitigate the Threats

This chapter argued the tech industry's approach to innovation leads to unreliable outcomes, and second, advancing automation is inherently unpredictable. These effects are hidden behind an industry awash in confidence. Visionaries and entrepreneurs abound, all claiming to have the answers. Brilliant, intimidating, and often charming, they believe they can see the future, but the truth is, they can't, and nobody can. As argued here, things change quickly, and what seems like a sure bet today can be a failure tomorrow.

Consider this: in 2022, blockchain and cryptocurrency innovations were hot. Like today's GenAI craze, tech vendors, fintech startups, and instant experts pushed new products. *Fortune* magazine's August/September 2022 issue featured Sam Bankman-Fried, the founder of cryptocurrency exchange FTX, on its cover. They presented him as the next Warren Buffett or J.P. Morgan. Less than a year later, Bankman-Fried was in jail.

There is no ambiguity surrounding the dangers going forward: automation will grow more sophisticated and opaque, less understood internally by the company and externally by the public and regulators, all of whom will not be able to keep up with the tech industry. The more we rely on automation, the more we must trust senior leaders to set up the right guard rails, governance, and transparent culture. This means they must cautiously and meticulously listen to the engineers, designers, and testers of these systems, and these people need a big seat at the table during decision-making.

Despite various researchers, analysts, and the press presenting warnings pertaining to AI, the message is not getting through. Forrester's research found that only a small percentage of companies have reached the maturity required for Responsible AI or have hired Chief Trust Officers.[11] Businesses will continue experimenting with emerging technology; that is inevitable. However, in doing so, they should listen to the engineers, broaden the community of stakeholders, and maintain a humble posture (see Figure 1-2).

What We Can Do	Why It Matters
Recognize the tech industry will introduce new automations before they are ready.	The ability to scale successes and mistakes is unprecedented.
Understand that future automation is based on probability with unpredictability.	Potential outcomes of emerging automation will be harder to foresee.
Encourage leaders to listen to diverse voices that include AI specialists and external communities.	The broad approach helps anticipate less predictable outcomes.
Question reliability of automation with potential negative effects. Insist on human checkpoints.	Unpredictability is inherent in emerging automation and requires human checkpoints.
Ensure training for humans keeps pace with automation's progress.	HITL works only if a worker knows how the automation works.

Figure 1-2: The tech industry requires humans in the loop.

CHAPTER 2

AUTOMATION: WHERE WE ARE HEADED

THIS CHAPTER DELVES INTO THE history of automation, tracing its evolution from the Industrial Revolution to the present day and beyond. It identifies three distinct phases: industrial, intelligent, and human-capable. You might wonder why we delve into this past. The answer lies in the context and perspective it provides. By understanding automation's journey, we gain valuable insights into its future trajectory and impact on the workforce.

This brings us to an important question: what do we mean by automation? Simply put, automation is when technology is used to minimize human effort. Think of it as a big tent encompassing aspects of physical automation, such as robot welders and factory automation, but also simple spreadsheets used in an office, or personal applications such as home monitoring. Computer vision, machine learning, and natural language processing fit within the automation umbrella and hundreds of software and hardware categories.

In 1946, the term "automation" first saw its use in the automobile industry to describe the increased use of devices and controls in production lines. However, its history began significantly earlier, dating back to the machines that drove the Industrial Revolution. Oliver Evan's 1785 automatic flour mill might have been the first automated industrial process.[12] Bucket chains and conveyor belts drove the mill, resulting from a decade of tinkering. While operating continuously without any human intervention, it was the first time that a mill also operated without dependence on waterpower.

Once the Industrial Revolution began, it gathered steam (pun intended) and continued to add machines of all kinds. Soon after, "How you gonna keep them down on the farm" entered the vernacular as youth left to work in mills and factories in fast-growing cities.

Although it is accurate to use the term "revolution," it is necessary to blur your eyes when doing so. For most people, it was hardly a revolution. Human change caused by automation was gradual, drawn out, and fit into most people's lives without any stress. In fact, if you did not move to a city, your life may not have changed.

The term "revolution" is more appropriate for where we are going. The pace of today's automation and the effect on workers will be disruptive. Millions of middle workers will be displaced. Digital elites will be forced to take human-touch positions, and traditional full-time employment will decline as many opt to become "work-life pioneers." These workplace shifts will take place in a few years, not over generations as in the industrial period.

Carl Benedikt Frey rang an early alarm bell in 2019. He used a machine learning algorithm to estimate the ease with which 702 American jobs could be automated. He and his Oxford University partner Osborne concluded that, over the next decade or two, 47 percent of jobs could be performed by machines.[13]

This pace of automation's advancement is unprecedented. By contrast, early innovations in steam, electrical, petroleum power, and factory operations were adopted slowly and steadily. But even then, the arrival of automation caused people to fear for their jobs, like today's concerns.

The now-famous Luddites were named after Ned Ludd and were nineteenth-century English textile workers. They smashed the new textile machines with sledgehammers, claiming that they were used in "a fraudulent and deceitful manner" to replace them. You can sympathize with them: many owned small labor-driven workshops that could not compete with modern machines, akin to how today's independent hardware store can't compete with Home Depot.

The self-employed textile workers shut down their shops and applied for factory jobs. However, few such jobs existed: automation had eliminated them. Military support and jail time were necessary to suppress the Luddites, a term used today to denote anyone opposed to progress, especially technology.

Workers continued to fight over wages, child labor, and work conditions and continue to do so. However, in the end, industrial automation created new industries, improved the availability of goods, and raised many boats, including a strong middle class in Europe and the US.

Three Phases of Automation

My automation timeline breaks down into three phases, each a significant leap forward (see Figure 2-1). First came industrial automation, laying the groundwork with its relentless march. But recent years have seen a surge in so-called intelligent automation, where software tackles low-value tasks that once required humans. Now, we're hurtling toward human-capable automation (HCA), the ultimate collaboration, where human and machine strengths are combined.

Note that the three phases are not sequential. Each continues to develop independently. New technology seldom replaces the old. The shiny new technology spreads like a virus with great fanfare, the old technology forgotten, ignored, and ridiculed. But a closer look reveals that the old automation continues to be useful and relevant. Email has not replaced postal mail. Your last ATM withdrawal was likely managed with Cobol software running on IBM mainframes.

Like cockroaches and Keith Richards, technology never goes away.

Industrial Automation

It has been a long journey and best viewed through the Industry 4.0 framework that plots how human factory labor was gradually reduced through four phases,[14] but I will take some liberty and summarize the big steps.

The path was gradual indeed. Water and steam powered new machines and led to the slow transition from farm to urban factory work. Standardization and assembly lines, pioneered by Henry Ford, revolutionized manufacturing, diminishing the role of the skilled craftsperson. Factory robots and more advanced electronics were added. Industry 4.0's "intelligent factory" leverages advanced data exchange, cloud resources, and AI to streamline operations, minimizing the need for direct human involvement. Dr. Paul Miller is a vice president and principal analyst at Forrester covering digital manufacturing, and explained that industrial trends show little regard for workers:

> Industrial workers could soon have less freedom than their machines. Machine-operating employees in many countries have more rights and protections than ever before, but they also have less ability to make decisions about how they prioritize and complete tasks. They are micro-managed, constantly tracked, KPI-burdened, a mere machine appendage, and a precursor to a dystopian future.

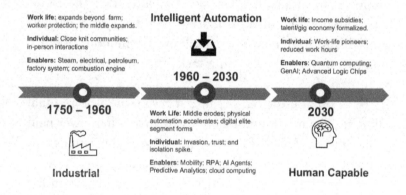

Figure 2-1: Automation phases overlap.

Intelligent Automation

Intelligent Automation (IA) began in the 1960s and primarily focused on data-driven office tasks. It evolved from the simple automation of accounting and payroll functions to RPA bots that replace human tasks. Other widely used and equally valid names for this period include cognitive automation, intelligent process automation (IPA), or hyperautomation.

The IA periods use software to automate tedious, repeatable, and low-value tasks. The fast-food worker enters an order into a point-of-sale machine a hundred times a day, for example. It can be performed by a robot. Automating these repetitive, low-value tasks, or simple human workflows is IA's sweet spot.

Software bots, built with robotic process automation (RPA) low-code tools and several other technologies are employed to attain this. Gartner estimates that the IA or hyperautomation software market is already at $600 billion. This form of automation will extract millions of work hours from these lower-value tasks that humans currently perform daily.[15]

IA is often criticized because it results in little residual value. It primarily minimizes costs by extracting lower-paid human hours. IA can also eliminate entry-level positions that help individuals break into a company. How many "rags to riches" stories have we heard where the hero starts in the "mail room"? A team of MIT professors referred to this type of technology as "so-so" automation since they extract hours from human toil while creating few new jobs.[16] Others have termed them "the boring bots" since they perform simple, unexciting tasks.

Unfortunately, businesses think these technologies are far from boring. For example, for some, the maintenance costs of an RPA software bot can amount to $25,000 annually, replacing two humans performing low-value tasks, such as manual verifications, data entry, cutting and pasting among applications, and answering simple questions with a chatbot or virtual agent. In later chapters we will see IA's disruptive influence particularly on middle workers.

You can trace IA back to the 1960s. Across many offices, secretaries would quietly type outside a door or take dictation in the office, just as portrayed in the television series *Mad Men*. In time, these secretaries moved to a typing pool. By the 1990s, word processing contributed to their decreasing numbers. And by 2010, personal tools like Microsoft's email, OpenTable, TripAdvisor, Travelocity, Orbitz, Google Docs, and Google Calendar turned professionals into their own secretaries and finished them off.

The peak of IA was the pandemic. Digital transformation before that was a slow grind. Legacy systems, procedures, and stubborn organizations stood in the way. But the pandemic hit like a rogue wave in 2019, and IA found the high gear it needed. At the height of the pandemic in 2021, Satya Nadella, CEO of Microsoft, summed it up well: "We just saw two years of digital transformation in two months." Pragmatic automations were the pandemic winners, while the pause button was hit on discretionary spending for AI and more transformational projects. Pandemic darlings like RPA startups had off-the-chart valuations but may be roadkill on the highway to AI and the human-capable period.

Human-Capable Automation

Science fiction writer William Gibson would say, "The future is already here—it's just not evenly distributed."[17] This means you can find it, but it takes some looking. Changes can be seen in small segments and examples. For instance, even in

2001, if you had looked carefully, you could find a small set of individuals addicted to their BlackBerry phones. They had swagger, disrupted meetings to check emails, and annoyed their spouses by depriving them of attention. People even called the now-crude devices "crackberries." Think about it. This was six years before Apple introduced the iPhone and ten years before mobility exploded. Now, most of us fall asleep with our devices nearby. In other words, if we look closely today, we may get a glimpse into the future.

HCA is where we are going, and we don't have to look hard to find it. Higher-level human functions like decision-making, physical agility, and conversation are already integrated into apps. we use at home and work. These automation take on more human-like characteristics and alter our relationship to machines. Gibson would point to evidence of the HCA future in self-driving vehicles or GenAI infused bots that generate meaningful interaction and advice. HCA makes possible a future where technology enhances everyday life and benefits society as a whole, to not simply automate existing tasks but to harness the combined strengths of humans and machines.

An illustration may help convey the point better. In the IA period, tech was created to mimic human behavior and repetitive fundamental activities. These are demonstrated as Levels 1 and 2 process patterns in Figure 2-2. For example, at Level 2, a bot would take over a keyboard task from a human by opening a window, copying some data, and pasting the information into an open application. In the manufacturing world, robotic arms have replaced most human welders. The robot arm repeats ten steps hundreds of times a day—a Level 1 sequential pattern. In these examples automation copies basic human tasks. Automation enthusiasts like to say the IA period takes the robot out of the human and many of these tasks are beneath human capabilities and talent, which must be directed toward more advanced tasks.

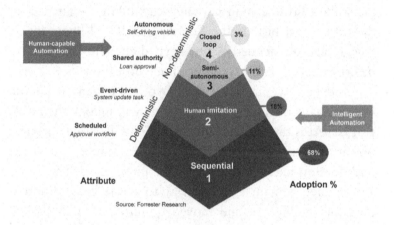

Figure 2-2: Human-capable automation will accelerate Levels 3 and 4 process patterns. Figure courtesy of Forrester Research.

The HCA period takes intelligence up a notch to Levels 3 and 4, which enter the non-deterministic world of AI. While Level 3 systems use AI with human oversight, Level 4 processes rely on AI to drive autonomous or "agentic" systems Human tasks are still off-loaded to the machine, but these now include the less repetitive ones, like conversation, analysis, decision-making, and navigation. These HCA functions present entirely new ways of doing things.

It's the UI Breakthrough Once Again

It's always that new user experience that creates the hockey stick-like adoption for the next automation push. The DOS operating system in the 1980s made personal computers popular, giving millions an easy way to interact with them. Netscape's browser and crawling capabilities, launched in the 1990s, gave birth to the Web. Apple's 2008 I-Phone interface, replaced Blackberry's tiny keypad and allowed Apps to be downloaded, and led to our phone obsession.

And here we are yet again. Two key advancements in how humans interact with computers will unlock the HCA era. GenAI is the big one. OpenAI's ChatGPT used a simple prompt interface to allow us for the first time to exchange and develop ideas, with human-like intelligence. The innovation gave humans a simple way to access Level 3 and 4 machine intelligence and moved us into the HCA period ahead of schedule.

Natural language processing marks the second breakthrough in user interface design. Similar to the limitations faced during the pre-literacy era, when only a small elite could read and write, computer systems today are only accessible to a limited group that understand complex coding languages (around 27 million), but imagine the impact if this number expanded tenfold, to 270 million.

That's where we are headed. NLP will democratize access to computing power. HCA has kicked off a new period of "computer literacy," where people can speak directly to machines, and with that interaction vast numbers will be able to leverage automation's power, accelerating its impact both good and bad.

HCA is a big change. Although thousands of automated processes occur in enterprises today, 86 percent are Level 1 or Level 2. In the HCA period, the goal is to transfer as many processes as possible to Levels 3 and 4.

As such, we can distinguish between the two periods in the following manner. While IA improves the efficiency of things we already do, it doesn't change how we do things. The HCA period we are entering provides opportunities to innovate and create new ways of working. It also presents a new set of workplace challenges.

In some cases, the changes will be barely noticeable and gradual. Crude chatbot sessions of the previous era are being replaced by machines that can carry a more complete conversation: AI begins to make real decisions such as granting a loan or advising a judge on the right bail amount for an offender. AI bots create art, write news stories, and give advice at work and for relationships. Digital smarts are embedded in the physical world to facilitate autonomous delivery to our homes, robot janitors to disinfect offices, and robotic security officers to roam hallways and office parks. Compared to IA, it's the difference between lightning and a lightning bug, to steal a line from Mark Twain.

Three Forces of Automation Distinguish the HCA Period

Three primary drivers will transform the relationship between automation and humans: control, scale, and convergence (see Figure 2-3). These are the main enablers of the workplace shifts and challenges that follow.

The first driver is the shift of control from humans to machines. In previous periods, automations simplified work, but humans still were in charge. Nail guns saved wrists from long-term damage, but carpenters still determined the appropriate position for the nail. This will be less the case going forward.

The level of danger will depend on how quickly the shift happens. Economists in the book *Prediction Machines: The Simple Economics of Artificial Intelligence* are confident it would be rapid. The central argument was simple enough: AI will shift human decisions to machines since it would reduce their costs.[18] This trend will be as disruptive as the internet that lowered the cost of a "search" to near zero. Look at the consequences that we witnessed: newspapers never recovered; the yellow pages disappeared; and the music industry changed forever. No question: machines will make more decisions for us and in the process, we will cede more control to them.

The second driver is a new formula for computing how companies grow or scale. During the previous phases of automation, a company expanded by adding more land and physical assets. They invested more capital, and more importantly, added more workers. This was the traditional formula for company growth we might have learned in early economics courses.

Scale operates differently today: Apple, Alphabet, and hundreds of other next-gen companies use a digital scale that employs a different balance of land, capital, and labor. There is a need for only a small number of digital elites with skills in social media, data science, machine learning, and specialized automations. Cloud resources replace the need for land or building, and capital investments are relatively low. This new form of scale builds automation with common application platforms, cloud infrastructure, and mobile networks. Digital scale allows companies to grow rapidly with fewer middle and human-touch workers.

A third enabler of HCA is digital convergence, where automation brings the physical and digital worlds together in new ways. Products, equipment, buildings, and supply chains in the physical world are already embedding digital smarts. The interaction of analytics with this intelligence causes convergence and produces smart buildings, autonomous delivery vehicles, and robotic waiters and security guards. Full or partial digital immersion based on metaverse principles is one example of convergence.

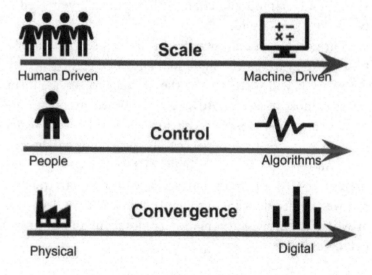

Figure 2-3: The three forces of human-capable automation.
Figure courtesy of Forrester Research.

CHAPTER 3

THE SELF-SERVICE TIME BOMB

TOO MANY COMPANIES FOCUS THEIR automation efforts on replacing people. As an employee, you'll see that this is one of the threats to your job. And as a customer, you will do a greater proportion of the work that employees used to do yourself, as you interact with imperfectly designed machines for everything from self-checkout to customer service. To understand and counter these threats, you need to be aware of this trend.

Put simply, our current path toward self-service automation is too quick to eliminate humans. At the current pace, automation will force all but the affluent to service themselves in most situations. Advances in physical automation—or if you want a simple word for them, robots—threaten humans with creepy experiences, and psychological discomfort. Automation is increasingly dictating our tastes and preferences. Your parents may decide your religious training, but we can decide what automation to accept. So, let's look at where self-service automation comes from and what you can do about it.

Self-Service Automation Hell

I like to arrive at the airport early. The new layout is crisp and clean. It seems somehow different since my last trip.

Self-service kiosks are lined up like little soldiers, flashing for attention, waiting for instruction. My mobile device is already packed away in preparation for security. But I dig it out, enter the password, and then scroll through a hundred emails to find my confirmation number. On the kiosk, screen after screen comes at me with a mix of security questions and upsell opportunities, which I easily identify and ignore.

After four attempts to print a baggage tag, my eyes (filled with immense hope) hunt for a human. Alas! No matter where I look, I find only the flashing machines and other confused passengers. I hoped to attach the baggage tag correctly and then drag the heavy suitcase to the bag-drop area. I planned on wrestling it onto the scale that tests for weights over fifty pounds. I anxiously hope the scale is having an off day as my bag is dangerously close to the limit. I've entered self-service hell.

I travel frequently. An airport can show you how the one percent lives. I glance at a well-dressed gentleman as he enters a queue reserved for high-ranking loyalty members. However, there is no queue, to speak of. The agent is ready to serve. The gentleman smiles and addresses the quick, efficient, courteous waiting human behind the counter. Welcome to a world where only the digital elite get human support. It's a worrisome trend—if you are affluent, you will get the human touch; if not, you will be relegated to self-service. The great unwashed must struggle to service themselves with automation.

In the end, I found an employee to sort out the bag printing challenge. Once she appears, frustrated travelers line up to get her help. Having failed out of the self-service path, I need to wait. That's the penalty for customers who don't fit the automated box the company has reserved for them: a slow, excruciating wait.

Digital Transformation Is Popular, but Often Leaves Customers Behind

According to surveys of businesspeople, companies are increasingly keen to embrace "digital transformation" to increase efficiency and cut costs. Forrester, my employer, has scores of analysts helping clients facilitate digital transformation. Despite the stated goals of improving the customer and employee experience through automation, the outcome is always the same—we as customers do more work.

Bill Burr is one of my favorite comedians. He perfectly captured the frustration of self-service automation in one of his routines. Imagine him ordering a sandwich: turkey, lettuce, tomato, and mayonnaise. The employee repeats it back to him, leaving out the mayonnaise: "Turkey, lettuce, tomato." Burr corrects him, "And mayonnaise!" The employee nonchalantly replies, "The mayonnaise is, uh, over there."

Burr raises his voice in exasperation, "Well, go over there and, uh, get the mayonnaise! I paid for 100% of the sandwich, and I expect 100% of the sandwich to be made. I'm sorry they fired the mayonnaise guy, but I'm on this side of the counter! The guy that pays for the sandwich and you are over there; the guy that makes the sandwich." To conclude, Burr expresses his ultimate fantasy: "I just want to climb up the greasy corporate pole to get to that 'eyes wide open' party and strangle the corporate yes-men who make these decisions!"

Self-service automation has been on a roll for one hundred years or more. During the 1880s, small products like postcards, gum, and stamps were sold through vending machines. In 1986, CheckRobot Inc. installed the first modern self-checkout (SCO) machine in a Kroger grocery store. And it's not just retail-oriented self-service. Interactive voice response (IVR) systems—voice menus—began to appear in the 1990s. They provided bank balances, routed your calls, and responded to basic queries. Websites have integrated hundreds of self-service options. Virtual agents or chatbots siphon off customer requests from contact centers. Electronic menus, QR codes, contactless payments, and mobile ordering continue to advance at an unprecedented rate.

Businesses now seem to be in a rush to replace humans with automation, even before they understand the downsides in most scenarios. Take self-checkout. In 2013, there were only 191,000 SCO units worldwide. The number is predicted to skyrocket to 1.2 million by 2025.[19] You could probably run for president on a platform to eliminate SCO in retail stores; you might not win, but you'd certainly garner a passionate following. Some customers swear by the convenience, but others resent these devices. One study found that 75 percent of customers had difficulties with the technology and at least 80 percent sought assistance at least once during the self-checkout experience.[20]

Here's what's wrong with the current SCO trend: It requires customers to do all the work. We are turned into unpaid employees trying to figure things out on our first day on the job. We do our best to execute unfamiliar tasks while navigating imperfect technology. One retail pharmacy clerk I found was shocked at the number of people who needed

SCO-based assistance. The machines treated customers like small children, dictating directions and treating them rudely. The kiosk instructs you to scan your items, place them in a bag, and when to insert your cash or card. One customer couldn't figure out how to put cash in the machine:

> The customer stood there clueless and fumed for five minutes. They yelled at the machine, called it stupid and screamed at no one in particular, so I eventually came back and said that here is where the cash goes. So, like yea, I was petty, but they were rude and not using their brain. I was supposed to train customers to use a robot that will eventually replace me. Not a good feeling. If you can't tell, retail is not for me.[21]

The retail industry is pushing this self-service technology on us, whether we're ready or not. They tout their automation as all-encompassing and comprehensive and in reality it falls short. Self-service options are often mazes with incomprehensible instructions that don't resolve issues quickly. While sometimes it is better and more convenient for customers to self-serve, sometimes, we rely on self-service to do too much.

We have reached a digital tipping point where the cognitive or physical challenge outweighs the benefits. Anxiety, frustration, and doubt, which are common, are too high a price to pay. The tasks we are supposed to perform are unclear. The instructions and information presented lack credibility and relevance. Customers lose confidence and trust in the process. In short, our ability to resolve an issue when it arises—as it often does—becomes hopeless.

Humans have had enough. Companies are finding they need metrics for "click rage." As a measure of frustration, they count when a customer clicks or taps on an element on a website or app. Customers are starting to actively avoid the SCO option. We'd rather wait in a long line for a human cashier.[22] Can you blame us? Humans are faster and more skilled at checking out customers. Retail clerks know all the arcane codes for items and are expert baggers.

Some humans are fighting back privately, and, in some geographies, we may be getting assistance from the government. In Spain, for instance, companies that don't provide customers with human assistance within a reasonable time frame are fined.[23]

Companies hope to reduce frustration through smarter automation. They hope AI will evolve to anticipate needs and act on them, serving us proactively. In their dreams, computer vision will recognize the avocado and no longer require the elderly lady to enter a code into the machine. And we will get there. In mid-2024, Mashgin, an AI-based self-checkout startup with 4,700 locations (many in sports arenas), briefed me on its approach. It departs from traditional barcode-reading, and instead uses computer vision technology.

Beyond that, SCO kiosks will be made obsolete by Just Walk Out (JWO) platforms like Amazon. Take what you need off the shelf and leave.[24] Eliminate those moody human cashiers. And why not get rid of those entitled customers altogether? Have them order online, and a robot will pick and pack it for delivery by a self-guided vehicle or drone. Someday, maybe, but techno-enthusiasm and the search for profit are pushing too hard toward self-service.

What can you do as a customer? Push for legislation mandating human assistance, as in Spain. Rate stores online and be clear when you've given low ratings for lack of human help. Conversely, rate stores with human clerks better. Write company management and suggest a customer advisory board to clearly what loyal customers expect from both humans and automation.

If you are a retail clerk, you can't do much yourself. But you can make progress together with fellow employees by unionizing, as two hundred thousand workers have in recent years.[25] Make maintaining jobs in the face of automation a worker demand, as the writers did in their strike against the Hollywood producers. Unions provide support and advocacy for workers and help negotiate for better wages, benefits, and working conditions. A pandemic-emboldened workforce, the growing wealth gap, and automation fears have created a more positive attitude toward them. Prospects to organize non-union workers are better than they've been in decades.[26]

Humans Are Not Ready for Many Forms of Physical Automation

Humans will play a critical role in how any automation is accepted, and this is far from new. In 2014, Nicholas Carr's *The Glass Cage: Automation and Us* warned that automation needs a firm place for the human and must complement each other rather than compete. Richard Baldwin's *The Globotics Upheaval: Globalization, Robotics and the Future of Work* (2019) argued that automation and human labor will occasionally interact negatively. These views capture the broad implications of advancing automation while emphasizing the need for careful human-machine design.

What's happening in the trenches? In 2023, I led research to compare the progress toward mainstream acceptance of different categories of physical automation (think real robots). We interviewed employees, consumers of technology, and tech vendors across eleven automation categories to judge the barriers and determine the timelines for acceptance. We found that people assimilate automation through six phases of adoption (see Figure 3-1). Fully accepted automations must enter the adoption window. Some technologies race to the window. For instance, voice assistants graduated from Unthinkable to Popular quickly. Others, however, will take longer. The difference lies in a human's psychological comfort level.

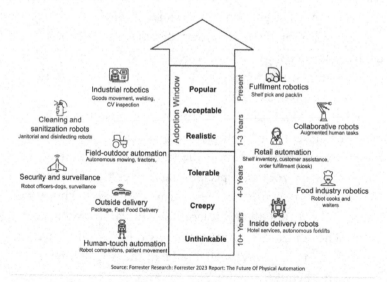

Source: Forrester Research: Forrester 2023 Report: The Future Of Physical Automation

Figure 3-1: One third of physical automations are creepy or intolerable.
Figure courtesy of Forrester Research.

My research team and I then placed the eleven areas of physical automation—think classes of robots—across a timeline, analyzing near-term, mid-term, and long-term trends. Some interviewees debated the timing of each robot category, but all agreed: how an automation coexists with people will be decisive.

For example, everyone agreed that fulfillment or warehouse robots are fully accepted. Humans no longer dominate warehouse fulfillment workspaces; they do their best to stay out of their way. These robots mostly scoot along the floor like a Roomba vacuum that cleans up after supper with the kids, but new ones are on the way that may not be as acceptable.

Amazon introduced two new service robots, Sequoia and Digit, in 2023. These are full humanoids with arms, legs, and faces. A released picture shows Digit with a cup of coffee in hand. Our research shows that robots that look like us are less acceptable, even "creepy" and "unthinkable" in some contexts. Digit and Sequoia will struggle to get along with their human sidekicks.

Cleaning and sanitation robots, on the other hand, became "acceptable" during the pandemic. Humans are happy to give jobs that meet the three D's—dull, dirty, and dangerous—to robots, especially ugly ones that don't look like us. Robot security officers struggle as well. Those we interviewed found them "tolerable" but far from "acceptable." The android security officer, or the drone buzzing around the mall, always seems to be in the way. Humans do not accept them yet.

Robots have even further to go for most human-touch workplaces like hospitals. No family member wants to hear bad news about a loved one from a robot. However, they can help with non-patient facing tasks to reduce nurse burnout and tackle hazardous cleanup. Natalie Schibell, a principal analyst at Forrester, predicted that in health care through 2032, humans will dominate over automation. So, we need humans for the time being.

What does this mean for companies adopting robots? As good as automation looks in a promotional video, it cannot be forced upon humans without carefully reviewing the psychological effects. Humans are not yet ready for many forms of automation, and coercion is not the solution. We need this human perspective on automation now more than ever.

What happens when companies violate this principle? Disaster.

Consider that the three biggest events in life are marriage, birth, and death. Each event is filled with anxious moments, tradition, and religious overtones. These events celebrate our most human attributes: finding a mate, procreation, and life's end. When we lose a loved one, rituals guide us to lay the person to rest respectfully. Family and friends follow traditional mourning rituals and events to honor their loved one's life. Well-worn traditional steps put the loss in perspective.

This is no place for a robot. But the Nissei Eco Co., a plastics manufacturer with a sideline in the funeral business, elected to try to do so anyway. The company hired the child-sized robot Pepper, made by SoftBank Group Corp. They clothed it in the vestments of Buddhist clergy and programmed it to chant several sutras, or Buddhist scriptures, to mourners.

This seems insensitive to me, and I suspect to you as well. Certainly, some find public speaking intimidating and would welcome a machine to take over. But in this case, Pepper kept breaking down during practice sessions. The same human-oid robot botched jobs at nursing homes and failed to connect with fans at baseball games. It was, in short, somewhere in between "unthinkable" and "creepy." This robot appears to be a solution looking for a problem that doesn't yet exist.

In general, there are few use cases for these robots in public spaces, and they can trigger creepy emotions. The most successful physical robots to date are ugly and designed for a specific task. They are more effective than skinny bipedal robots with arms, legs, and a head.

What does this mean for you as a worker? We can forgive employers who use robots to perform dirty, dull, and dangerous tasks that few employees would tolerate. But we must raise objections to robots clumsily intruding into spaces better left to humans, like funeral homes and base-ball games. Industrial robots are fine. But humanoid robots fail on emotional dimensions and likely will continue to fall short.

Automation Risks Stifling Our Creativity

Los Angeles likely has more original screenplays than home-less people on its streets, but they aren't likely to be produced. Why? Because production decisions are likely made based on historical risk-return data. Machine-learning-based calculations now determine the fashion, music, and movies we see.

Algorithms will recommend we produce what already exists with minor tweaks, whether it is a formula for a plot, a catchy tune, or a short-sleeve fashion that has worked before. The result will be repetitive; if we liked something in the past, we would probably like it in the future. In this paradigm, how will humans produce new ideas? Automation degenerates our culture into a homogenous, sterile sea of profitable sameness.

Take superhero films, for example. Could there be a more tired formula? A regular person gets superhuman abilities, encounters evil, faces challenges, and then prevails in the predictable climactic battle, largely with characters invented by comic-strip authors during the Depression.

The movie industry has been criticized for overusing old intellectual property for years with no effect. Lately, more sequels have been produced than original movies. But maybe that will change. Superhero film fatigue among US adults is up six points as per a 2018 survey.[27] The studios may soon have to revert to old-school human thinking: roll the dice to find that next *Forrest Gump*, *The Wizard of Oz*, *The Godfather*, or *Psycho*.

Streaming content is even more formulaic. Content produced by and streaming on Netflix, Amazon Prime, and Disney+ is as boringly similar as if an algorithm designed the plots. Viewers are overwhelmed by the number of choices, according to a Nielsen 2021 survey. This applies to the shrinking music market too. Three major record labels produce two-thirds of the music consumed in the US. They use similar risk-reward analytics to prioritize and push a few mega-stars and pop hits, leaving little room for new talent. Is this why so many millennials are hooked on boomer music produced before they were born? Book publishing is a similar story: most are published by the Big Five, and there's a formula for what they produce.

The resolution of the 2023 writers' strike may be foreshadowing the future. It addresses a pile of the usual wage and benefit issues. But, for the first time, protection from AI was on the list of demands. Writers don't want their scripts used to train AI models. They don't want to be hired on the cheap to review and tweak a script a robot created. They don't want robots to create them. It looks like they have won their battle against AI, but what about the rest of us?

This resolution gives me hope for workers in creative industries and overall. Replacing writers, retail clerks, or nurses with AI will likely generate what we've seen so far: formulaic, limited, and flawed results that will annoy the humans who must deal with them. But writers are adopting AI to assist them—fix mistakes, summarize research, and identify inconsistencies. When the humans are in charge and the automation serves them, the results are better than either can deliver alone.

Keep these challenges in mind if you are in an industry where kiosks, robots, or AI are coming in. Learn the technologies. Embrace their power. And ensure that your managers understand that humans would still rather work with humans—especially humans augmented by automation—than face only machines. We'd rather not wander around airports because we can't figure out how to get a kiosk to print out a luggage tag.

Workers will benefit from an uproar against self-service automation, an almost certain "techlash" is on the way. We will recognize that automation is great at repetitive tasks, but human talent, such as empathy, problem-solving, and creativity, is often necessary. Service jobs especially will become more important, more nuanced, more available, and better paid. Develop your interpersonal skills to add that human premium. Workers who have them will be in high demand, and it's already started.

BMW knows the performance, reliability, and style of cars will converge, and they will have to sell a "driver experience." A human now delivers a loaner car to your house and inspects and cleans your vehicle. In Apple's retail stores, you get a high-touch human experience. I am amazed at how personable, articulate, and digitally skilled the average support person at the "Genius Bar" is.

People are getting fed up. They do not want to be pushed around by automation. Companies will realize their success will be driven by the memories or experiences surrounding their offering. The future lies in what surrounds the product or service. And that's you.

What We Can Do	Why It Matters
Gauge your tipping point for self-service automation and don't be afraid to opt out.	The ability to opt out is one of the five principles of the White House's 2022 AI Bill of Rights.
Don't let automation be forced upon you. Reject unthinkable and creepy experiences.	Acceptance of physical automation will go through six phases. You get to determine adoption.

Don't succumb to a machine's idea of acceptable ideas, fashions, and entertainment.	Emerging artists need a chance. They risk getting buried by an AI-driven culture.
If you can, be willing to pay more for a "human premium" to combat self-service trends.	Supporting companies that use humans in creative and engaging ways encourages their use.
Support legislation to mandate human availability for customers.	Businesses force automation on us. Without resistance, only the affluent get the human touch.

Figure 3-2: You have a choice on the automation you accept.

PART II

The Workers

We do not have a great track record in predicting the future, particularly in rapidly evolving fields like technology. Examples of misguided predictions could fill this chapter, but my favorite dates to the 1939 World's Fair. The Futurama exhibit predicted that all Americans would own flying cars by 2000. Other examples form an embarrassing litany of human misjudgment.

Many financial experts predicted the housing market bubble wouldn't burst, leading to the devastating 2008 financial crisis. Brick-and-mortar stores were doomed due to e-commerce. Bank tellers and branches would be gone due to ATMs and online banking. We have been predicting widespread unemployment due to automation for over a hundred years.

Confirmation bias and overconfidence, like two mischievous goblins, often trip us up when we try to predict the future. We cling to information that confirms our existing beliefs, ignoring evidence that contradicts them. People are prone to see what they are looking for. A Forrester veteran once warned me:

Some thought leaders wield data like a drunk uses a lamp post—for support, not for illumination. Don't fall into that trap. Approach predictions with a healthy dose of skepticism, seek out diverse perspectives, and let the evidence guide your conclusions.

Good advice, but in my view, the most insidious bias an analyst faces is "novelty bias." Our media landscape craves disruptive predictions—the bolder the better. No one hungers for the mundane assertion that the future will mostly resemble the present, perhaps with a few minor tweaks. You won't land a keynote slot at a tech conference by predicting slow and steady progress. Yet, for most innovations, that's what happens. Instead, paint a picture of a transformed world, even if the evidence for a dramatic shift is shaky.

Future of work predictions are easy prey for the "novelty bias." Predictions of massive job loss or robots doing backflips will always get headlines. Forrester predicts seventy-five million jobs in the US could be automated by 2025, primarily in retail, transportation, and administrative positions. McKenzie estimates up to eight hundred million global jobs could be displaced by automation by 2030. Frey and Osborne's famous 2013 study projected up to 47 percent of US jobs are at risk of automation by 2033. These views get attention because, like the four-car pileup, they scare us.

Three Divergent Views Dominate

Intense disagreements about the social and economic consequences of automation rage on, dividing even the most esteemed minds. To drive this point home, I've organized thought leaders into three groups: Historians, Technologists, and Dystopians.

Historians are often academics from technology, labor, social science, and economic fields. They draw from the longest and richest data set available and apply the most academic rigor. They are quick to remind us that the job destruction forecasts have always been inaccurate. Many argue that previous automations were absorbed seamlessly and often created massive new industries and jobs in their wake. They point to the data and the "help wanted" signs on every street corner. In other words: don't worry about it.

Yet not all historians agree. The title of Jason Resnikoff's 2022 book says it all: *Labor's End: How the Promise of Automation Degraded Work.* Progressive thought leaders like Aaron Benanav in *Automation and the Future of Work* argue that only a disaster can result from automation in the hands of twenty-first-century capitalism, and only a new kind of social consciousness can provide hope.

Technologists are a second collection of diverse opinions. They include industry analysts like me, consultants, AI thought leaders, and tech executives, who tend to be positive, since they will benefit and prosper from technological advancement. For example, Andrew Ng, the inventor of TensorFlow, an open-source AI software platform, claims that AI will do more for humanity than electricity. They see robots lurking around every corner and cannot wait. This optimistic outlook, reminiscent of Ray Bradbury's utopian visions or the effortless convenience of Star Trek, imagines a world transformed by technology. McKinsey Research estimates that GenAI alone could add the equivalent of $2.6 trillion to $4.4 trillion a year to the world economy, roughly the equivalent of Germany's gross domestic product. Of course, companies will require the support of many consultants to do so.[28]

ChatGPT's emergence in 2022 was the spark that gave new life to the Dystopians, igniting a wildfire of anxieties about automation's march on jobs. Karl Marx probably started the dystopian ball rolling in his 1867 *Das Kapital*. He claimed that new forms of mass production would alter society in favor of the owners of capital. Over a hundred years later, the late Professor Stephen Hawking warned that AI could mean the end of humans. He said: "It would take off on its own, and re-design itself at an ever-increasing rate. Humans, limited by slow biological evolution, couldn't compete, and would be superseded."[29]

The dystopian path mirrors the bleak landscapes painted by Philip K. Dick in "Do Androids Dream of Electric Sheep?": robots will take most jobs, before heading to the streets, as portrayed in a zombie apocalypse. The wealthy people who own the machines will exploit everyone else, who eke out dreary lives, making frayed ends meet, akin to the world famously pictured in the 1982 movie *Blade Runner*, with crumbling infrastructure, collapsed social order, decadence, and decay.

Facing the same automated future, these three intellectual powerhouses offer visions more disparate than branches of a machine learning algorithm. We can't even agree on whether technology will affect society at all. According to Technology Determinism (TD), a theory developed in the 1970s, technology change directly affects social change. Yet, several studies oppose this view. Social Construction of Technology proponents, for example, argue the opposite, that society shapes technology.[30]

For the record, I sit between these two camps. I agree with TD proponents that automation undeniably shapes our behavior. But my optimism about societal control and influence is guarded. Commercial interests often steer automation decisions, leading to far-reaching, often unforeseen consequences. We need robust safeguards and thoughtful planning to ensure technology enriches, not exploits, our lives.

The Heart of the Matter: Job Transitions

Global job loss predictions due to automation are vague and unhelpful. It's a guessing game nobody wins, and even perfect foresight doesn't tell us how to prepare. We need a more nuanced conversation. Automation's impact is undeniable—it will touch nearly every job. But before we get lost in the big picture, let's zoom in on the individual worker. How will they adapt? Which segments will experience the most disruption and reskilling? Who thrives, and who faces an uphill battle? Focusing on this micro level—how automation transforms how we work—is crucial. Only then can we equip workers with the essential skills, resources, and guidance to navigate this inevitable shift. (For those who prefer a broader view, Figure 4-1 summarizes the transition effects for our four worker segments.)

The Middle Will See the Most Decline and Dispersion

The overall number of middle jobs will dramatically decline. That's why the job-growth loss block the is labeled high growth. IA, the low-value technology described in Chapter 2, is the main culprit and labeled "major". HCA will have a "moderate" effect. Most middle workers will become human-touch workers or work-life pioneers. On the positive side, some middle workers will take on work that the digital elite do today (discussed in Chapter 4). This is why the chart shows "moderate" growth for new jobs.

Worker Segment	Job Gains And Loss	Automation Effect	
		Intelligent Automation	Human-capable Automation
Digital Elite	Strong Steady Gains	Modest	Strong
Middle	Significant Loss	Major	Moderate
Human-touch	Exceptional Gains	Modest	Moderate
Work-life Pioneer	Strong Steady Gains	Modest	Moderate

Figure 4-1: Ten Year Worker Growth Prospects and Transition Effects*

*Job projections are taken from Forrester's "Future of Work" Forecasts. Transition effects are detailed in the worker segment chapters.

Human-Touch Workers Will See Job Growth

Millions of human-touch workers will be needed to provide premium service and human accents in many roles. Job growth will be "exceptional". Physical automation will help them have safer, cleaner, and better-paid jobs in areas like janitorial services and security. Movement to middle positions will be modest but available. Device and problem-solving skills will keep the robots running. Auto technicians will benefit from machine guidance that allows them to take on more complex repair assignments, for example. IA and HCA will have consistent but "modest" effects compared to other segments.

Digital Elite Positions Will Expand but Face Transition Challenges

Unlike the middle, the more advanced HCA is the disruptive culprit for the elite. Much research, programming, decision-making, analytic reporting, and creative tasks will move to automation. They will depend on their human and critical thinking (CT) skills to maintain their lifestyles. Some jobs will be lost to middle workers aided by AI, but overall, the demand to help companies transform into digital and scaled businesses will increase their numbers. They will experience strong steady job gains with modest losses.

Work-Life Pioneers Shift Toward Flexibility and Freedom

Within five years, a four-day workweek could become the norm, alongside a surge in alternative work lifestyles, fueled by a growing population of work-life pioneers, individuals who break free from the traditional nine-to-five grind. HCA and IA play a supporting role in this transformation. By automating routine tasks and offering flexible work arrangements, these technologies help work-life pioneers pursue their ideal work-life balance. Automation also supports those with specialized skills and a passion for craftsmanship. Artisan and niche products and services can find a wider audience online, allowing individuals to turn their hobbies or talents into viable careers.

All four segments face future work challenges due to automation. The true test for all workers will lie in navigating them. The following four chapters begin by explaining how technology will affect their work and offer specific advice. We get our hands dirty. We talk to workers in their environments and to their bosses.

CHAPTER 4

CHAPTER 4

HOW WORKERS IN THE MIDDLE[31] CAN AUTOMATION-PROOF THEMSELVES

A TRADITIONAL TAXI, WHICH SOMEHOW survived the Uber and Lyft onslaught, picked me up one day. That ride was my first encounter with Enzo. My destination was Boston's Logan Airport. Enzo's vehicle was a basic Ford sedan that had seen better days. No fewer than three red warning lights were on, as if to proclaim, "Your car is living on borrowed time." Enzo was past his prime as well, and a few days past his last shave and shower, but he was happy to recount his experiences.[32]

Two years ago, on one of his cab trips, he noticed a machine shop had opened less than a mile from his house. A curious guy with an appetite for change, he was always on the lookout for anything. He'd been a machinist for twenty years and hoped to pursue a career in that profession again. He was excited to see machine work returning to the US after so many jobs were lost. As he told me:

I was fifty-six years old and no rookie, but I managed to get hired. I had changed some—added a few extra pounds [he laughed], but the machines had changed a lot more. They had gotten very high-tech. The work had changed. There was now a lot more to do in the prep, setting up the machine for the job, putting in codes that the computer executes. These new CNC [computer numerical control] machines are just the opposite of the old ones I knew. With those, you had to be good with hand wheels and levers. If not, you could get hurt or mess up the job. Today's machines want you to speak their language—or G-code—which tells them things like feed rate, speed, RPMs, and location.

At the shop, a kid working toward his college degree tried to help him by explaining the setup and the testing process. However, Enzo was not interested in learning about the new machines, and he hated going to work every morning. Each time he input the codes, he was scared he might break something. He had been a top performer for decades at a top shop. But in this changed context, he was a slacker.

Eventually, he went to the foreman and resigned. The foreman tried to talk Enzo out of it. He liked Enzo since he kept to himself and worked hard. But for Enzo, focusing on something he wasn't interested in or good at proved difficult. So, he asked the foreman, "Can't I just run the machine?" But the foreman shook his head. He needed someone end-to-end. So, Enzo quit and went back to his cab. Driving it was relaxing and he didn't need a lot of money anyway. He summed it up: "I take care of my family and stay out of trouble. That's what a good *paisano* does."

Here's what Enzo teaches us: the laws of the jungle will apply to you if you're short of needed digital skills. Just as lions separate the slower antelopes from the herd and take them down, middle workers like Enzo will become fair prey in the service economy. Millions of middle-class jobs will shift. In this chapter, I will argue there is a positive place in the future of work reserved for humans in the middle, and I will tell you how to get there. You don't want to be an Enzo, wandering around looking for fares. I will describe how automation affects middle jobs and then outline strategies to help you thrive in the new environment.

The Truth Your Employer Doesn't Want You to Know

Fireflies light up for one good reason: they are in pursuit of dates. But the females of the genus Photuris have not-so-romantic intentions. They copy other fireflies' flashes to attract the males of those species. When one such male arrives, this "femme fatale" firefly pounces, first sucking his blood and then devouring his insides. It is important to understand that the firefly is not vicious or evil. There is no emotion involved, just nature working its magic.

In a similar fashion, businesses have evolved to seek profit, not to provide attractive jobs for workers. Their intentions are not evil, however it may appear. As profit-seeking entities, they invest in automation regardless of whether that investment may hurt their workers. More than 50 percent of enterprises surveyed by Forrester have set up centers of excellence (COEs) to rapidly deploy automation, with their stated goals emphasizing improved customer or employee experience. However, the underlying drivers are always the same: increasing revenue and profit. That puts your job at risk.

Because your well-paying middle job is a prime target, many like you will find yourself out of work, regardless of the business's good intentions. One midsize mortgage bank, for example, now has thirty-six fewer people in the loan department, although this wasn't the original plan or what they told the workers.[33] The software robots were built with the promise that they would be helpful, simplifying the work while making it more interesting. And they did that. They fill out disclosure agreements, collect data for risk assessment, and enter data into a cryptic loan origination system, then a machine algorithm generates a credit score.

Previously, these tasks were done by high-school graduates for reliable paychecks and health benefits. That's no longer the case. The bank had hoped, and told employees who helped with robot design, that additional loan volume would prevent layoffs. Their "change management" program lasted about forty-five seconds. When that additional volume didn't materialize, the bank let dozens of people go; their salaries were an expense no longer needed.

Jobs in the middle will be the first to go. The automation technology to replace them is here today. It doesn't require the "moonshot" approach like many AI projects. A simple and unsophisticated bot can be built in weeks to perform well-structured repetitive tasks. As a result, cubicle jobs in the middle are emptying humans out now, making it particularly challenging to explain the value of these robots to skeptical workers at risk.

For example, Jim is a major health insurer executive who sat down with his middle employees and explained how the software robots operated. He explained the software ran on servers and took over desktop tasks. They would update the reports for them, verify relevant lists, and send emails attaching the right documents. He portrayed the robots in a positive light. They will only do what you hate to do. They will free you to spend more time with customers. Your job will get better. He truly believed this, and why not? Consultants and senior management assured him this was the case, but all he heard around the office was that these robots would replace them. So, he thought about the robots from his employees' perspective.

> I get it now. Employees assume management has the worst intentions. It's not their first rodeo. They have seen the top floor come up with one story after another for years, but at the end of the day, management just made life a bit more miserable and saved money somehow. We need to think this automation thing through. We need a better story, but that means understanding the actual implications, and nobody knows. Not management, not the high-priced consultants, and not the workers.

Management in these cases wasn't being intentionally deceptive. It's more accurate to state that they don't know how the planned automation will turn out. Random acts have unpredictable consequences.

The Invisible Robots Are the Real Threat

On March 28, 2021, CBS' *60 Minutes* broadcast a segment titled "The Next Generation of Robots." They interviewed me to offer perspective on the effect of next-generation robotics on the economy and workforce. Even before they could pose any questions, I asked David Levine, the associate producer, why their segment featured hardware robots when the invisible ones, in the form of automated software, are taking over the workforce. He met my comment with a glazed look and polite smile. I explained that software that takes a phone call, a decision-making machine-learning algorithm, or robotic process automation that updates a general ledger are in fact robots. These software robots were substantially impacting the workforce, more than any other hardware robot.

Levine's silence reflected that my comment was not aligned with the story they wanted. They were keener on showcasing human-like robots from Boston Dynamics doing backflips, dancing to hip-hop music, and demonstrating exceptional athleticism and agility. But something important was overlooked. The latest robots, despite their backflips and sprinting, did nothing useful.

With media coverage like this, you might think an army of robots—metal heads glinting in the sunlight—will soon take over your job. There is no doubt that robots and physical automation are advancing, but they are far from being ready to affect your job in the middle. Even in the case of Enzo in the machine shop, the software within the machine replaces the human. The robot you can't see should be your concern. Popular media has not gotten the message. When people think of robots, they still imagine a human form, like C3PO in *Star Wars*. Or they think of a machine designed to perform a task, like a driverless delivery vehicle or a machine racing around a warehouse. Software robots are different. They are invisible and more agile. They can learn faster and benefit more from accumulated knowledge than their hardware cousins. In the next decade, these robots will reshape middle jobs.

By 2027, most workers will have a personal software robot. The AI assistant will always be by your side, a constant voice in your ear. You will complete tasks with a voice command, without switching between different apps. Infused with GenAI, these software assistants will handle thousands of hours of administrative tasks, take customer calls, and, over time, become smarter than the humans they support.

There is a need for workers like Enzo to get comfortable with these advancing tools. They will need to "own" them, learn to customize them to fit their needs, and ultimately use them to design new automations. As a skilled worker in the middle, mastering these tools will be your ticket to remaining and thriving.

AI Will Make the Robots Smarter

As an exercise, the employment website Indeed subjected an AI chatbot to a job interview. They sat down ChatGPT and grilled it. While this interview lacked the normal back-and-forth tension, they asked the typical questions: what skills are you best at and where are you the weakest?[34] ChatGPT was more honest than most job applicants. The AI was confident in some areas and showed humility in others. It admitted that its vehicle operating, leadership, and personal care skills were poor, but rated its communication, language, and technical skills excellent, for example.

Indeed's research team then matched the ChatGPT answers with fifty-five million 2023 job postings to see which ones would be most affected. The bad news is the GenAI program said it was "good" or "excellent" at most of the skills middle workers like you have. Indeed's research put sales, technicians, customer service representatives, administrative assistants, and shift managers on the top ten list of jobs most at risk to AI. If you are in one of these or similar roles, you need to reboot your career.

Here's what these jobs have in common. They depend on skills to summarize, interpret, and perform tasks based on sorting through piles of data in corporate systems, documentation of standard operations, or external websites. In these jobs you are an intermediary, broker, go-between, or agent between disorganized piles of information and the customer.

Your job exists because a human brain is required to make sense of it all—but that will be less true going forward. AI can navigate these big piles better than you. Excel jockeys that perform acrobatics with formulas, macros, pivot tables, and charts will become lost souls. IT and operations roles that carve data and reports from enterprise systems like SAP and Oracle will thin out. These jobs require a mix of technical, communication, and business skills, all competencies that AI aced in the interview.

If this sounds like your job, get ready. AI will reduce the number of workers in those roles.[35] It will not be the android or physical robot that pushes you out of your cubicle. It will be a smaller number of humans superpowered with GenAI enhancements.

Middle Managers, Prepare for the Great Flattening

If automation trends continue, Amazon and other scaled digital companies will soon resemble an hourglass: the digital elite will remain at the top, lots of less skilled people will work at the bottom, and a thin middle will exist that robots will mostly own. The automation will run in the cloud and will likely take over your middle job that manages human tasks, schedules, and logistics. If you are a middle manager, you should raise the white flag and investigate upskilling options.

Recognize that in many positions, work-from-home trends make you more dispensable; your physical presence is no longer necessary and sometimes impractical. Virtual meetings are now the norm for many organizations. Collaboration technologies like Microsoft Teams, Cisco Webex, Slack, and Zoom promote peer-to-peer communication and free information exchange. They reduce the need for managers to put in effort to keep everyone on the same page. The result? Flatter organizations and fewer middle managers.

Algorithms are now better at managing things than you: they do not get locked down, do not get ill, will not transmit a contagious virus, and are unlikely to sue a company for poor working conditions. They can sort out warehouse, inventory, supply chain, and a host of other human logistical issues. In machines and vehicles, sensors transmit signals that algorithms can use to manage operations at low cost. They produce sophisticated dashboards with a sea of metrics, enabling decisions driven by predictive analytics. What does this mean? Simply put, if you are a middle manager with a clipboard, you will soon discard it. As I'll soon explain in more detail, the best strategy to prepare is to improve your skills. Either take training to move up to the digital elite or become adept at managing AI tools to do the work you and your colleagues used to do.

The Gigafication of Middle Work

As algorithms take many middle management jobs, they will assign tasks, set deadlines, and evaluate performance, assuming all the responsibilities of a human manager. In this way, they will manage workers just as algorithms manage Uber and DoorDash drivers today.[36] Because mobility, GPS, and analytics have worked so well at efficiently managing gig workers, the same techniques will also spread to other industries. It may be the legacy of the gig economy to show how to use automation to organize work for humans.

This will lead to further "fracturing of work," a term used by Noam Scheiber in the context of the 2023 writers' strike.[37] Rather than hiring full-time writers, Hollywood will employ contractors for microtasks and then piece them together. Fracturing like this breaks jobs into lower-paying, degraded pieces, not unlike what Henry Ford's assembly line did to blue-collar workers in the early twentieth century.

In our context here, I would call it the "gigafication" of work with automation the important enabler. Thought leaders have been tracking the role of technology in carving up work for some time. Books like *The Gig Economy* by M.T. Casey (2014) and *The Rise of the Robots* by Martin Ford (2016) argue that technology will fragment jobs and increase freelance work.

A darker question arises going forward: if algorithms manage fragmented work as in the gig economy, will workers be treated in a less personal and more transactional way? Will your employer have the same non-relationship with you as Lyft has with its drivers? Imagine a world where a former job becomes a series of impersonal transactions mediated by cold algorithms. GenAI will add richer context beyond the simple automations used in today's gig economy. Is this the reality that awaits workers as the gig economy expands? From a worker's perspective, will income become less predictable with no human recourse for grievances? Put simply, will we inherit the less appealing aspects of gig work? Is this where automation will take us, and if so, will we like it?

Rich Lane can help answer this question. His perspective is unusual. I've never met anyone who has held jobs as a digital elite, middle, and human-touch worker. He worked at Splunk, a company that predicts problems in advanced computer systems, has also held various middle technical support roles, and has been a human-touch worker in the gig economy. Here's how he describes it:

> My dad was a Korean vet and worked in the same factory for over thirty years. When I was a kid, he would take my brother and me there and we thought it was just so cool, big, and important. All that huge machinery and people running around, but he told me, "This place is dirty. It's noisy and smelly. You're eating dust and dirt for eight to ten hours a day. You need to do something better." I was nine years old and had no idea what he was talking about.

Much later, when Lane was an adult, his dad fell sick, and his brothers couldn't help. They had kids and worked hourly jobs, while he had neither. And that's when Lane entered the gig economy to work for Amazon. He delivered packages, all shift work and the luck of the draw. You grab a delivery the same way an Uber driver grabs a fare. It's hard for some, but Lane was good at it and could get four hours of delivery credit in just two, effectively raising his hourly rate. There is little human presence in this work. As Lane describes:

> An algorithm is your boss. If you do one thing wrong, some metric will catch you, and you're just gone. It's not like they say, "Hey, you're a good driver; we'll give you another chance." There's zero loyalty, no human to speak to, and no appeals process. They have so many people trying to get the job, they don't need [to keep any one individual]. They need to keep the machine going with as much unskilled labor as they can get.

> The gig economy only works for people with partners that have real benefits or as a side hustle. Few of my buddies could get enough work to hold on to a middle [class] lifestyle—the house, kids, and education. The gig life is not great, but neither are a lot of company jobs either. These firms need to be more introspective. They should say, "Yeah, we're an insurance company. It's not cool and sexy, but we can make it so people don't hate to come into work." A few of my friends have just given up. They just want a job. I'd say, "You know you'll never get anyplace there." And they would say, "That's OK. I like leaving here at five. Go home, play with the kids, have a beer, watch a ballgame. I'm good with that. That's how I want to lead my life."

Automation will make traditional middle jobs look and feel more like gig work. As Lane reveals, this is not a positive direction. In his experience, employers exploit gig workers with low wages, long hours, and no recourse for grievances. Income is unpredictable and unlikely to match what a solid middle job provides.

In addition to financial insecurity and stress, working alone or with less human connection can lead to social isolation and loneliness, a topic explored in Chapter 10: Isolation. Gig workers miss out on the traditional nine-to-five workday, employee badge, regular paycheck, company events, softball team, March Madness bracketology, and workplace romances. Chillingly, data from 131 US incidents shows that 11 percent of mass shooters were gig workers.[38] Making matters worse, the rise of GenAI threatens to squeeze even more gig workers out of the market. A review of freelance job listings reveals a significant decline in available positions: writing jobs are down 33 percent, translation jobs 19 percent, and customer service jobs 16 percent. The culprit? GenAI.[39]

Here's How to Automation-Proof Yourself

We have examined how automation will eliminate, transform, and disrupt middle positions. These are the most unintended or random effects of automation, and you will have to contend with them. Now, let's discuss what you can do to survive the onslaught of automation and thrive. By focusing on these six areas, you can position yourself for success in the age of automation.

Become an AI Operator

Many top jobs are held by those with more education than you. In Chapter 6, we define them as the digital elite. The good news is that GenAI and supporting automation will provide detailed instructions for less credentialed workers, like you, to do a percentage of the digital elite's work. But to do this you must become an AI operator.

For example, there are 350,000 US paralegals with a US median salary of $56,000. Most have an associate's degree. The National Bureau of Labor estimates a 14 percent annual growth rate for this role, higher than most categories. While GenAI will take over many routine tasks they perform, it will also allow them to focus on legal analysis, strategy development, and client relationships where human judgment shines.

Paralegals will eat into the lawyers' work, and that is your opportunity. ChatGPT passed the bar exam, so why pay a lawyer six hundred dollars an hour?[40] A paralegal with good chat prompting skills may suffice. New law firms are emerging that use GenAI to provide legal services at a fraction of the cost of traditional law firms. These firms rely on a pyramid model, with a few licensed attorneys at the top and a team of GenAI-trained paralegals at the base. In simple terms, if you are a paralegal today, GenAI alone will not take your job, but those who know how to use it are likely to—so to retain your role, you must become an AI operator.

Here's another example. Charles Schwab has thirty-four million active brokerage accounts. Fidelity had forty-two million. How do they plan to support such vast numbers? Chapter 6 answers that: they will invest in automation to achieve digital scale. This may sound modern and advanced, but it boils down to this: only the wealthy will get top-tier human assistance. These firms' investment websites and commercial ads show a retiree being soothed by a certified financial planner or licensed investment manager, but the vast number of clients makes this scenario increasingly rare. The bulk of human support will be provided by middle workers like you without four-year college degrees.

And that's your opportunity: newly minted middle workers, supported by GenAI, will replace that financial advisor with an MBA and a low golf handicap. Robo-advisors will craft investment advice and financial roadmaps. Don't take my word for it. Scan today's open positions at these firms. The number of "client service specialist positions" at the larger brokers continues to grow, and guess what? There is no degree requirement. They are looking for you.

Automation will alter how health care is delivered. Tech-savvy nurse practitioners and physician assistants will build careers under a machine's direction. Even before GenAI, these positions were expected to grow by 37.4 percent and 36 percent, respectively, over the next ten years.[41] GenAI will increase these percentages. Consider this. According to a recent study, ChatGPT can already give better advice than human physicians. Its replies were preferred 78.6 percent of the time over human doctors. The chatbot's responses were rated as higher quality, and even more startling, higher in empathy.[42] So a nurse with an AI assistant will do much of the work doctors now do.

The three middle opportunities described above are a sample of those that will emerge. Look for jobs like this if you work in a field where AI-infused invisible robots are coming. You will need to make a move. Learn to understand and manipulate AI instead of listening to the typical advice for struggling middle workers, "Learn to code." That advice is obsolete. The Turing bots built from GenAI that I describe in Chapter 6 will make coding skills less important. The next programming language will be human. To prosper, or simply retain your position, you must become an AI operator. As a bonus, you can take work and income currently reserved for the digital elite.

Here's how to do it. First, understand the significance of "prompt engineering." It is not a new job category, nor will you see job openings for it, but a set of skills you will need for emerging jobs like those mentioned above. AI models in the future will resolve customer issues, guide research, and manage human work patterns, but only if you ask them in the right way. You must know how to create clear, concise, and informative questions to make them effective for the roles described above. That's what prompt engineering skills help you do.

Online resources are available to help you become fluent in prompt writing techniques. Prompt writing courses on platforms like Coursera, edX, and Udemy are a good start, but hands-on experience is essential. Use open-source AI tools like OpenAI's ChatGPT, Google AI's Bard, or Hugging Face's BLOOM to try different prompts and observe the responses. To nail one of these new positions, you will need a portfolio of prompt engineering projects. Organize them by the type of work you want to do. You can post these on job search platforms and use them to apply for jobs like those described above.

Become an Automation Creator

As automation erodes the number and value of middle positions like yours, you will need to demonstrate new forms of value. You can buy some time by specializing in a niche area that is not easily automated, but this approach is passive. It attempts to fight or hide from automation. Consider the proactive alternative: join the automation party and become an advocate and creator.

Think of it this way. At work most of us are consumers of automation's value. Someone we probably never met did something clever with software or hardware that made our job easier and more efficient. What if instead of being a taker of automation, we became a maker, curator, inventor, or organizer that supports automation?

Automation creators have the best chance of survival going forward. To be one, you must develop skills to develop and maintain bots, digital workers, AI Agents or other automations that can improve firm efficiency. As automation lowers your value, develop skills in creating, improving, or maintaining it.

It's not as hard as it may sound. A billion-dollar low-code software market rides on your success in becoming exactly that, an automation creator.[43] The term "low-code," coined by Forrester Research in 2014, refers to a development environment used to create software through principles of model-driven design, automatic code generation, and visual programming, eliminating the need for trained programmers. If the tech industry gets its way, you can create and maintain automation without formal training.[44] If you can text into your phone, you can develop software.

Here is what I've seen work: make friends with someone in IT to help choose the right low-code platform for you. Most companies already have one or at least a plan for getting one. Airtable can build custom databases and workflows; Microsoft Power Automate can fire up bots around your office apps like Outlook and Excel. Bubble allows you to build a complete website application. By using these tools, you spend less time on tech and more time on the process which you know best.

Low-code development tools are a great way for middle managers and workers to maintain their positions. And it works. I've seen accounts payable managers create bots to do parts of their jobs and become invaluable team members. You can too. Most importantly: embrace constructive ambition and don't be afraid to experiment with these emerging tools. Tutorials, documentation, and online courses are readily available. For most of your career you have been a consumer of automation, the recipient of its value. To succeed now you need to be an automation creator.

Lean into Your Human Skills

I recently spoke with Sally, a middle worker in a well-known telecommunication call center. You know, the type of call where you thrash around in a phone tree for a while, enter information that gets lost along the way, and then you get someone to help you in Sri Lanka. Her team has a mix of onshore and offshore workers.

She told me her manager was in trouble. He told his bosses the new chatbots would reduce 10 percent of contact center employees, but that's not what happened. Not even close. While there was a drop in the number of calls made to the center, the calls getting through were harder and took longer. So, he had to hire more people. Sally has an attitude about it:

> What happens when chatbots or virtual agents start taking customer calls? I'll tell you what happens [she laughs]. The calls that get through become really hard. You think a stupid bot searching through some lame database can handle the crazy conversations we do? I had this confused person the other day tell me all about how her sister-in-law somehow screwed up the account—way too much information. The bot, even with AI, would have no chance.

> These new bots take the easy ones we used to get credit for. We don't get paid enough for what we must deal with. They pay us rates that were OK for handling Level 1 simple stuff like an address change, but we are in Level 3 land all day. Longer calls and much harder. We deserve more.

Sally is giving us today's view of chatbots. In short, they aren't ready to be unleashed upon customers, despite that misconception among businesses. She also reveals that automation is not distributing its value fairly. It is taking some of their work away, but she is not benefiting. She anxiously hints at what is around the corner:

> Our cubicles get more turnover than a "hot sheets" motel [laughing]. The average employment time for one of us is about nine months. Here's the thing: an

agent is not any good until four months in. With thousands of employees and these retention rates, that is frightening math. You just can't keep a solid team up to speed. But these new bots will be a trained agent on the first day and with AI they will train themselves.

If you have a position like Sally, recognize that chatbots will get better and replace most of you, despite how bad they are today. Christina McAllister is a senior analyst at Forrester covering contact center technology and processes. She believes the GenAI effect will be dramatic and describes the agent transition this way, "Agents will be moved more to the background, to help identify and deal with lapses in communication and discord in "agentic communication".

To survive, you will first need fluency with digital devices and software apps. Health aides must enter data and manipulate apps in an electronic medical records system. Retail clerks will use smartphones to process returned items, and manufacturing workers will use augmented reality to control robotic factory systems. Digital skills will remain important, but your best bet is to lean into your communication skills and a quality less talked about: personality.

Your personality is remarkable, unique, and difficult to replicate in a machine. We started to speak to each other 150,000 years ago. Over time we developed unique verbal and nonverbal skills to understand and persuade each other. Early humans who couldn't distinguish a friend from a foe during an encounter didn't last long. Next-generation bots will likely get a lot of answers right, certainly more than they do now, but they won't possess personality characteristics such as sarcasm, humor, intuition, and instinct.

Here's why that's important. For any business, future success will depend on creating positive customer feelings. They will differentiate less on product and service features, and more on the personality and feelings surrounding them. So, it's important to be yourself and let your personality shine. You could say it this way: a company's future margins will be driven by customer memories, and you are the force that will create them.

The best way to distinguish yourself from a robot is to understand the customer's perspective and care about them. Leil Lowndes' book *How to Talk to Anyone* contains familiar platitudes, but the critical one for you is, "Be a great listener."[45] When a customer feels you are interested in them, concerned about their long layover in Dallas, or sympathetic to their trials with a defective washing machine, they will likely give you a positive review or buy something. They can spot a phony a mile away. Keep a book like Lowndes' close at hand and glance through it once a week.

Of course, you can enhance communication skills with ongoing education and online tools. Commercial platforms like Coursera, Udemy, and Alison offer free online courses on communication skills, such as "Communication Strategies for a Virtual Age" and "Improving Communication Skills." However, workers hoping to learn these skills may respond better to online communities like Reddit, which provide a supportive environment for practicing communication skills with feedback. One reason given is that subreddit groups bring together workers in similar jobs who can share experiences and advice.

Diversify with Side Hustles and Personal Brands

The pandemic was a disaster for small businesses. More than half a million failed because they lacked the cash reserves or borrowing power of the corporate chains. Millions of workers bid goodbye to dreams and vibrant lifestyles. Visit any town and you will still see vacant store windows. Imagine the effort and vision that went into the grand opening, where now only a "For Rent" sign remains. Workers left positions in restaurants and bars that shut down, concert venues that no one would attend, or movie theaters too scary to enter. Some had no choice but to work for larger chains or take side gigs.

Yet millions turned their passions into side hustles and businesses. Automation certainly helped. Low-cost, low-code, do-it-yourself apps allowed entrepreneurs to establish a comprehensive brand in a few days. Any idiot could build a digital storefront. Tattoo artists, key lime bakeries, pet care, help for lost dark souls, commissioned poetry, the occult, lifestyle journalists, metal sculptures, fitness gurus, and shops for alternative clothing—and that's just a small sample.

Without question, a percentage of our youth have rejected the traditional forty-hour week required by traditional work. They created new businesses that have several things in common: they are first and foremost digital; they leverage social media; and they form loose connections with suppliers and partners.

Here is an interesting example. Pandr Design is a boutique studio based in Southern California. It builds custom art pieces to boost the social media presence of a business. Imagine huge murals, painted walls of buildings, and large, amazing art displays. The winning formula: two women, lots of talent, constructive fear, and Instagram. California native and burrito lover Roxy Prima runs the company with her colleague Phoebe Cornog.

Roxy is a trained graphic designer working for a firm with many stale stereotypes. Her job bored her. Despite several promotions as a designer, she failed to break through the senior management glass ceiling that so many women encounter. She knew her talent and drive were more than they could deal with. Then one day it all boiled over. She ditched her office job that had her locked behind a computer screen all day and turned to a pencil and a big paint brush. During my conversation with her, she talked about the reasons behind her transition:

> I wanted to prove just two things: One, you could make money doing what you loved. I wanted to combat the "starving artist" stereotype. Two, that women could build a successful business. Sometimes we go into Home Depot to buy gallons of paint. The contractors don't know what to make of us. But Instagram was the key. Once I got to a thousand followers, the ability to network just grew. We could post our best work and gain traction quickly. And best of all, we don't work with clients we don't like. No question, there is just a lot less stigma to going out on your own now. It is much more acceptable to not have a traditional job. Even my parents are now believers.

Starting a business is never easy, and it can be especially challenging for women. But by learning from the journey of Pandr Design, you can increase your chances of success. Pandr chose Instagram, the right social media platform for their target audience. These two women moved from stint to stint in their work, creating bursts of exciting moments that they posted. They narrowed their target audience and gave them high-quality content. They were visible, authentic, confident, and passionate, sharing their art without fear. They focused on marketing their brand and talent and replaced loyalty to a company with a passion for what they do.

Fight for Your Work-From-Home Status, If You Value It

During the pandemic, millions of middle positions switched to work-from-home (WFH) and have remained so. If this was you, you likely improved your work-life balance. Sadly, your bosses now want you back in the office, so you must fight to stay home. Cathy feels pressured to return to the office:

> [My boss] Callie, yeah that's his name, doesn't care a whit if working from home makes my life happier and easier. His goal is to protect the beloved office culture that lets him escape the kids for forty hours a week. No, I really don't miss the office [she laughs]. The guys kept the office temperature just right for a meat locker. My NorthFace is always a good look. Loud talkers that should have worked as longshoremen on the docks, nosy cubicle mates, that chronic interrupter: "Hey! Can I get your eyes on this for a sec?"

Entitled coworkers leave their dirty coffee mug in the break room. I also long for the strong odors from the shared microwave, that Middle Eastern or Indian delicacy or late afternoon scorched popcorn. I've been in my own environment for two years and these distractions are hard to take. They want to take this away and stick me in a cube in a marginally ventilated room. Not happening.

Companies still struggle with the right WFH policy. Some want you back in the office but worry about employees leaving. Most have moved to some form of hybrid status. Others hint that they will pay workers less if they want to retain their work-from-home lifestyle.

Women like Cathy worry they will lose the "invisible work" points that provide a second dimension of value. These are important things we take for granted: comforting a colleague, remembering birthdays, coordinating lunch, circulating a goodbye card, or showing a new employee how to make coffee. According to sociologist Rebecca Erickson, women do more of these tasks than men. Their job description does not mention this emotional labor, and the biweekly paycheck does not compensate for it. First, fight for your work-life balance.

You should focus on doing a good job, and that's it. Automation can help. Bots can take over routine and repetitive tasks that will free time for more strategic and creative work. As a result, you will become more valuable and have more leverage, which may be required. Less enlightened employers will see little difference between a home and contract worker, except that the latter is 15 to 20 percent cheaper. You may be the first to get terminated in uncertain times. Firing Hal, whom you haven't seen in nine months, is always easier than firing Bill, who is in your carpool. Bots can also remind you and draft personalized emails to stay connected with colleagues and clients and offset those lost "invisible work points."

Automation to support remote work keeps advancing. Become an expert. Agility with shared documents and advancing collaboration platforms will make you stand out. They now record and summarize meetings. Help figure out the best use of this content, for example.

Keeping your WFH status will be a fight. Advocate for policies that support WFH with your manager, HR department, or employee resource group. For example, employees should get the necessary equipment and software to work from home effectively and be paid the same as their in-office counterparts. Suggest productivity tracking tools to make your case. Storm clouds are forming, but by taking these steps, you can hold onto your improved lifestyle.

Constructive Ambition Is Essential for Success

Invisible robots will disrupt middle jobs that require people to work in cubicles, including those in finance, accounting, procurement, and contact centers. Today, the US workforce employs approximately twenty-one million cubicle dwellers.[46] Forrester's 2019 Future of Work model predicted that 80 percent of those jobs would be eliminated by 2029. Although the report raised a few eyebrows at the time, its predictions now seem spot on. Software robots are already replacing these jobs today, even before the latest GenAI kicks in.

If you are a middle worker, there's a lot you can do. To begin with, don't fight the invisible robots. They are coming for you and you can't win. You can do one of three things: have a bad attitude and resist the new automation, remain neutral and stay out of the way, or be that volunteer who jumps to the front of the line to help. Only the volunteer will succeed.

Here's my favorite example of the third option. As I was walking from my hotel to a tech conference venue, someone shouted at me from a bench, "Are you Craig Le Clair?" My first reaction from watching too many movies was, "Who wants to know?" He then told me his tale:

> You helped me a lot, and I wanted to let you know how. I was a newbie, just six months on the job. I printed out one of your research reports on the way to a meeting on the upcoming automation project. Within fifteen minutes all conversation had died. People were looking at their devices, so I just started talking and reading from the headings of your report and somehow, I made sense to managers in the room. They made me the project lead. That was four promotions ago. I'm now a senior director.

His actions are, basically, a template for what you have to do. Listen for clues on the latest automation project being discussed around the workplace and be prepared to act. A good term for this is "constructive ambition," a willingness to embrace and overcome obstacles and take chances, an intrinsic desire to learn, grow, and master something.

According to Angela Duckworth, you will need one other quality: grit. In her book *Grit: The Power of Passion and Perseverance*, Duckworth defines grit as a combination of passion and perseverance. It's less about talent or luck but rather a strong interest in something and determination to stick with it even when faced with challenges. She found that gritty individuals are more likely to achieve their goals.[47]

You Are Not Alone

Millions of workers have shared experiences like those of Enzo, Jim, Sally, Stephen, Rich, Roxy, and Cathy. They worked tirelessly, dreaming of a better future for themselves and their children. They envisioned owning a suburban home, driving a late-model car, and retiring comfortably. They believed that hard work would pay off and that their children would have access to a better education and achieve more than they had. These ambitions are less achievable than when Ronald Reagan was president. Automation has made these goals more difficult but not impossible. There is reason for discouragement but also hope (see Figure 4-2).

What We Can Do	Why It Matters
Recognize that the human footprint you leave in your wake will keep robots out of your cubicle.	The only way to compete with invisible robots is to leave evidence of your humanity everywhere.
Look for careers that emerge due to automation. Develop constructive ambition to grab them.	While your skills may be challenged, automation will open jobs for millions of middle workers.
Take control of your career path. Management will not know how to advise you.	Despite best intentions, management and advisors don't know automation's likely effect.
Forget "learn to code" but refine your general digital and prompt engineering skills	AI operators will need to ask AI tools the right questions and be digitally fluent.
Become an AI operator. Look for new jobs that will emerge because of automation.	While your skills may be challenged, automation will open millions of possible positions for you.
Recognize human skills are your critical asset. Enhance them with education and online tools.	You need to emphasize your communication skills and try for positions seeking them.

Middle managers, prepare for "the great flattening." Train to be automation creators.	Automation creators will thrive as automation reduces middle management jobs.
Do not fall for the misconception that the gig economy has the answer for you.	The current gig economy model will not work for many middle positions that require full benefits.
Diversify by initiating a side hustle and creating a personal brand.	You can no longer depend on a single employer to ensure your family's well-being.

Figure 4-2: Middle workers have the biggest challenge.

CHAPTER 5

ROBOT COWORKERS WILL BENEFIT HUMAN-TOUCH WORKERS

RAMONE WILLIAMS IS THE OWNER of Tastee Spoon, a Caribbean Jamaican restaurant and food truck serving authentic, unique cuisine in Atlanta. If she can afford a robot restaurant worker, almost anyone can.[48] But her journey of employing a robot started out as a joke. She was at home and got yet another text from one of her staff saying they weren't coming in, and she said, "Damn! I wish I had a robot." And then she thought, *Why not?* After conducting an extensive Google search, she eventually found RichTech Robotics. When she contacted them, she said, "Don't send me any BS, just a link where the robot is being used, not just as a novelty."

Although their references were solid, most of their robots were employed in fancy Las Vegas joints. She laughed and told them, "You don't get dressed up to come to my place." So, she bought one, and a month later it was in the restaurant. Well, *almost.* The kitchen staff and the front store people were outraged and expressed their concerns about their jobs. So, for a while she hid it in her office.

"I decided the robot might get sprayed with hot cooking oil if it went back to the kitchen, so we had it go to the server's window, grab a meal, and deliver it to a table."

The robot was named Irie Milley and handed customers water and greeted them at the door with, "*Waa gwaan*," a Jamaican greeting. He played the "One Love" Bob Marley tune, and strolled through the restaurant, and when blocked by someone, said, "Hey, don't get too fascinated with me, I'm just trying to do my job," or, "Are you trying to get me fired?"

Ramone was surprised by how it affected the business and her people. "Waitstaff can walk two or three miles a day, but not ours, not with Irie Milly around. No more going back and forth to the window to see if something is ready to be served. But here's the surprise: the wait staff makes more in tips. They cover more tables and spend more time getting to know the customer.

"It's become a thing. We have customers coming from all over and now operate with less staff. An autistic child visits Tastee Spoon to see Irie once a week. Others are upset when the robot doesn't bring them something or when they leave with no chance for a hug."

Ramone's decision was driven more by a quality-of-life issue than cost reduction. A bad employee can create a stressful environment, contributing to constant worry. You are always letting someone go or hiring someone, and this consumes a lot of valuable time. It is the worst part of running a restaurant. But Irie is there at 10:29 every day. Staff shortages and turnover is why robots in restaurants will increase and not just for the big, scale chains but for small stores like Ramone's. Whether they will use physical robots, like Irie, will depend on how well they work with other humans.

The service sector is the largest of our four worker groups, with more than 2.5 billion worldwide. While middle-worker counterparts face severe challenges due to automation, human-touch workers are poised to reap the most benefits. However, this impact will vary across different occupations, and certain actions are necessary to capitalize on these opportunities.

The purpose of this chapter is to direct you to the more promising careers and steer you away from those that are not. A key view is that automation will make one area better for you than another. Skeptical colleagues have challenged me: do you think a typical human-touch worker will read this? Fred Goff is the founder of JobCase, a career and support social platform for human-touch workers. He would tag this as a snobbish and condescending question. He would say his people solve problems and can benefit from support and guidance.

To better understand the impact of automation on human-touch workers, we first examine job categories, identifying the winners and losers. Automation for some occupations will create opportunity and provide improved worker experience. Finally, we explore six specific changes in skills and attitudes that will aid in navigating the changing employment landscape.

Automation in the Form of Physical Robots Is Inevitable

Investment in physical automation or robotics is accelerating. In a 2022 study, Forrester identified over five thousand startups targeting human-touch automation. Areas include robots for food preparation, retail and warehouse robotics, android security officers, robot janitors, and delivery drones.

Why the acceleration? For one, technologies continue to advance, making them more versatile, intelligent, and capable of helping human-touch workers. AI has allowed them to learn, adapt, and make decisions autonomously. They can better navigate obstacles, manipulate objects, and interact with humans.

The pandemic also made us more accepting of them. Humans seemed more dangerous than robots. Consider that before COVID, sneezing wouldn't raise many eyebrows. You would often receive a "God bless you." Even post-pandemic, you are more likely to see your friends dive for cover. In an unexpected turn, we became more comfortable with robots.

The hotel industry makes this point well. The next time you order room service, you may receive a text on your phone rather than a loud disruptive knock on your door, or so Savioke's CEO Steve Cousins hopes. This San Jose company develops service robots, and according to Cousins, the perspective of hotels has transformed. Before the pandemic, the hospitality industry believed a human touch was essential to ensure optimal customer experience. But that has all changed. As Steve likes to say, "Robots don't sneeze." He points out other advantages: they sidestep the awkward tipping ritual, cut delivery times, and are not embarrassed to encounter an unclothed guest. They are also upskilling. Why not vacuum on your way up to a room or deliver coffee from Starbucks in the lobby?

Automation Will Improve Your Job Safety

The pandemic has had a lingering effect on the corporate psychology surrounding risk and safety. This means business now has a commercial incentive to make jobs healthier and safer. You will benefit from this if you seek employers that have invested in automation.

The surge of automation in the meat and poultry industry is one example. It was already a challenge to recruit workers willing to stand in several feet of blood and take an electric saw to a freshly killed animal. And two things happened: technology underlying robots improved and became less expensive. For example, years ago, robots could go to an exact location and pick up a sausage. However, the sausage had to be placed exactly right. Now, they can "see" the item, orient themselves, and pick it up. A robot can pick up two hundred sausages a minute off a conveyor belt. A single employee can only pick up thirty to forty sausages per minute.

COVID-19 also made our food supply chain vulnerable. Thousands of workers were sickened, leading to the shutdown of many plants. Colin Usher, research scientist at Atlanta-based Georgia Tech Research Institute (GTRI), sums up the new attitude well: "The idea is simple; people are the vector for introducing disease and should be removed or mitigated as much as we can."[49]

The rise of robots in many physical environments is accelerating. They are used to cut animal carcasses, encourage exercise, disinfect facilities, and wash windows in high-rise buildings. In Ireland, drones are used to monitor sheep. This is all positive for you. Evaluate your next career move based on the degree of automation an employer has applied. Understand its specific effect on the job.

Another example is the warehouse, which employs far more workers. For decades, warehouse pickers faced a brutal reality. They snaked their way through vast warehouses, often clocking up to 10 miles a day on foot, pushing heavy carts overflowing with goods. This wasn't just tiring, it was dangerous. Workers, desperate to save time, would overload carts, leading to accidents and injuries. A worker would swing a cart around a corner and break someone's ankle. Some warehouses even referred to these loaded carts with the grim nickname "widow makers."

Robots are taking over many physically demanding warehouse tasks, reducing daily walking distances to a more manageable 2-3 miles. As one worker shared, "Now, when I get home, I actually have the energy to play with my kids or cook dinner." Safety has improved. Kait Peterson is the Senior Director of Locus Robotics. She reports that some of her warehouse customers have had an 80% decrease in injuries. This translates to fewer workers getting hurt and missing time with loved ones.

The rise of robots in many physical environments is accelerating and will improve the workplace. They are being used to cut animal carcasses, encourage exercise, disinfect facilities, and wash windows in high rise buildings. In Ireland, drones are used to monitor sheep.

Physical automation is positive for you. As you consider your next career move, take control by researching an employer's automation plans. Don't hesitate to ask about them in the interview. It shows initiative and positions you as someone who embraces positive change. But go beyond a general question. Dig deeper to understand how automation will affect the role you're interviewing for.

The Job Winners

At one point during the pandemic, the entire country stepped out to clap for many of you who risked your lives to prepare our food, provide basic health care services, and work in infected stores. They sent thousands of you to the 2021 Super Bowl. Yet after the brief curtain call, diminished respect returned. It took an epic worldwide crisis to raise our respect for you, and only a vaccine to reverse it. Heroes were again perceived as burger flippers.

Forget flipping burgers! Here's a glimpse into job categories with more potential. These roles offer diverse career paths and the promise of respect and growth. Advancing automation makes these jobs safer, cleaner, less tiring, and higher paid. Look for jobs that share these characteristics. Take an active role in shaping your future—explore these options and discover how your skills can thrive in the evolving workplace.

Security: A Future-Proof Career for Human-Touch Workers

Those being pushed into service jobs struggle to make ends meet while also yearning for self-respect. A security guard, or security officer (SO), patrols and protects businesses and personal property from theft, vandalism, and other illegal activities. This job category employs more than 1 million US workers who earn between $16,000 and $24,000 a year.[50] The turnover rate is 130 percent a year, which is among the highest. Armed guards, bank guards, bodyguards, mall security staff, bouncers, security officers, and transportation security screeners guarding airport exits fall into this category.

If you have limited education and experience, these jobs are available, but they do not count on them to boost self-esteem. Olek Sumoski, who was referred to in the introduction, came to this country from central Europe.[51] It's fair to say he has developed an attitude:

> It's a thankless job, sadly. If you work at a store, customers might accuse you of following them, when really, you're just walking around because you're bored. I'm sure they're making robots who can do my job. But I worry about the armed positions; humans decide today if they should put a bad guy in his place. Robots are ones and zeros, black and white. How will they decide?

He tells us this: these aren't great jobs. Given an option, people will try to do something else. It is my hope and opinion that future security professionals will challenge this antiquated viewpoint. Want to see what that future looks like? Visit Wes Swanson, CEO of NOVVA, a data center company that provides large corporations with high-end ultra-secure computer facilities.

They operate on 1.5 million square feet of space on a one hundred–acre campus, on the shoulder of the majestic Wasatch Mountain Range, in West Jordan, Utah. He began the operations with drones that fly in thirty-mile-per-hour winds to monitor hot and cold spots on the outside perimeter of the data center.

At five thousand feet elevation, things get cold. However, these drones have a climate-controlled house. When they return from a mission, the door to their shed opens so they can enter their warm charging station. It's a sound investment: $150,000 covers costs for three years and includes a backup drone. He would require three to four people to complete the same set of tasks and yet, they wouldn't be as good. You can't record 4K videos from someone's eyes.

The robot dogs roam around the data center. They read the LED panels on the servers to monitor temperature and other indicators. Wes admits to being a Sci-fi buff,

> The neatest thing is the way the dogs greet guests. They charge up to them pretty fast to confirm their identity via facial recognition. If the guest is not in the database, the dog signals central security. He doesn't attack them—in fact aggression of any kind is not a programmed function. Our next project is to get the dogs to talk to the outside drones to coordinate incidents. A lot of my people (workers) like these gadgets, but over time, human security positions will be reduced. This is obvious to anyone familiar with this technology.

Ralph Parks agrees. He is head of security at Woven Planet, a spinoff of Toyota Research Institute (TRI). His security team has three robots, one for each building floor. He named them Moe, Larry, and Curley, with Moe, of course, placed on the executive floor to be with the other bosses.

The robots check on Wi-Fi, read LEDs on servers, identify monitors with screens left on, determine if the building is too hot or cold, and even disinfect for COVID. Parks uses robots as extensions to traditional security officers:

We are in California, right. Lots of weird things happen. We want robots to be our first line of defense. Sometimes a homeless person with mental issues will bang on the door. He might think you are from outer space and pull a knife. The robot should be the first on the scene.

Parks has learned important lessons: you must inform people about what robots do. This must not be done half-heartedly. The explanation should be exact, and the company must work with legal regarding privacy issues:

People do stupid things (chuckle). They don't realize the robots are recording after hours. I've seen people do embarrassing things you wouldn't believe and don't want to hear, and not realize they were on camera. I'd call and say, "Hey dude, you're on video."

Here's what you can do. Recognize that robot dogs, drones, and human replicants offer opportunities going forward. First, they take some positions, but the remaining security tasks get better: less boring screen monitoring and less walking around. For the next five years, these security robots will still be short of a full deck of cards. They will continue to fall into mall fountains and occasionally run over small children.[52] Moreover, a few people find them creepy. They are far from perfect and need your support. Best of all, required tasks to work with the robots are more skilled and improve self-esteem and paychecks.

But there is work to do. You must learn to use specialized software and hardware to monitor the performance of robots, identify problems early, and prevent downtime. You will improve your skills to keep the robots running smoothly with routine maintenance, such as cleaning, lubrication, and inspection, and troubleshooting and repairing problems. You can work with others to develop and implement safety protocols. These tasks are all better than Olek's daily life.

Take a Fresh Look at Janitorial Jobs: They Will Get Better

Robot janitors are now "acceptable" in our physical automation timeline shown in Chapter 3's Figure 3-1. This means they are short of the adoption window but close. Companies spent significant dollars to keep facilities safe as the pandemic took over the world. In 2019, Walmart purchased 3,600 robot janitors based on the BrainOS® AI software platform. The robot floor scrubbers are equipped with sensors to clean spaces around customers. Hundreds of janitors were let go, although their names were passed on to the robots. Defending this move, Walmart executives argued that it was too hard to find workers and they would prefer for their people to help customers anyway.

Janitorial jobs will get better for you with the use of robots. How could they not? The robot takes over repetitive and physically demanding tasks, reducing sweeping, mopping, and vacuuming. They have other advantages that give your job more substance: they can detect and treat atmospheric issues and generate a disinfection report. With a mobile device interface, you can control its work. You will be free for more complex tasks, such as disinfecting high-touch surfaces and responding to emergencies. They reduce the risk of injury and sickness and can clean hazardous areas such as hospital rooms.

Higher wages should result from increased productivity and greater skills required to manage the automation. They automate many time-consuming janitorial tasks, so you can clean larger areas in less time. As a result of this human-machine combination, your employer should have lower overall costs per area cleaned, and you should reap some of the benefits. You will be required to learn new skills to monitor and operate the robots from a device. The upskilling places you in a more skilled category of worker.

In short, this is a good area for upskilling and growth.

Automation Can't Solve the Aging Crisis, but You Can

Japan is the oldest country in the world. Diapers for adults now outsell those for babies. By 2025, the country will record a shortage of 380,000 eldercare workers, though other studies have stated that the figure would be closer to 500,000.[53] The Japanese government is funding robot development to solve this inevitable issue and views it as a commercially exciting area. Similar government-led investment enabled Japan to assume a leadership position in the machine tool industry in the 1980s, and it worked.

About five hundred Japanese eldercare homes already use robots to conduct games and exercise routines and guide scripted dialogues.[54] The government certainly helped: Panasonic developed Resyone, a bed that splits in two, with half transforming into a wheelchair. Cyberdyne's Hybrid Assistive Limb is a powered exoskeleton suit that helps caregivers lift people. Those who require assistance when walking can grab hold of Tree, made by Reif, which crawls along the ground and offers balance and support to those who need it. Robots can now talk for hours to entertain the elderly and act as their companion. All these initiatives had government backing.

Japan is mastering automation to solve the eldercare problem and create an export market. But here's the obvious question—wouldn't it be easier to import care workers from less-developed neighboring countries with high unemployment and struggling populations, like Indonesia and the Philippines?

Many would say yes. However, it's just not a route that Japan would take. For over two hundred years leading up to the late nineteenth century, Japan's borders were closed to foreigners, a policy called *Sakoku*. It is more open today, but the legacy mindset still lingers. Thus, Japan prefers technology to solve its eldercare problem over people.

The takeaway is that robotics innovation is poised to help us care for the elderly. Japan is just an example, but it will take a decade to put a dent in societal needs. As good as the engineers in Japan are, and despite the targeted government investment, we need people to solve this problem. Japan is taking the correct long-term view, but for the foreseeable future, it will not work.

Here's what you can do.

Recognize the world population is quickly aging. In many developed countries, there will be more grandparents than grandchildren. There will be a shortage of care and companion workers, creating an opportunity, if not a necessity, for automation and you. Automation will not solve this worker shortage, specifically when it comes to the dearth of companions, CNAs, nurses, and other human-touch workers. Robot helpers are expensive and may be too rough for fragile-skinned elders. At least currently, patients are more comfortable with humans than robots. For the next ten years, humans will do more to solve this worker shortage than automation. This will lead to higher wages and better job opportunities. The world needs you and should pay a fair price.

The Job Losers

Automation will affect human-touch jobs differently. In some cases, it may lead to a decline in job opportunities or make your role more routine. For other positions, automation might have a neutral impact, making it harder to advance in your career. These job categories highlight the potential downsides of automation for human-touch workers. However, this doesn't mean success is impossible. It means you may need to work strategically. While automation might not directly benefit these roles, you can still carve out a successful path through hard work, skill development, and a proactive approach.

Ignore Warehouse and Fulfillment Jobs If You Can

The pandemic forced us to develop our digital skills, and online shopping boomed. Amazon, now claims a staggering 50 percent of all US goods purchased. As e-commerce surged, so did warehouse and fulfilment jobs. By mid-2023, Amazon employed a massive 1.5 million people, solidifying its position as the second-largest commercial employer after Walmart.

The online push resulted in a tremendous investment in warehouse automation, and not just Amazon. Robots in warehouses and the fulfillment supply chain are here today and will increase. Forrester's Future of Physical Automation Report had them fully accepted.

In short, robots will own the warehouse. As a result, warehouse and fulfillment jobs will not be your best bet going forward. Humans will do their best to stay out of the robot's way. They might be repaired by you, but they will be managed but orders coming from e-commerce or other automation. Amazon can tell you an item will be delivered the next morning because their e-commerce front end speaks directly to the floor robots. Humans will have a declining value for any warehouse or fulfillment supply chain job.

Let's peek into the warehouse. These jobs include delivery, various fulfillment, and warehouse roles, which are easy to get but brutal to retain. Amazon uses the soft-edged and respectful term "associate" for someone who may work seven to five shifts as a warehouse picker. Thankfully, this is not as pandering as Disney's term "cast member" for someone slinging hot dogs to tourists.

At Amazon, a picker works in a metal enclosure where a flat screen flashes images of products to put in bins, destined for another part of the warehouse. Everything is brought by robots at a quick pace and is monitored by machine intelligence. An employee must average 360 items an hour or one item every 6.7 seconds. This worker at Amazon is part of the fulfillment assembly line, which essentially translates to a human robot. As a result, there is pressure to keep working consistently with as few breaks as possible. Workers describe this entire system as pure hell and both mentally and physically debilitating.

The bottom line is warehouse automation is progressing at a rapid pace. As of 2022, there were approximately 1.5 million warehouse workers in the United States responsible for receiving and storing goods, picking and packing orders, and shipping products to customers. The potential for job displacement due to automation is high. Studies have projected that automation could displace up to 40 percent of these warehouse workers in the United States by 2030. The automated warehouse will need specialized skills such as robotics repair, programming, or data analytics, but far fewer workers will be needed. Your advice is simple: avoid the warehouse if you can.

Avoid Food Service If You Can

The day started like most. Ron, the manager, entered the fast-food franchise one hour before opening. He brewed the first pot of coffee and waited for the early shift. They transform the bleak space with uncomfortable seating into a customer-tolerable environment that encourages people to stay. His team has been unhappy of late. He had to cut back more hours, and Jim had another kid he couldn't afford to raise. Janet's landlord is now charging interest for her late rent. He pushed these thoughts aside and began to wonder where they were.

He grew nervous as the opening time approached and then anxious as he stared at his unanswered text messages. Ron was being "ghosted" by his workers. He called the regional supervisor who reported that workers were no-shows at many locations. It was certainly the moment he dreaded: the workers had finally had enough.

In the next decade, new jobs associated with food preparation will exceed 2,500,000, according to the US government. Many workers actively seek better opportunities, driven by a lack of adequate wages and benefits or a desire to escape demanding work environments. In a desperate attempt to retain staff, one McDonald's franchise resorted to offering iPhones to employees with a six-month commitment.

A waitress was working at this insanely popular breakfast spot. Her first table was an adorable old couple. The woman ordered the duck hash special, and he wanted two poached eggs on toast. So far, so good. But when the food arrived the guy went ballistic, merely because the waitress forgot to bring a tablespoon for his eggs, and according to him, everyone knows poached eggs are served with one. The waitress of ten years had never heard this rule.

> I apologize profusely and tell him I'll go grab him a spoon. "No!" he yells. "My breakfast is ruined now!" and then, this grown adult throws his plate of food at me and storms out. His wife gives me a sympathetic smile as she slinks out behind him, and I work the next eight hours with egg yolk stains all over me.

It's not only customers that lack respect for you but also your managers. The story starts with a regrettable email. Wayne Pankratz, a former executive at an Applebee's franchise, drafted it in March 2022. The tone of the email was upbeat: good news, gas prices are up; inflation is raging; our workers live paycheck to paycheck; they will be desperate for more hours; we can lower wages; the labor market will soon turn in our favor.

Wayne sent this email to several other executives but didn't realize he had copied one of his restaurant managers, twenty-three-year-old Jake Holcomb in Lawrence, Kansas. The email confirmed Jake's worst fears regarding how management viewed workers. He quit on the spot but only after printing out stacks of the email, which he placed on tables all over the restaurant. Before he stormed out, he declared all food for customers and employees free. We can list thousands of incidents across industries like airlines, retail, and hospitality, but food service seems to take the cake (pun intended). Here's a pertinent question: can we blame human-touch workers for seeking a better life?

Automation will not solve the respect problem but can help with worker safety. Jacob Brewer is the chief strategy officer for MISOROBOT, a food preparation startup. He feels worker safety is often neglected in the industry:

> Today everyone talks about rising labor costs and staffing issues, and I get it. The average fast-food employee is paid $5,400 [a] Month. Flippy, one of my MISO robots, only costs $3,000 a month all in. We call it Robot As A Service, or RaaS. The math works out well, but the real value is worker safety and toil. Tasks like flipping burgers, frying fish, and pouring hot liquids are dangerous and horrible jobs. Restaurant work is often the first job for many, with kids doing dangerous tasks.

While Flippy might help in the back-of-house operations, what about the front? Restaurant experts argue that meaningful automation of table and bar service is not viable due to the often chaotic state of most restaurants. They have a point. Unstructured layouts, unpredictable situations like spills or rowdy customers, and constantly rearranging tables can be a robot's worst enemy. Ramone's robots at Tastee Spoon, while increasing your table service capacity, likely won't significantly reduce your workload in the short term.

Here's what you can do.

If you must work in food service, take care of your mental health: low self-esteem, low pay, long hours, lots of pressure, and job insecurity have always made it essential. The hospitality and restaurant industry reports the third highest rate of heavy alcohol use (11.8 percent), illicit drug use (19.1 percent), and substance abuse disorder (16.9 percent). Clinical depression affects at least 10.3 percent of food industry workers.

The suicide rate in the industry is alarmingly high. The nonprofit Giving Kitchen has worked to reduce it for almost a decade. They commonly hear food service workers stating, "If I don't get help, I'm going to kill myself." Giving Kitchen's staff are trained in suicide prevention. If the cell phone vibrates and someone needs help, human-touch workers are ready.

Recognize that the robots will not rush in to help you. Many humans still want the traditional dining experience. A nice dinner isn't complete without a human manager to complain to and a server brimming with local lore and kitchen insights. Grabbing that QR code and viewing the menu on your phone may still be sensible, but many don't want it.

Practical Steps You Can Take for the Future of Work

The previous section identified jobs likely to thrive in the age of automation. These roles promise improved working conditions, greater safety, and expanded opportunities. This does not imply that individuals cannot succeed in any of the industries mentioned but rather emphasizes the importance of understanding how automation will impact each sector. Now, let's delve into six actionable steps to enhance your experience in your chosen field.

Emphasize Your Device Skills

At one point, there were ten million job openings in the US and about six million workers who could work but chose not to. Most of these openings were meant to employ human-touch workers. That's almost two job openings for every worker, which was an unprecedented disconnect. So, what's going on?

Three factors contribute to the shrinking pool of workers for these jobs: stricter border policies implemented during the pandemic limited the number of workers who traditionally filled these roles. Additionally, many workers laid off during the pandemic weren't idle—they honed their digital skills and found alternative income through online platforms, contributing to the rise of the gig economy. Finally, some former workers no longer find these service jobs appealing, suggesting a shift in job preferences. These combined factors create a challenging landscape for employers who previously relied on a readily available workforce for these positions.

Ben Wolf is the chairman and CEO of Sarcos Robotics and had an interesting take. While acknowledging that we have a worldwide human-touch worker shortage, he explained it was not for the reasons many think. "Millennials want a job that lets them work on their devices. That's what they do best. They are happy to give the universal salute to unsympathetic bosses and difficult working conditions."

The smartphone has become the great equalizer. Over six billion people, or roughly 85 percent of the world's population, own one. Forget education level; the future is bright for those who can leverage their smartphone skills. Apps will allow you to complete small tasks, such as transcribing audio, taking surveys, or tagging images, all on your device. Customer service jobs allow you to answer questions, resolve issues, or provide technical support from a device. They can help you run errands, deliver food, or assemble furniture. Businesses hire people to manage their social media accounts, post content, respond to comments, and engage with followers. Task-based marketplaces will allow workers to post their skills and services, and if you are clever with your tool, they will hire you. By using your smartphones effectively, you can improve job prospects and earn a better living.

Smartphones and modern UIs make work better for younger workers and those transitioning from other countries. Newer warehouse robots come with modern tablet interfaces. These are familiar and intuitive, allowing you to use your devise skills. Even better, some interfaces recognize a worker's native language and adjust automatically, creating a more comfortable work environment.

Even video gaming skills can be an asset in the workplace. Robotic surgery is already commonplace, where doctors use hand-eye coordination to guide a robotic arm to make an incision. Robot janitors, security androids, or drone deliveries will follow similar interfaces and become opportunities for human-touch workers.

Video gaming skills can also help improve your problem-solving skills. College students who played video games for at least three hours per week demonstrated superior multitasking and problem-solving abilities compared to their counterparts who did not.[55] Human-touch workers who cultivate video game and general device proficiency will gain a competitive edge in the job market and experience more fulfilling work experiences.

Build Tactical Automations to Make You More Efficient

Automation can help make your job better and higher paid. There are hundreds of tasks that can be automated. For example, a healthcare companion can configure a medication reminder app to ensure patients take their medications on time and correctly. Wearable devices can track vital signs and activity levels. If you are a delivery or limousine driver, a transportation scheduling app can arrange appointments.

The automation tools you need will get easier to use over time. Previously described low-code tools, soon to be enhanced with GenAI, are designed to build automation like these for regular workers. These apps can free up your time for companionship and more personalized care. Automation can also help you demonstrate your value to your employer and customers. This may involve tracking the time you save, the number of errors you reduce, or the improved quality of the service you provide.

Be Open to Radical Job Shifts

Dominique Ansel invented the cronut and has recently launched a new delight called the Cookie Shot. Five bakers happily continued to make this delicacy at the bakery inside Caesars Palace in Las Vegas until the robot baker arrived. I spoke to Aravind Durai, founder of RobChef, the company that created the robot, and he told the baker's story.[56]

> They were shocked how well the robot worked. It retrieved a cookie shot from a shelf, filled it with chilled vanilla milk and delivered it through a rotating door. The robot was a novelty, but the real boost in sales came from their work ethic. The bakers stopped work at ten PM, but the robot just kept on going and could serve the crush of midnight fans exiting "The Colosseum" from the Adele concert.

> Unsurprisingly, Cookie Shot sales boomed. Caesars and Ansel were thrilled but the bakers were not. They filed a grievance with their union. In response, the casino sent a training plan to equip the bakers with the knowledge required to configure, maintain, and enhance the robot.

> Durai explained that the bakers had been transitioned to robot technician roles, but it's far from ideal. "They trained hard to become a chef, and then gave it all up to do tech support for a robot, but it may be better than the alternative."

> Jobs for telegraph workers lasted for three generations, from the 1840s until the 1940s. Yours will not. The problem

you face is one day you are doing x, and the next day you will be asked to do y. The pace of automation requires a new way to roll with the punches. True for middle and digital elites, but more dramatic for you.

Build an Emotional Connection with Your Robot Helpers

While research is ongoing, emotional connections between human and robot coworkers could hold promise. Potential benefits include a more positive work environment, boosted motivation, and improved communication. We will explore in later chapters how robots can personalize training and offer helpful feedback. A well-managed emotional connection with a robot coworker could lead to a more positive and productive work experience.

It's important to remember that robots lack true emotional intelligence. Ethical considerations are also crucial to ensure robots don't manipulate human emotions. Canadian researchers turned the tables on the usual "roboethics" negative concerns that robots pose.[57] They built a simple robot and called it Hitchbot. This robot used GPS, a limited vocabulary, and a highly amicable personality to hitchhike across the world.

He did not look threatening. The arms and legs were pool noodles and the head was a clear cake container. The body was a simple white bucket. People could seamlessly move the robot as it sat on a child's car seat. Someone would pick up Hitchbot, plug it into the car's lighter for power, and start talking. They might take it home for dinner or out for coffee. Travelers' reactions were warm with interactions posted on social media. Everything seemed okay until Hitchbot reached Philadelphia, the city of brotherly love.

A group of thugs decapitated and smashed him to pieces. Hitchbot's last message was, "I still love humans."

Despite the bad ending, Hitchbot's experience shed light on our future relationship with robots. Today, many workplaces have begun to name their physical robots with human names. In other words, we can develop positive relationships with them. This, however, may not hold true in Philadelphia.

Look Beyond Wages: Focus on the Good and Bad of Automation

This chapter shines a light on the significant opportunity that awaits human-touch workers. Automation is poised to help them more than their middle counterparts. Many human-touch jobs will evolve, demanding greater skill, nuance, and agility—qualities that robots simply cannot replicate. From complex problem-solving to tasks requiring physical dexterity, your intelligence and physical abilities will remain highly sought-after in the automated workplace.

The key to success lies in evaluating jobs for their potential for upskilling and growth. Imagine security officers supervising and managing robotic teammates, or janitorial robots paving the way for higher-skilled cleaning positions. To seize these opportunities, take action by enrolling in robot maintenance and repair courses or workshops, volunteering for robot research projects or internships, pursuing careers as robot technicians or engineers, or exploring other robotics-related roles. By actively upskilling, you position yourself as a vital player in the future of automation. This translates to greater job security and opens doors to potentially higher salaries and a rewarding career path.

Beyond the roles we've discussed, countless career opportunities await human-touch workers. Regardless of your chosen path, the focus should shift beyond wages and benefits, which will naturally adapt to market demands. Instead, the key lies in understanding and actively pursuing the challenges and opportunities of automation's advancement (see Figure 5-1).

What You Can Do	Why It Matters
Security is a winning field for human-touch workers. Physical automation will reach adoption soon.	Good transition opportunities await security officers to monitor and maintain robots.
Take a fresh look at janitorial jobs: they will get better.	Robots will replace many "D" jobs (dirty, dull, dangerous). Fewer but better jobs emerge.
Recognize automation's impact on health care is long term: millions of workers are needed.	Expect higher pay and use automation to raise your value.
If you can, avoid warehouse and fulfillment jobs. Robots will own the warehouse.	There will be limited growth and few transition opportunities for fulfillment workers.
Look for employers that invest in automation to improve safety.	Automation and safety: robots will make your jobs safer.

Look for tasks that leverage your device skills. They will provide more options than ever before.	Mobile skills are needed in the gig economy and for traditional work.
Be open to radical job shifts. True for all work groups but physical automation is dramatic.	Several physical automation categories are approaching the adoption window.
Look beyond wages: focus on the good and bad of automation.	Markets will control your wages. Automation will drive your future work experience.
We can develop relationships with robots that help us in the workplace.	Eleven physical automation categories are advancing. We must learn to work with them.
*Time frames for physical automation are taken from Figure 3.2 in Chapter 3 and based on the Forrester 2023 Report: The Future of Physical Automation.	

Figure 5-1: Human-touch workers can get help from automation.

CHAPTER 6

A DIGITAL ELITE CLASS TAKES OVER

I MET PHIL AT A conference where he scheduled a time to brief me on his company. Their specialty is creating virtual agent software, the sometimes clunky chatbots that aim to replace the human agent in call centers. The briefing is more important to Phil than to me. His goal is to get me excited about his emerging company and influence me to write a positive review in the next report.

These briefings follow a similar pattern and have one thing in common: they are boring. A review of the binomial theorem in nineteenth-century France might be more interesting, but Phil's enthusiasm is contagious. His view of business casual dress is more refined than mine. You could slice cheese with the crease in his trousers and his Italian shoes cost more than my entire outfit. He sits down and slides his device on the table to let me know the clock is ticking. His PowerPoint deck fires up and he starts with how well the company is doing.

As a startup venture, they have few customers and little revenue, with profit a long way off. He boasts about their ability to raise money from investors and explains they are one of a kind, disruptive, loaded with talent, and on a valuable mission. Throughout my fifteen years as a technology analyst, I have met and been briefed by hundreds of Phils, who, like those in the nineteenth century who stumbled into the railroad business, have found their niche in the next big thing.

He exaggerates and does not go deep into any technical area, like many on the business side of the tech industry. He has no idea what a neural network is or how GenAI works, but is good at sprinkling these terms throughout a pitch, but even Phil admits this is a problem.

I have been in tech for twenty years and I've never seen a lower bar for truth than the conversation around AI. The marketing buzz is just insane and generates confusion about what it is. My PowerPoint slides paint a cool picture, and if a prospect challenges me about whether my AI claim is realistic, I just say, "Well, yeah that's true but this is only a PowerPoint slide." Maybe it is a hangover from the Trump era, where words do not matter as much as they used to.

As an analyst, it's hard to believe that hundreds of these dumb software products woke up one day with AI and are suddenly brilliant. What is more difficult to accept is the tech industry's blind eye to the impact of automation on workers. To Phil's credit, he admits his work will eliminate jobs.

Oh yeah, the jobs thing. Sure, our solution eliminates jobs, but I do not dwell on it too much. A lot of the software we install does stuff that people hate to do, like creating reports or updating some database, or answering dumb customer questions. They should go do better things, and if we don't automate their work someone else will anyway.

The digital elite have a troubling attitude. They are dangerously overconfident, with a lack of empathy for the effect automation on middle and human-touch workers. This chapter first defines the digital elite and the role automation plays in this expanding segment. Automation is a threat to everyone, including the digital elite. The second part outlines what you should do.

Automation Is Building a Digital Elite Class

The digital elite consists of hundreds of technology-oriented managers, executives, software developers, and tech entrepreneurs. They are also non-technical people who hold jobs at the top of the work pyramid. Knowledge workers like lawyers, executives, marketing specialists, and business leaders depend on technical innovation to advance their careers without writing a single line of code.

James Burnham proposed a similar class in his 1941 book, *The Managerial Revolution*. He described a new population of workers that had formed to manage the size and sophistication of the twentieth-century economy. In short, a new ruling class. Like the digital elite today, training, education, and technical qualifications distinguished them. In 1977, social scientists John and Barbara Ehrenreich coined the term professional managerial class (PMC), which became shorthand for white-collar and left-leaning liberals in the early twenty-first century.[58]

Digital elites are a similar breakout but viewed through the lens of automation. This provides a needed separation from middle and human-touch worker roles. Opportunities, challenges, and advice differ and will grow more distinct over time. I needed the digital elites category to make these points clear.

Trajectory and growth are other reasons for separation. Forrester's 2019 Future of Work Model introduced the term. The study found that automation will bring about both positive and negative consequences, creating new employment opportunities (dividends) while also leading to job displacement (deficits). The digital elite work category was predicted to grow substantially over the next ten years, outpacing all twelve work categories. The question is what direction they will take the winning lottery ticket.

Consider this example. A small group of digital elites at OpenAI decide on the filters used for output created by their cutting edge GenAI. These filters are critical: they prevent sexist and racist bias and misleading, inaccurate, harmful, or unethical content. Yet, the public has no idea who these wizards are, or the hundreds of decisions they make. Their ideas of ethics are built into the model with no public input, review, or transparency. If a book has been banned, you know who is responsible and understand his or her often distorted logic. A handful of near-invisible people control the technology that affects a good portion of the eight billion people on our planet.

Digital Scale Is the Breeding Ground

In the 1950s, Eisenhower appointed former General Motors CEO Charles Wilson to his cabinet as Secretary of Defense. Wilson famously said, "What's good for GM is good for the country."[59] And he was right. GM was not just a jobs engine; it was a *spectacular* jobs engine. At its peak forty years ago, GM employed 618,365 Americans, including 511,000 hourly workers. The automaker used to produce many of its parts in-house when America made things. They dramatically lifted employment and wages. Sadly, our most valuable companies today lack this trait. No one can say what is good for Apple is good for the country. It is fairer and more accurate to say, "What's good for Apple is good for Apple."

The rise of the digital elite is a defining feature of our time. In this section, we explore how digital transformation has led to the emergence of individuals who leverage technology and expertise to succeed in the workplace. The argument is as companies use digital scaling, land, capital, and labor will be balanced differently, with labor being less important. Fewer service and middle workers are needed. Digital elites are essential but in smaller numbers (see Figure 6-1).

The investment needed to start or expand a company is different as well. Who needs to open a factory to create a business? Many digital startups begin by simply opening a laptop, not a factory. Sweat equity has replaced traditional capital investment. Airbnb and Uber own no property or cars, lease their office space, and consume needed technology as cloud services. Capital, land, and, particularly, people aren't fundamental to their growth. Look at today's most valuable companies. Apple, Amazon, and Alphabet (Google) generate around $1 million per employee. The average for most companies is $230,000 per employee. The more automation, the more productive the employees are and fewer are needed.

Traditional businesses are trying to scale similarly, and it's only a matter of time. Forrester helps them select the best technology and practices to do so. Sales orders will flow through digital pipelines, untouched by humans. Instead of having one hundred sales executives, twenty marketing people, and tens of accounting, finance, customer service, and administration workers, you have a handful of digital elites to design, develop, and maintain the system.

Now, even new brick-and-mortar stores can open with few or no people. Forget awkward smiles from kids in their first jobs and "Do you want fries with that?" conversations. The first autonomous McDonald's opened in 2023 outside of Fort Worth. Orders are delivered on a conveyor belt accessed through a drive-up window. Cooks and packers toil inside the store and never have to speak to a customer, perfect for introverted cooks who like their customers rare (as in interaction, not cooking style).

Want a more high-tech example of digital scale? The Amazon Go store referenced earlier uses computer vision, facial recognition, sensors, and mobile apps to eliminate humans from the store. There are no cashiers or bored security guards. You enter the store with your Amazon Go app, pick up what you want, and leave; that's it. The store is managed via a dashboard from an office park. These two examples show where the digital scale will take us and you, the digital elite, are needed to come up with the new process and technology.

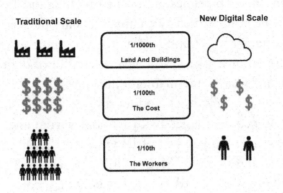

Figure 6-1: New forms of digital scale require fewer
middle workers and more digital elite.

Many of our most valuable digitally scaled companies
started in major tech centers. California is the biggest and
for decades provided opportunities for middle workers.
Solid middle jobs grew in aerospace and defense industries
and with companies like Hewlett Packard and Intel. Middle
workers built homes, bought cars, went to the beach on
weekends, and sent their kids to well-run public schools.
That was then. Today, California has high taxes and housing
costs and challenged schools. Regular people can no longer
afford to live there. In LA alone, sixteen thousand people
call their cars home. Digital scale has made the California
tech industry successful, but it no longer provides the same
opportunities for service or middle workers.

Political resistance to digitally scaled companies is growing. The justice department and many states are suing Google
for monopolistic behavior. Rising progressive star Zephyr

Teachout, in her 2021 book *Break Em Up*, argues that the only way to fight the ravages of digital scale is to stop mergers, break up the big corporations, and regulate the big tech companies as public utilities. Economist Jan Eeckhout, in his book *The Profit Paradox: How Thriving Firms Threaten The Future Of Work*, ends with a similar argument. He argues companies use technology to gain market power and suffocate the world of work, and we (the citizens) should share more directly in their success and govern their power. Despite political headwinds and anti-trust legislation, digital scale will continue. There is no stopping it.

From Phone Lines to Algorithms

Bill works in the high-stakes world of institutional brokerage, where big money fuels the trading of financial products. The past five years have witnessed a dramatic acceleration of volume across all sectors, driven by machine takeover. Now software looks for price gaps and automatically makes the trade, with human review if there is a problem. He used to spend over four hours a day on the phone, breaking only for the occasional ninety-minute lunch. Now he monitors activity from a dashboard.

He thinks nervously about the new talent the firm is hiring. They seem different from his current buddies, the forty-plus gang. His generation of traders were probably good high-school athletes and rough around the edges. In a crowd, they have presence. They could get the bartender's attention at a crowded venue to get their clients a drink. They aren't dumb. Strong in practical math, their faces tell a story of grit and hard-earned experience. They possess a keen understanding of people, though complex analysis might not be their forte. They came of age when most of the work was human to human, but those days are past.

Bill concedes these new guys seem intellectually more gifted. They were pruned from that small slice of high STEM achievers. They maybe went to math or programming camp as a child, and certainly were in advanced placement courses. They are great at math and statistics, with the latter being more important for AI going forward.

Their social skills are weaker, probably considered nerds in school. Conversations aren't their forte. They tend to focus on their screens, offering concise responses when prompted, but they don't need these human skills. Digital scale has made most of the transactions machine to machine. Their ability to replace humans with machines, further automate their jobs, and take automation to the next level matters most. They either write code or give instructions that can be coded into an algorithm.

Bill believes social skills matter less as businesses become more digital. The high-end of the digital elite spectrum will do well, but those who blend human and technical skills, like him, will not. If your job is a form of negotiation, either a complex sale or financial trade, you may be displaced, unless you can ramp up your STEM skills. Financial transactions are now done mostly by machines talking to each other rather than traders or advisors screaming into the phone. Personalized solicitations, recommendation engines, next-best action, and GenAI chatbots will replace many human-to-human tasks you now do, with professional social skills less important.

Here's What You Can Do

In the face of automation's relentless advance, digital elites must adopt specific strategies to safeguard their careers. First, the unpredictability of automation will require unprecedented career flexibility. You can also maintain a hybrid work presence to maintain a human component to your work, support mentoring, and innovation. Third, cultivate a strong professional network to expand opportunities and access critical information. Fourth, continuously acquire new skills to remain competitive in the evolving digital landscape.

Beyond practical measures, digital elites must cultivate empathy and appreciation for human-touch workers, recognizing their vital contributions to society. Additionally, they must acknowledge the role of collective taxation in funding infrastructure and education, which has laid the foundation for their success. By embracing these broader perspectives, digital elites can foster a more inclusive and equitable digital society.

You Sit on a Goldmine: Recognize Your Automation Power

Your future success hinges on your ability to unlock digital growth for companies, and here's why. Forrester surveys indicate that digital transformation remains a top corporate initiative, even after the pandemic. It's simple. Businesses that use automation to scale digitally will outperform those that don't. And with it, the levers of power and influence increase for you.

You can help them move to cloud-based solutions, subscription models, self-service automation, online consultations, and mobile apps. And you don't have to be in IT or have a technical background. These initiatives mostly fail from process and people issues, not technology. Figure out who is accountable for the automation strategy and where it sits in the company. The automation center of excellence or a chief digital officer is a good starting point.

Recognize that automation is your long-term opportunity. You will prosper as an enabler of automation. It's simple: every enterprise needs you. Enterprises Forrester speaks to are desperate to automate their operations. Corporate boardrooms are filled with consultants, extra spring in their steps, lecturing executives on how their competition plans to use AI and digital scale to put them out of business.

The pitch is simple: digital scale and autonomous operations are the only ways to deal with future "systemic risks." Automation can build resilience in operations to make a business operate like a self-driving car. Deloitte, for example, one of the top global consulting firms, reported record revenue of $64 billion for FY23. Most of this work is helping transform companies into digital- and automation-first enterprises.

For example, behind the scenes in the tech community, analysts who work with the insurance industry roll their eyes. The industry clings to outdated technology and conservative practices, even though most of their work revolves around information management, a field ripe for innovation. Hundreds of software programs work to onboard a new client, settle a claim, send a bill, create a policy, and handle exceptions. But most were built decades ago. Manual and paper-based workflows, Fax machines and real signatures are still common. It might have a chatbot or telematics system that charges insurance by the mile, but the main claims, billing, and administration systems probably run on software developed in the 1980s. An insurance executive recently said to me, "My last COBOL programmer just died of natural causes."

The point is not to beat up on our beloved insurance companies, but to make a simple point: every company needs what you have to offer. Insurance companies, maybe more than most, but they all need to get their digital act together. They will not prosper unless they can support an on-line business, employees who want to work at home, analytics that organize their supply chain, and a good mobile experience for customers.

Here is a simple way to think about your digital power. Imagine you're drowning in student loan debt with ramen noodles, your best friend. Yet, armed with a few digital skills you picked up playing Minecraft, you could make a small change to a website and thousands of online shoppers can find a new sparkling water product. The local grocery store clerk has no such digital reach. They might heroically move the new "hint of nothing in particular" La Croix to eye level but affect only a handful of confused shoppers. You can make a single tweak to a website, and suddenly thousands are sipping this mysterious beverage.

Digital skills and acumen give you an outsized power with a *Wizard of Oz* like aura. In other words, you move the levers behind the curtain that control the automation we rely on to deliver food to the door, communicate instantly, navigate, work from home, or run our businesses. The rest of us take this power for granted but don't know how anything works or what in God's name we would do if it was unplugged one day.

Ironically, once the curtain is pulled back and the LED lights on the computers dim, it would not be you, the digital elite, that would save us, but those who know how to feed, clothe, shelter, and aid people without automation. Heroes they would be. A massive cyberattack could be our next systemic risk and put this to the test.

Your Network Will Be Your Net Worth

A few years ago, I was in a bar at Penn Station late one Friday afternoon, waiting for my train back to Boston. Many of you have been there. Noisy, gritty, low ceilings. Like much of the mistake called Penn Station, it lacks charm and human connection. But on this day the atmosphere was celebratory. It was the end of another week and the packed room felt like a drink or two was well-earned. It was there I met a crafty old salesman named Harry. His blue eyes sparkled as he told me his story, how the Empire State Building had changed his life.

The Empire State Building is the most iconic landmark in a city full of them. It is no longer the tallest, but arguably the most famous building in the world. It has appeared in over ninety movies, launched the career of King Kong, and to this day, dominates the New York skyline.

As a sales guy, Harry was given a peculiar territory. It consisted of just one floor, the eighty-fourth, in the Empire State building. For thirty years his life revolved around that one floor. He commuted into Midtown to roam those corridors, make small talk in the elevator, support office workers, always careful not to slink into the floor below. His talent was building relationships, getting to know people, being genuinely interested in them, and helping them even when he received nothing in return.

He was an IBM salesman, and not a good one. From office to office, he went but could not make a sale, but he made friends, and then his fortunes turned when the IBM Selectric typewriter came out. It's hard to think of it as a disruptive technology with today's supercharged tech innovation, but when the internal "golf ball" replaced the individual typebars that swung up to strike a ribbon, many new features came with it. The ball could be changed to alter fonts, and an erase or type-over function was now in play. You may not find any of those details interesting, but the point is that suddenly, everyone wanted one. IBM Selectric typewriters and their descendants eventually captured 75 percent of the United States typewriter market and gave Harry a comfortable middle-class life.

Harry succeeded due to his ability to build and maintain relationships. For you to prosper in the age of automation, you must as well. You can understand customer needs better than any chatbot. You can ask probing questions and listen carefully to the answers. You can negotiate deals better than any chatbot. You can build rapport with colleagues and find creative solutions to problems. You can handle complex human interactions, where a customer or fellow employee needs to be educated about the product or service. An AI bot can list features, but you can explain how they connect and perform in aggregate.

Your challenge going forward is to build relationships without as many face-to-face interactions. The boondoggle express of years past is gone. Zoom, Microsoft Teams, and Webex have become second nature and now seem almost natural, so dismissing the optimism of the travel industry, business trips will decline. The lifestyle of optimizing loyalty programs, expense account dinners, and hotel room service will not return in the same way. The WFH reality of the pandemic period confirmed that chief financial officers, with their perennially raised eyebrows, had been right all along. A lot of corporate travel was questionable. And now it will not be approved.

Here's what this means for you. You will need to build strong relationships with your associates even without the round of golf or pub crawl after the conference. The basics of building relationships remain. Be supportive: offer help and advice when needed and celebrate a colleague's success. I've found that helping someone in their career with your network builds the best loyalty.

But reduced travel and face-to-face time means you need to be more intentional about the process. Without body language, facial expressions, and with limited time, you must overcommunicate. Host virtual social events such as happy hours or game nights. Breakout room features, available on most platforms, can create intimate follow-up sessions that make everyone feel special. Virtual meetings are super efficient so waste time with casual conversation, follow up with emails and texts, and care about what's going on in their lives. And although trying at times, stay on video.

Cultivate Workplace Experts

The future of work demands specific expertise. It has always been valuable, but now is critical to stay relevant and adapt to a modern workplace brimming with automation—with both its magic and chaos. Expert advice can clear away confusion and propel you towards becoming an expert yourself. Digital elites, more than other segments, must build a portfolio of experts.

Finding the right expert in the chaos of automation is your first challenge. Cultivate experts who have tackled recent automation challenges and seek out rising stars. Don't assume the 50-year veteran holds all the answers. The 29-year-old who just cracked a critical automation hurdle last week might be more valuable. There are many who act like experts. Don't be fooled! Back-office workers comfortable with Excel pivot tables might inflate their title to "data scientist." They are not.

Clarity over complexity is a key indicator. Clear, concise explanations are a hallmark of knowledge. Genuine experts avoid jargon and acronyms that only serve to confuse. They can adjust their communication style to your understanding. Jargon is a red flag to weed out a fake expert. Muddled words, jargon and acronyms often reflect muddled thinking that does not understand the problem. The real expert is not frustrated by your lack of understanding and can adjust to your level to explain things. And GenAI can do that as well and can be helpful here. Use them to validate information received from experts.

Yet once an expert is found, many people hesitate to reach out to them. They fear appearing uninformed or are anxious about wasting the expert's time. Put these fears away. Experts often relish the opportunity to showcase their knowledge and help others. At Forrester, we have hundreds of analysts like me, but often one area of technology will get hot, and everyone wants to talk with the analysts writing about it. Take GenAI for example—it's the "hot topic" currently. When Robotic Process Automation was hot in 2019, I was the go-to person and would talk to anyone that would listen.

There are a few tips that can help. First, respect their time and do your homework. Respect goes a long way, but they appreciate diligent pre-work even more. Don't approach an expert without reviewing available resources. If someone approached me to speak about an area I cover, but had not read my previous research, my enthusiasm to help would be lower.

Second, focus on learning, not just getting answers. Shift your focus from seeking a quick solution to satisfy deadlines or appease your boss, to mastering a CT approach. The goal is to understand the problem, its key variables, how they interact, not just have a solution handed to you. Finally, express your gratitude for their time. A heartfelt email or a small token of appreciation, like a bottle of wine, shows you value their expertise.

The Office Still Matters: Build a Hybrid Presence That Works

The post-pandemic work transition has been difficult, complicated, and not the same for all industries. By Forrester estimates, 51 percent of firms have adopted a hybrid model,[60] meaning millions of you will not return completely to the office. Major corporations will reduce their office footprints and draft new policies led by our most innovative companies like Alphabet (Google), Apple, and Salesforce. In a touch of irony, Zoom ordered all employees back to the office: it made a good August 2023 headline, but you must read the details. It only applied to workers within fifty miles of an office and only for two days a week.

For the most part, you love flexibility. You were so accustomed to "being there" in that office every day, you failed to notice the better alternative: not being there. You now love saving commute time and expense. The average commute time to New York City was claimed to be thirty-seven minutes in a recent study, which seems low. This must have included the homeless, who could leave their refrigerator cartons and walk a few blocks to pass out leaflets to tourists. During a low point in my career, I had a commute to New York, but unfortunately it was from Boston. I left Monday morning and returned Thursday evening, exhausted. It was useless to complain. My New Yorker colleagues thought I was an amateur, sitting in some aisle seat on a thirty-five-minute flight to LaGuardia.

Their nightmare commutes had defined my friends' lives for decades: subway problems, train signal malfunctions, track fires, packed buses, and tunnel congestion with debris falling from ceilings all peppered their stories. But surprisingly, every commute story started the same way: "You know, it's not that bad, I drive to the station in Jersey, hop on the train, take the short ferry, a quick bus ride uptown, and a short walk and I'm there. I can do it in ninety minutes some days."

For many, those days will not return, or if they do, they will be only a couple of times a week. And you are probably WFH-ready. You have your office backgrounds the way you want them, upgraded the art on the walls, and adjusted lighting and Zoom filters to remove that washed-out or baggy-eye look. Disasters trying to learn five or six different collaboration platforms are over. You are finally fluent with important controls and protocols. Chats only go out to those they are intended for. You know to stay mute except when you address the group.

Remote work has increased productivity and well-being, particularly for isolated tasks but less for innovation, a potential problem for the digital elite. At home it is difficult to collaborate and share ideas, engage in informal conversations, and brainstorm.[61] Let's face it: the virtual world is no substitute for face-to-face meetings. Apple points out that its greatest innovations came during in-office collaboration, with small teams working furiously. John Lennon and Paul McCartney composed early hits nose-to-nose with guitars touching or banging away at the same piano.

Here is an often-repeated example. During the 1960s, Lockheed Martin was under pressure to complete the space shuttle but needed to reduce its weight by two thousand pounds. Engineers spent week after week trying to slim down the bulky spacecraft. Several times a week, an HR manager would walk by their conference room, a cup of coffee in hand. He wondered what they were doing and finally poked his head in and asked. They explained the dilemma. He looked at the scale model and asked, "Why is it white?" They responded that space vehicles are always white, to which he replied, "Look, why don't you paint that giant fuel tank black?" They ran the numbers, and guess what? Painting it black reduced the weight by a ton.

Physical collaboration allows unexpected voices to chime in and random encounters to occur, making an office a breeding ground for innovation. Even tech-savvy digital elites recognize the value of the office. Jacob is a late-thirties development manager for a software company. He looks forward to having the group return to the office but is unsure whether that will ever happen.

> Software development is driven by release dates, often two or three big ones a year. You are always behind. Test loops reveal last minute bugs. Management fights to get new features squeezed in. The greatest productivity comes in the last few weeks before the release. This is best done in a supercharged physical location where we are all together. Programmers side by side, getting in sync. You need a party vibe, late nights, beer, piled up pizza boxes. This is where a lot of innovation happens.

Innovation is only one part of the WFH rubric cube. Many younger workers are loaded with debt, crammed in with Dad and Mom, or work from a cramped apartment. They would be happy to go into a cool office setting. Remote work makes professional development difficult: a career heart-to-heart is difficult through Zoom. Employees may miss an opportunity to speak with an executive in the break room, which could have led to a new project. These are a few concerns you may have but they may be secondary to social aspects. Jacob continues:

Virtual work is also a social wasteland, a problem for my young staff. Some have moved to New York, an unfamiliar city, for their first job. The traditional workplace is their hope to find friends and arrange social events. Instead of putting on that new killer outfit for work, they are trying to choose between yoga or sweatpants.

Cushman and Wakefield's study of WFH trends supported many of these points. There is no surprise that a giant commercial real estate broker expects current office vacancy rates to improve.[62] And maybe they are right, and you will be summoned back to the office.

Here's the bottom line: maintain a hybrid work presence, if practical. Even if you can be totally remote, avoid becoming too reliant on working from home. Beware of the long-term pitfalls described in this section. Take isolation, decreased productivity, and a loss of creativity seriously. You can develop a unique and memorable style of work. Remember, your personality needs to be that colossal footprint of Godzilla that scares automation away and keeps it in its place.

Build Data Mastery

Recognize that automation will churn out mountains of data, painting a detailed picture of sales, productivity, and finance. They will expect you to be proficient in the software that makes sense of all the numbers. Mastery of dusty spreadsheets and clunky formulas will not be enough. In tomorrow's data-driven landscape, you must unlock insights hidden within the numbers. Those who can translate raw data into actionable stories will win.

And you can, with the right skills. Mastering data visualization tools like Microsoft Power BI or Tableau (now under Salesforce) is no longer nice to have but essential for many digital elites. Use these tools to transform data into captivating visuals that showcase your analytical prowess. Basic PowerPoint or Google Slides with one data chart after another will fall short. Advanced features that show smooth transitions, strategic data visualization, and engaging storytelling techniques will grab and hold attention. Consider Canva or other online design studio tools to craft professional-looking visuals.

But your challenge doesn't stop there. Collaboration skills will be assumed, so be ready to share, comment, and iterate your data insights with your team, leaving the "email back-and-forth" as a relic of pre-pandemic times. Never underestimate the power of visually stunning graphics to tell a story.

Tools like GenAI become your allies, helping you weave data from spreadsheets, databases, and AI-powered predictions into clear narratives. Remember, advanced Excel skills are still valuable. But to truly stand out, embrace the future of data analysis. Become a storyteller with numbers.

And here's how to do it. Understand the significance of "prompt engineering" as a set of skills you will need for the tasks mentioned above. AI models will help with these goals but only if you ask them nicely. You must know how to create clear, concise, and informative questions to make them effective. That's what prompt engineering skills help you do. Many courses are available to develop these skills, but the elite need to go well beyond this. You must actively assume the role of data managers, curating the information GenAI needs to support your work effectively. You can spearhead efforts that provide GenAI with the documentation to needed for success. You can help design checks and balances to validate the model's output.

Digital elite will be under pressure to do more with less. Mastering LLMs and adjacent data skills will be essential to succeed. Those that do and embed them into their work streams will outperform you. Donning their metaphorical Superman capes, many have already darted into the phone booth for a quick change. According to Forrester Research, an estimated 6.9 million knowledge workers in the United States will be using Microsoft 365 Copilot by the end of 2024. This represents approximately 8 percent of the total knowledge worker population in the US, and that is just one AI toolset.

Here's the main point: to stay ahead of your peers, data management skills must become an integral part of your professional repertoire. Realize you are in an automation race with your peers; They will develop skills to create content, do research and gather information, generate code for a new automation, or analyze data for a report. They will manage documents, spreadsheets, and presentations. Therefore, developing expertise in data collection, organization, and curation is essential.

Beyond Data Mastery: You Need to Tell Stories

One key skill to combat automation's disruption? Storytelling. Look no further than the Bible's Good Samaritan parable.

This timeless story challenges prejudice and compels action through empathy. Similarly, personal narratives shared in media are shifting attitudes towards LGBTQ+ communities. In the face of automation, storytelling's power to connect and inspire will be crucial.

Imagine explaining a complex idea to a colleague and seeing their eyes light up with understanding. Now picture captivating a client with a compelling narrative that seals the deal. Storytelling isn't just for helping your toddlers drift into sleep—it's a powerful tool that can make you more valuable at work.

I have seen too many dry presentations overloaded with bullet points, the audience on their devices within five minutes. Try to explain things visually with infographics or diagrams. Humor can break the ice and make complex topics more relatable. Most importantly, weave in human examples—stories of success, challenges conquered, or lessons learned. Forget drowning your customer in reliability data. Transport them to a blissful beach scene. Imagine them, cool drink in hand, completely worry-free—because your service ensures 99.9% reliability.

Research reveals a fascinating link between storytelling and human achievement.[63] Groups with skilled storytellers experience greater cooperation, higher levels of procreation, and a stronger sense of community, leading to increased acts of service from peers. In essence, storytelling fosters connection, understanding, and action—all essential ingredients for workplace success.

Keep Learning, Be Curious: Don't Let AI Do Your Thinking for You

If you got this far, you might think all things are terrific for you. Not so fast. The super elite, like machine learning and data science experts, are safe and in demand. Various estimates forecast jobs well into the millions for those with analytics skills.[64] But how about other elite jobs subject to advancing automation?

Robots help doctors and anesthesiologists perform common surgeries or tasks. News agencies will use AI bots instead of people to gather and synthesize information from websites. Law firms have replaced many paralegals and associates with e-discovery and research robots. ChatGPT recently passed the bar exam. It didn't have a perfect score, but will you need that $600-an-hour lawyer? Financial analysts are being replaced by software that finds patterns in financial data. In short, digital elites are vulnerable to advances in automation like everyone else.

AI is reshaping the job market, automating tasks and potentially shifting positions held by digital elites. However, full-fledged AI leadership roles are likely to remain rare for the foreseeable future. In a move that would make yet another forgettable sci-fi thriller, an AI-powered virtual humanoid robot, has already been appointed CEO of Fujian NetDragon Websoft, a subsidiary of a Chinese video gaming company. Announced in 2022, Tang Yu, is probably the world's first robot CEO, and this was before GenAI.

Tang Yu is personified as a woman and seems to be working out. In 2024, she won the "China's Best Virtual Employee of the Year' "award at China's Digital Human

Industry Forum (the title of which raises some concerns itself). Interestingly, she required assistance to physically accept the award.

This appointment garnered the expected media coverage, but despite arguments that AI will make more objective decisions than humans, they are not ready to take senior-level positions. These involve nuance, ethical considerations, and unforeseen circumstances that AI is not trained for. Yet companies will experiment. Innovative tech companies might appoint an AI "leader" to showcase their cutting-edge technology. A financial startup might create an AI figurehead to highlight innovation in algorithmic trading, but CEOs are safe for a while.

No, the challenge for digital elites will be the proliferation of AI Agents that operate at the director and VP levels. As a reminder, AI agents are software trained to make decisions, and interact with data or other systems autonomously. The tech titans and hundreds of startups have raced to announce GenAI-based platforms to build them, with Microsoft's Co-pilot the best known.

Forrester listed AI Agents as one of the top ten emerging technologies for 2025. These include consumer-facing agents, like customer self-service chatbots, and consumer-owned agents, like digital doubles for online shopping, and employee support agents or digital coworkers. Digital Elites will be challenged by the latter that do creative work, provide data analysis, plan scenarios, investigate fraud, and prepare reports. These digital coworkers will be disruptive.

Let's delve into the world of second-tier elites like programmers, system administrators, and IT operations roles. Many will slip into the uneasy middle or even the human-touch segment. Here's why: technology such as GenAI or low-code development platforms aim to turn every working soul into a creator of software applications. These tools allow regular workers to build applications without knowing a programming language.

These capabilities are advancing rapidly and eventually the tech vendors will get it right. And to help, every generation of new workers has better digital skills. These trends mean that current programming jobs may be eliminated or severely commoditized. Thousands with general programming skills may find themselves slipping into the uneasy middle.

Forrester analysts Diego Lo Giudice and Mike Gualtieri coined the term "Turing bot" in 2020. The most popular task TuringBots automate is code generation from developer comments and well prompted requirements and design artifacts. He predicted 10 percent of software developers' effort would be done by the Turing bots. At the time, just three years ago, many called that notion ridiculous. With recent GenAI developments, Lo Giudice now predicts Turing bots will take over 30 percent of the effort. He points out it's not just writing software, but GenAI will help with ideas, design, and documentation. Developers will have a "Turing bot in the loop" during the entire software development lifecycle. Lo Giudice puts it this way:

> Turing Bots have landed on planet Earth. They are fast, friendly, and work while you sleep, and they combine multiple AI technologies to automate large swaths of the software development process.

The rise of cloud-based applications like Salesforce and ServiceNow also cuts technical jobs. When companies move software to the cloud, they share that version with many companies. The SaaS provider maintains it. These providers handle updates and maintenance but reduce the overall number of technical jobs required.

Software positions are one example, but a similar pattern will affect hundreds of jobs. It's a difficult transition. You became a digital elite by committing information to memory, probably with advanced degrees to prove it, but with GenAI, you may think you don't need to store or learn as much. You may think your accumulated skills are no longer necessary. It will be easy for you to offload your knowledge retention, memory, and task execution to Gemini or ChatGPT.

Think carefully before you go all in. You will probably change jobs every three to five years. You will need to emphasize creativity, problem-solving, and your ability to make connections. You need to remain sharp, and too much dependence on AI may dull your mind, a form of digital dementia. I'm not kidding. As early as 2011, Harvard researchers coined the term "the Google effect." Put simply, it is cognitive impairment from overdependence on technology.[65] GenAI will raise this to a new level.

Here's what you can do. Don't let AI diminish your desire to learn or your curiosity. Too much dependence will leave you more vulnerable to replacement. Position yourself to benefit from automation but keep it in its place.

Support Human-Touch Workers: The Unsung Heroes

The elite need human-touch workers more than ever. Affluent lifestyles need their physical agility for the hard tasks that living well requires. I was with a group of successful millennials, all riveted on their phones. A young woman was making an Amazon order for a single small box of Burt's Bees lip balm. This would be picked from a bin at the warehouse, loaded onto multiple vehicles for delivery, and arrive in two days. All done by human-touch workers, and the elite will need more of them.

And here's why. Physical automation (lifting, climbing, gathering, walking) is still expensive to build and maintain in a robot. You can train a child to put a bolt in a different spot in a second; the cost of programming this change into robots is still high. Don't take my word for it. Prasad Akella is CEO of an AI startup called Drishti, who has spent time on factory floors.[66] The simplest human things, like taking a pen out of your pocket, are hard. He points out that most humans still perform factory work. To make the point, he says:

> Take that smartphone out of your pocket. How many robots helped build that? I'll tell you. A big zero. Probably around one hundred humans, most likely in China, built that phone. And here's what bothers me. A lot of robot forecasts are out there but the people that do them have never been on a factory floor.

Here's what you need to consider. Physical automation to support service work will take time except in select areas, as argued in Chapter 5 For example, three of our twelve physical automation categories are still in the "unthinkable" and "creepy" stages well short of our adoption window. At the same time, the digital elites' numbers and wealth will grow. They will need more dog-walking services, personal organizers, shoppers, delivery, and nail salon services. Demand will grow faster than the pool of workers taking these jobs. Physical automation will help, but not enough. It is important to pay these workers more and respect their talents and help.

Empathy: Get Some Bread and Sop Up Some Gravy

Income inequality has been a talking point for progressives for years. Robert Reich, Bill Clinton's Secretary of Labor, is in his fourth decade warning about moral and economic dangers. Prominent academics like Thomas Piketty have in-depth models to explain how we got here. To Elizabeth Warren, big business has made their money on the backs of the poor: banks target them; big Pharma pushes opioids to them; and scams on Wall Street continue. She does not mince words, "Many CEOs improve profitability by laying off workers. They have shimmied to the top of the greasy pole get all the rewards, while everyone else gets left behind."[67]

Dramatic, perhaps, but our national wealth continues to expand, yet the number of pockets it flows does not. Our GDP in 2021 was a whopping $23 trillion, a good $6 trillion ahead of China but increasingly the money ends up in fewer hands.[68]

Conservatives do not deny our wealth gap but are more relaxed about it. Their argument is life is unfair and has always been, and the wealth gap was even bigger during the Gilded Age. The lord of the manor used peasants to farm the land; the tribal chief sent underlings into battle.

If we try to fix wealth inequality through government policy, it will hamper our economic and innovation progress. Look at world history: no country, civilization, or tribe has achieved true equality at any level of scale or affluence. Progressive economies, like Cuba have a high percentage of equals, but they are mostly poor. In all these attempts, government leaders remain a bit more equal, and shadow economies evolve to game the system. If someone gets wealthy, well, good for them. That's just the American way. Innovation results directly from our desire to be less equal, to be better than the other guy. And look what it has brought us: longer and better life spans.

A variety of factors put us in the current state, that have little to do with automation. Historical racial segregation, governmental policies, a stagnating minimum wage, outsourcing, globalization, and the declining power of labor unions, are well-researched topics, but automation will not help. Darrell West, in *The Future of Work: Robots, AI, and Automation*, concludes, as does this author, automation will exacerbate income inequality:

The United States and the world are at a major inflection point. The increasing adoption of digital technologies and frequent changes in business models have fueled a dramatic change in the U.S. Employment landscape and an increase in economic inequality. Inequality in turn threatens the political process by making it difficult to address underlying social and economic issues.

You, as a digital elite, are better equipped to prosper but here is something you can do to address this issue, and you can begin tomorrow: show empathy for the human-touch workers that support you and middle workers that will struggle. Empathy is in short supply and the digital elite are often given a pass. Empathy and high technical competence are just assumed to be opposite traits not found in the same person.

Wellesley College is an elite women's college a few miles from MIT. Organized social events have been commonplace for a hundred years. You might hear this joke from hopeful Wellesley students before an event: "Your odds are good, but the goods are odd." We accept that the technically astute will be the least patient with "users," the least concerned about how automation affects a human, and short on empathy. Does Elon Musk come to mind?

The digital elite can learn from John D. Rockefeller Jr., the only son of John D. Rockefeller, who founded Standard Oil. He came upon his empathy the hard way: he was the poster child for the 1914 Ludlow mining massacre, called by historians as the watershed moment in American labor relations. Twenty-one people, including miners' wives and children, were killed by a corporate-backed militia trying to break a strike. He was part-owner of the Ludlow coal mine and was blamed and vilified. Junior testified before Congress on the disaster and afterward was so depressed he stayed indoors, out of the public eye, for nearly two years.

Sometime later he went to live with the minors in Ludlow, to walk in their shoes. He said it was "the first time he sopped up gravy with bread." The immersion gave him empathy for the working man and set him on the philanthropic crusade that would define the remainder of his life. The digital elite should occasionally roll up their sleeves and walk in the shoes of the workers they depend on. It takes little effort to build empathy for those who will not obtain your level of success in the digital world.

Tip Your Hat to Government-Funded Innovation

It is a difficult balance. Tech industry innovation gives us lower prices, better health, and convenience. Treatment of automation's achievements would be a longer book than this one, if not a full library. It's important not to kill this progress, which is the envy of the world. Yet, it is important to be knowledgeable about the tech industry when forming your attitude toward policy and regulations that affect it. Much of this book tries to do that.

For example, here's a perspective few have. The tech industry's ability to scale digitally as described in the first part of this chapter, results directly from our tax dollars. This means two things: we might want something in return and, at a minimum, not be abused by advancing automation.

In terms of government research funding, the internet is a shining example, but it is not the only one.[69] Google developed its search algorithm with funding from the National Science Foundation.[70] The US Department of Defense funded GPS and Siri through nonprofit R&D centers.[71] Examples would form a book of its own. These technologies would not exist without the government's support and early purchases. The tools of digital scale—cloud platforms, mobile, social media, and AI—emerged from these public investments. Our tech companies owe their ability to scale digitally to our government's infrastructure investments.

I worked at Bolt Beranek and Newman (BBN) for eight years and had an up-close view. In the early 1990s the entire internet was run out of a small computer room in BBN's Cambridge, Massachusetts, facility, all funded by DoD's Advanced Research Projects Agency (ARPA). Good fortune allowed me to meet Ray Tomlinson, the inventor of email. He was not trying to make money or plan a new startup venture but wanted to do something interesting. And he did. Tomlinson figured out a way to send a message server-to-server across the internet but was stuck on one detail: the email address. The username or individual had to be separated from the hardware location or IP address. Perhaps with the help of some "refreshments," one evening while staring at the keyboard he noticed the seldom used @ sign and thought, "That might work."

This section and the Tomlinson story tell us two things: profit motive is not the only driver of innovation. Humans will experiment in pursuit of knowledge or fun. They always have. Secondly, recognize the contributions of taxpayers. Our most important steps forward have been aided by public funding. Understanding the tech industry DNA is important in forming your attitude toward policy and regulations. You have an important voice going forward, and an opportunity to use it. In summary, the digital elite have a great future but will also face challenges (see Figure 6-1).

What You Can Do	*Why It Matters*
Help companies build digital scale. If you can, you will become an essential part of their future.	Leading companies will be software-based and digitally scaled.
Recognize automation is your long-term opportunity. It will be a long slog.	Enterprises need people, process, and technical skills for digital transformation.
Plan for always-on, lifelong learning with three-to-five-year job changes.	Many of your jobs will be vulnerable to automation and may slip into the middle.
Don't expect GenAI to offload the things you need to learn.	Too much dependence on AI will leave you more vulnerable to replacement.
Recognize that automation puts pressure on your relationship and networking skills.	Automation will deemphasize what you know and perform your basic tasks.
A hybrid presence will protect your WFH lifestyle. Don't get too comfortable at home.	WFH will not expose your humanity due to a lack of face-to-face interaction.

Take good care of human-touch workers—you need them for health care, food, and support services.	Despite advances in physical robotics, service workers will continue to be in high demand.
Get some bread and sop up some gravy. You will benefit from automation. Not everyone will.	Greater empathy is needed for users and workers who struggle with automation's rapid advance.
Tip your hat to government-funded innovation. Support policy to control automation's advance.	Digital scale stems from our tax dollars. We deserve something in return.

Figure 6-2: The digital elite have the easiest path but with challenges.

CHAPTER 7

PIONEERS IN THE NEW WORK-LIFE MOVEMENT

WE ARE ALWAYS LEARNING FROM nature. Giant sequoias are the planet's largest and among the oldest trees. They depend on fire to reproduce, a negative event for most forest inhabitants. From the ashes the sequoia cones can release their seeds. As a result of the devastation, holes in the forest canopy allow sunlight to reach the young seedlings. Nature's disruption is the catalyst to jumpstart a new generation.

Likewise, humans often need a disaster to get them to address a problem. The pandemic's disruption gave life to deep-seated discontent with life more work- than people-centered. Health, both mental and physical, took priority over economic progress for the first time. During the lockdown, millions challenged long-accepted norms. Work-life balance, flexibility, and desire to work for purpose-led organizations, for example, became the priority for many.

People now have an open mind to change career direction to make a difference and be more fulfilled. Coming out of isolation and misery, many are now open to a mission-centered existence, where what people believe in and care about is more important than their net worth or material possessions. In summary, pioneers will pave the way for the future of work. Automation will provide the needed sunlight.

Joy Is the Whole Game Not Just the End Game

This shift in people's attitudes and behavior is evident. People want to play more and work less. Think about these trends: thirty-eight states now have laws broadly legalizing marijuana in some form. For the first time, marijuana smokers outnumber tobacco users.[72] Practicing meditation to reduce stress is now mainstream. In total, yoga, meditation, and mindfulness services are expected to grow to an $11 billion industry.[73]

The Entertainment Software Association reports that 61 percent of Americans play video games for at least one hour every week. But here is a surprise: three-quarters of players are adults, not teens, and 44 percent are female.[74] Incessant striving, lack of spiritual or moral substance, the can't-talk-now-text-me-later lifestyle has been losing steam. The pandemic with all its horror, gave momentum to this trend, and for many, a once-in-a-lifetime opportunity to reboot.

Millions now realize that in clearing that inbox day after day, we stayed too much on the surface, never digging deep enough into who we are or want to be. I treat this as a new and growing segment that deserves a name and a definition:

> *Work-life pioneers value possibilities, take risks, [and] focus energy and imagination to pursue a set of principles, [a] sense of purpose, and positive culture and community with less emphasis on income and wealth.*

Work-life pioneers want a more personal than work-centered approach to life. They may toil from home via Zoom, wearing sweatpants and a t-shirt. They will be middle workers reluctant to take human-touch worker positions or over-qualified, unemployed tech digital elite, marginalized by AI. They will be human-touch workers fed up with frontline work and unsympathetic bosses.

Work Attitudes Have Changed

Whatever position they hold, they share a common bond. Full-time employment and career paths no longer define them. In the past, a good career raised your marriage prospects and gave your parents something to talk about. A casual view toward full-time work might lead to discomfort, a loss of eye contact, and qualifications like, "My boy is still finding himself" or "My daughter is carefully exploring options." If you described yourself as a consultant, friends would politely assume you were unemployed and looking and refrain from further questions.

Hard-working families were idealized. Announcers laud the athlete who works hard off the field. Digital elites show off their epic work schedules. Even severely disabled welfare claimants must seek work: 2017 federal policy now requires that those receiving Medicaid, even though sick, meet work requirements to receive health benefits.[75]

These attitudes about work develop at an early age. Raymond did not want to be identified. He lost his job of ten years at a Midwestern bank due to automation. He told me work helped him grow up, become responsible, and show up on time. The threat of a poor job was his parents' ultimate weapon. His dad would say, "If you don't study in school, you'll be a trash collector or a ditch digger." His parents instilled in him a notion that has never left, that without regular work, he was less of a person.

We now have a crack in this parental foundation. Attitudes like those of Raymond's parents are changing. Non-traditional pursuits are more accepted. Rewards associated with tenure, or a traditional career path are less reliable. There has been too much downsizing, Wall Street–driven mergers, and acquisitions. Loyalty from the company to employee and the reverse has declined.

A worker's success depends less on an employer and more on reputation among peers, clients, colleagues, former mentors, and teachers. These networked resources are often deeper, more stable, and more committed than your managers and coworkers, who may be victims of tomorrow's merger. In short, working in different ways is more accepted, and in some ways, safer.

People also want to live more in the present than in the future. A pension at age sixty-five is no longer a goal if you could find one. Millennials will make up a strong percentage of work-life pioneers, mainly because they're now a third of the US workforce. They graduated into the Great Recession, entered a weak job market, and now face record student debt. They're ripe to select an alternate lifestyle.

And so are the Japanese. They even have a term for it, "herbivore," to describe men with no interest in getting married or finding full-time jobs.[76] The herbivores turn their backs on typical "masculine" and corporate roles. Japan now has 2,500,000 "freeters," or young people working only part-time. This trend isn't helping a declining birthrate, as many women refuse men who don't have steady jobs.

Baby boomers and late millennials are part of the trend as well. Ten thousand boomers retire each day, the population of a small city closing the door on decades of experience.[77] It is called the "silver tsunami," and we're not prepared. The departure of employees from companies and government can lead to the loss of valuable institutional memory and skills. Corporate amnesia is now a category in some risk-management frameworks.

Digital elite baby boomers have pursued contract work to supplement fixed incomes and enjoy social interactions, but only on their terms, thanks to the newly accepted WFH flexibility. Before addressing his tee shot at the golf club, one retiree quipped, "I still work 24/7. I shoot for seven months a year and try to work at least twenty-four hours a week."

Here is the bigger question: is retirement a concept that should retire? With longer life and more opportunities for work-life harmony, is retirement necessary in the twenty-first century? Jayne Burns of Mason, Ohio, would say it's not. You must keep moving and not sit around the house all day. The 101-year-old still works nine to five cutting fabric.

Igniting Passion: Work-Life Pioneer Journeys

Let's look at examples of successful people who entered the work-life segment. David White and Guy Kirkwood live on different continents but share an important direction. They both bucked the traditional work path and became work-life pioneers.

David worked in investments in New York but often felt alone. He was always a "momma's boy," so he moved back home to Atlanta. He continued in pension fund management and parlayed that into positions in the telecom sector. The dot-com bubble treated him well.

After the birth of his first child, White and his wife adopted a child from China and that changed his life. Holding the child, he realized that his professional work was not aligned with his internal drumbeat, which was children and their needs. He started to do research into foster care. One thing bothered him:

> I hated the fact that when a foster care kid moved, which might be four or five times, they packed their belongings in a garbage bag. Didn't they have enough indignities to deal with?

He started a campaign to get large luggage companies to donate suitcases and duffle bags. From that point, his life's purpose and internal drumbeat were in sync. He started Fostering Great Ideas, a "think tank" devoted to children's issues and foster care.

> The great number of children entering foster care is a reflection on the stresses from opioid addiction, that plagues all parts of society. Addictions can ruin the best-laid plans and throw a wrench into an otherwise functioning family unit. Coupled with the increasing loss of two-parent families over the last thirty years, undue stress will be with us for a long time. When will the pain end?

The David Whites of the world will accept a less reliable job and income to work from a farm in Vermont or Little Rock, Arkansas, and feel good about themselves.

I would label David Friedman a work-life pioneer also. His career started like many successful people: the MBA, a stint with Accenture, and then top positions with Razorfish, a leading digital agency, but at fifty-seven years old, he left it all.

David became obsessed with the harsh reality of autism unemployment, which he experienced firsthand. His son, bright and talented, faced invisible walls in the job market due to his neurodiversity. The stark statistic that 80 percent of autistic adults are unemployed, the highest rate for any disability group, became his call to action. Disillusioned with corporate life, David ditched the suit and embraced a new mission. Inspired by his autistic son's untapped potential, he founded AutonomyWorks, an outsourcing company that empowers hundreds of thousands of talented autistic individuals often overlooked by the workforce.

The movie *Rainman* depicts a character with off-the-charts intelligence. Given my limited knowledge of autism, I turned to David for clarification. Could one of these workers or his son create the next super algorithm? He said that is out there too, but the high-end cognitive work is a narrow set of the autism range. Mostly they just make good workers for the right task:

> The autistic maintain focus over time, are attentive to accuracy and details, and prefer to work on a small set of tasks consistently. They take a small set of things, and go deep, and want to be great at something. They also don't get bored, which is a problem with many young people today who get bored easily.

Like workers interviewed in previous chapters, David is worried about the invisible robots as well. He says they are closing in. His challenge is to find a task too complex for the bots to grab, and where an error is expensive. That will get more difficult over time.

The pandemic seems like a long time ago, but its role in creating work-life pioneers deserves a mention. Guy Kirkwood is fifty-one years old and lives outside London. As a young man, he spent four years as a Scots Guards Officer in the British Army, dealing with the "troubles" in Northern Ireland. He meandered through assorted tech jobs and hit on one that gave him some financial leeway. Yet he woke up one day in 2021 and decided to become a farmer.

Like everybody else in 2020 and 2021, Kirkwood spent a year and a half inside the house. And, like many, he found he could do his job better. Does it make sense to jump on a plane and eat horrible hotel food for a two-hour meeting? The ability to work from home gave him an almost supernatural ability to time travel. One day he had a morning meeting in Australia, a lunch in South Africa, and a tech event panel session in the American afternoon. All without leaving his living room.

His epiphany was being home with family is better than being on planes—and not just better, but terrific. He realized he loved his home and family and now put a high value on being with them. The quarterly grind to meet business goals suddenly felt hollow. This is part of why he left a good technology career, but the other part is harder to explain:

Farming connects you to where you are—the land. The French call it *"un sens du lieu,"* that sense of place. I think of it this way. When you fly over

England what stands out is the patchwork of fields and hedges, those clean horizontal and vertical lines. These were all once just forests, that slowly evolved over thousands of years with the vision and toil of long-gone generations. My eyes were first opened to a sense of home, and then to a sense of place, and then a desire to own my own land.

His technical background will not be wasted. He believes farming is ripe for change. The old farmer "plant doctor" will need to embrace data science and automation. Drones will capture aerial imagery for analysis; autonomous tractors will roam the landscape; and weeding robots will reduce pesticide usage.

You might think, "OK, nice examples, but in these cases previous work success gave them economic flexibility that is not available to most people." David's passion for children and Ken's desire to reconnect with the land were made possible by their financial security. We should examine whether this path is applicable to middle-class and human-touch workers, even though it may have worked for the digital elites above. We should also consider the impact of work-life pioneers on the overall happiness of a nation's population. To gain a broader perspective, let's delve into the French experience.

Is France the Laziest or Smartest Country?

Top executives at France's giant telecom company wanted to downsize the business by twenty-two thousand workers between 2006 and 2009. Not an easy task. Workers were state employees and hired for life, but executives were hired to find solutions, and a plan emerged. They resolved to make work life so unbearable that the workers would leave. The CEO told other company officials the employees would have to leave "by the window or the door."

Strategy may not have been their strong point, but execution was. At least thirty-five employees committed suicide, feeling trapped, betrayed, and anxious about finding new work. The former top executives of France Télécom were convicted of "institutional moral harassment," a first for a French company. The chief executive, Didier Lombard, spent four months in prison.

The captivating testimony shared in the aftermath of the suicides played a role in shaping France's current worker landscape. They have a statutory thirty-five-hour work week, with a move to thirty-two being debated. A "right to disconnect" law forbids employees from sending or replying to emails after work hours. The question is whether France is becoming the laziest or the smartest country, or both.

Let's look at the numbers. France is below average in terms of hours worked per year, ranking twenty-first out of thirty-seven OECD countries in terms of average annual hours worked.[78] Strong labor laws protect workers' rights to leisure time and overtime pay. A generous social safety net reduces the need for people to work long hours to make ends meet. Work and life are balanced. It's unfair; they already had the best wine and food.

France is the second-largest economy in the European Union, trailing only Germany, but is not setting growth records. They are not performing well by traditional measures. Taxes are insanely high. The digital elite complain they spend too much time figuring out ways to keep the government from taking their money. Many have given up and left.

The bureaucracy makes the simplest task infuriating. The level of innovation in business and technology is rated lower than in other countries of similar stature.

France is either a disaster or heaven, depending on who you talk to, but fortunately we have the "World Happiness Report" at least to argue about. The 2022 report looks at six factors to generate a happiness score.[79] The index is not without critics. How can the Nordic countries dominate when they lead in suicides and antidepressant consumption? Saudi Arabia receives high scores due to its high GNP per capita, but are women happy considering the restrictions placed on their freedom?

Given these and other concerns, the World Happiness Report is generally considered valid. France ranked twentieth in terms of happiness out of 150 countries in 2022, a good ranking. They worked fewer hours than the average country, and had more time for meals, recreation, and family activities. Ask an American who they are, and they will start the answer with their job or profession. In France, they do not consider their occupation their most important quality.

How to Become a Work-Life Pioneer

You don't have to move to France. You can still pursue this direction and we will tell you how in this section. Set your goals on joy as the end game, lower consumer spending, search for employers that align with your values, and seek employment in rapidly automating fields. While work-life balance formulas will vary greatly, these elements will always be present.

Seek Out Purpose-Led Organizations

The focus of workers is shifting to a company's triple bottom line, demanding social and environmental responsibility alongside financial performance. They may also be interested in certified B Corporations that obtain a minimum score for social and environmental performance.[80]

Work-life pioneers may avoid a corporation that owns coal production. Others may support the more conservative "freedom fighters" position on gun control. No single set of values defines them, but they will search for meaning in their work, a mission, something they can be passionate about. If they can't find a job they want, they'll try to create their own.

Attitudes have started to change. Outrage at companies that act in unethical ways is more common. Employees and customers are wielding their power: refusing to work for or buy from companies with tarnished reputations. And sadly, there are many.

Take the opioid crisis, a festering wound on our national soul. A trio of Sackler brothers immigrated to New York in the 1950s to become doctors but ended up building a pharmaceutical empire with OxyContin, an innovation in pain management. The Sackler family became billionaires, but their offspring were not satisfied. They pushed doctors to oversubscribe, a crime conducted on a massive scale, their greed leaving a trail of shattered lives. In a twelve-month span ending in September 2021, over eighty-seven thousand people died from opioid overdose and countless lives were ruined.

It's easy to become cynical: when a drug dealer on the street is arrested, they will likely do some time for a transaction that, no question, is illegal, but may affect only a small number of people. Sell a few "eight balls" or some ecstasy to a cruising millennial and it affects only a few. The small-time dealer is treated as a criminal, but for white-collar crimes you are lucky to see anyone punished.

The Sackler family paid no personal penalty for the opioid crisis. Honoré de Balzac, the French realist, summed it up well in the nineteenth century, "Laws are spider webs through which the big flies pass, and the little ones get caught." The opioid crisis and the financial fraud that led to the Great Recession are top examples. Virtually no one was punished.

Capitalism's engine of innovation churns out both wonders and pitfalls. Some industries and leaders prioritize progress, while others exploit it for personal gain. But you hold the power! By actively researching your potential workplace, you can choose an environment that fosters your happiness and aligns with your values.

Seek Employers That Will Take a Stand

Michael Jordan struck a groundbreaking endorsement deal with Nike for Air Jordan sneakers. This revolutionary partnership, the first to grant athletes a percentage of product sales, propelled Jordan to financial superstardom. Yet, he was criticized for weak positions on issues that affect minorities, and famously quipped, "Republicans buy a lot of sneakers too."

Staying silent on social issues is no longer an option for companies. A new generation of work-life pioneers demands action, not just paychecks. Companies that take a stand on issues they care about will win the war for talent. They'll attract passionate employees who are more likely to stay and contribute their best work.

Sticking with Nike, let's revisit Colin Kaepernick's protest. The NFL quarterback took a knee during the national anthem, sparking a firestorm across an already divided America. His act of defiance against racial injustice effectively ended his playing career. In a bold move, Nike stepped into the fray, featuring Kaepernick in a powerful ad campaign. With the tagline "Believe in something, even if it means sacrificing everything," Nike took a stand alongside Kaepernick, igniting a cultural conversation.

If you thought this was a huge risk for Nike, you underestimated them. Marketing analytics showed they would lose older customers, but they would gain millions of Generation Z, with their growing spending potential. They expect issues such as climate advocacy, environmental justice, and diversity will influence their buying decisions. Marketing research firms valued the media coverage at over $150 million.[81]

And it's not just progressive positions. Chick-fil-A's stand on Planned Parenthood appealed to conservative customers and workers. Businesses will be forced to take stands to appeal to a growing population of work-life pioneers, but they must get better at it. Budweiser took a strong LGBTQ position wildly out of sync with their pickup truck, hunting, and fishing customer base.

Lower Your Consumer Purchases

Product and marketing innovation since the 1950s has been amazing. Our autos, appliances, phones, and TVs are the envy of the world. Our possessions plotted our upward mobility like points on a graph. "Keeping up with the Joneses" became a common phrase in the 1970s and made sense at that time.

The Joneses lived on the same street, drove similar cars, and sent their kids to the same school. Their social status was similar. Word spread in the neighborhood when the new dishwasher arrived. But the Joneses next door no longer exist. Social media expanded the neighborhood to billions of lifestyles and by doing so, widened the sphere of observation and envy.

The extravagant consumption and lifestyles of the digital elite are now unavoidable. Mansions, upscale SUVs, private jets, and the Kardashian culture are in constant high gear. A few years ago, regular people wouldn't even know about the Hermes Shiny Niloticus Crocodile Birkin, a mid-priced purse for only $59,950. Shipping is free.

Even what is portrayed as middle-class on the average TV sitcom is a lifestyle barely achievable by middle workers. It takes a household income of $87,192 to live in Rego Park, Queens, home of Doug and Carrie Heffernan, the working-class couple on the *King of Queens* sitcom. This is well below the salary of a humble UPS delivery driver. Could the characters on *Friends*, few of whom had steady employment, afford those nice apartments in New York City?

A less material and work-centered lifestyle was a percolating trend, and then COVID gave it heat. We cut back on non-essential consumer purchases, stopped going out to eat or to be entertained, and to the surprise of many, we didn't miss them. FOMO, the fear of missing out, was replaced with JOMO, the joy of missing out. We took pleasure in gathering wood for the backyard fire pit or renovating that old chair decaying in the basement. For a moment, we ignored the ads on TV, pop ups on phones, and new consumer items. This lifestyle shift was fueled by a move out of urban areas, fewer possessions, and decluttering. It made us question why we were obsessed with working so much. The pandemic's lingering effects are debatable, but one takeaway is not: we can survive well without leaving home, going out to dinner, expensive travel excursions, new clothes and apparel, and a host of questionable consumer products.

Nick Mullins is a ninth-generation Appalachian and the fifth generation to work in the coal mines. Mullins believes that the constant pressure to consume is not helping.

> I've tried to protect our kids from the piped-in unreality of TV and social media where everything is done to excess. That was not the Appalachian way. But you can only do so much. It just seems we are barraged with marketing for a bunch of crap we don't need.

> We are told—go work your * off so you can buy all this stuff. If you do, you are being an American— contributing to society. This keeps the economy going and people working. But I realized this wasn't true. Most stuff was being made in China anyway. It's time for something different, to take advantage of both worlds: the self-sufficiency that allowed our ancestors to survive, and the new technological world where we use human advancement to become even more sustainable and perhaps—even happy.

No question, many of us have been on a treadmill, induced to work longer and longer hours, to support more consumer spending and falling behind in the process. If you want to become a work-life pioneer or achieve a better balance in life, resist the endless drumbeat of our consumer-driven economy. Most of us could get rid of half the stuff we own and not miss any of it, and we would still have more stuff than most of the world's inhabitants.

Automation Will Set You Free: Seek Out Industries That Get It

So far, we have seen how automation will accelerate the decline of the middle, be largely positive for human-touch workers and reward the digital elite. Automation can also support new attitudes and work/life balance for people across these segments. Maintenance of our standard of living will require increased productivity, and automation applied in non-random ways.

If you take a close look at the OECD work index numbers, the first thing that jumps out is Germany ranks number one in the fewest hours worked, 1,349 per year. Germans are known for hard work, so how can this be true? For one, they have strong workers' councils that keep employers in check. But here's the main point: they have high levels of automation and hence productivity. They work smartly.

Several Latin American economies also jump off the chart, including Mexico and Colombia. They are working their tails off (2,128 and 1,964 hours a year, respectively), far more than Japan, who work such insane hours they have a term, "karoshi," meaning death by working. Yet the data shows that on average Mexicans and Colombians work harder. Their factory, construction, food service, and farming tasks are manual and low-skilled. Automation does not provide them with smart ways to work. Low skill levels provide no leverage over employers. If a worker does not want to work long hours, they are easily replaced. They have little choice. Basic needs must be met.

Automation is the big story. The US, Germany, and Japan use it to work efficiently. Countries in Latin America are less automated. Manual steps that require physical and not cognitive skills dominate. In short, Mexico works hard but not in the smartest way. Corruption, crime, and poverty wreak havoc on the happiness index. It is easy to understand the desire to come to the US.

Embracing a More Fulfilling Work-Life Balance

The world of work is being transformed. Automation continues to advance, and at the same time our exploration and understanding of happiness deepens. We realize the traditional model of long hours and relentless productivity is no longer sustainable or desirable. Further, that the pursuit of happiness is not a luxury but a necessity for society to thrive. By embracing a work-life balance that prioritizes well-being, we can create a productive, joyful, and fulfilling world.

Put simply: we can work less and still achieve greater happiness. In fact, six of the top ten happiest countries in the world work the least. The key to achieving happiness going forward lies in working smarter, not harder. This means embracing automation to streamline tasks and free time for more meaningful pursuits. Automation, if targeted properly, is about creating new opportunities for creativity, innovation, and personal fulfillment.

Work-life pioneering doesn't have to mean a complete overhaul of your lifestyle, as in the case of David and Guy. It can be as simple as aligning yourself with companies that share your values or reducing your retail consumption to support purpose-driven endeavors. Even small changes, like dedicating more time to leisure activities, can make a significant difference in your overall well-being (see Figure 7-1).

What We Can Do	*Why It Matters*
Take a break from unnecessary consumption. We can work less and be happier.	Automation is part of the answer to work-life balance. Reduced consumption is required.
Companies will take a stand on social issues. Follow your moral compass.	More options will present themselves to combine your values with ways to support yourself.
Look for environments, geographies, and companies with evolved states of automation.	People will work fewer hours per year in highly automated industries and environments.
Don't let full-time employment and career paths define you. Stay open to the adjacent possible.	Attitudes are shifting to accept non-traditional work pursuits.

Figure 7-1: Pioneers will be a fast-growing segment.

PART III

Mental Health Challenges at Work

Chapter 2 told of anxious textile workers who destroyed the machines destined to replace them. That anxiety is still common today. Rumors of a software upgrade at work might cause a sinking sensation that your job is not secure, for example. That is only one form of workplace anxiety. I argue here there are many more with new ones on the way. We are just beginning to understand these more subtle forms of worry.

Research on how technology affects our mental state is ongoing, multi-disciplinary, and, in some cases, overwhelming. As a result, I've narrowed my focus to the mental effects of advancing automation in the workplace. Each chapter first highlights automation trends that create invasion, trust, and isolation effects. Advice is then proposed that may help. If successful, the three chapters will help us mitigate the negative mental effects of automation's advance in the workplace.

Why Pick These Three Areas

Previously we introduced the AI, Algorithmic, and Automation Incidents and Controversies (AIAAIC) repository. It identifies negative events associated with automation and helped build the scaffolding for this section.[82] Reported incidents represent automation's overreach, often launched without adequate testing or governance. It is the best database of random acts we have. In a perfect world, there would be no need for one.

AIAAIC reported negative effects from automation include biased decisions, privacy and ethics violations, car accidents, fraud, and disinformation. The list of potential impacts on our mental state is extensive but can be categorized into three primary areas: trust, invasion, and isolation. To group incidents into the three categories, AAIAC's risk labels and descriptions were used (see Figure 8-1).[83] Select stories are used in the chapters that follow to help illustrate a point and support constructive advice.

Some random acts will shake our feelings of trust in the workplace, trust a machine's direction, or believe what we are reading. Imagine thinking your boss was on a Zoom call, asking you to move $25 million. Turns out, in a recent incident, it was a deepfake impersonator and some convincing AI colleagues! A seasoned Hong Kong finance worker fell for this AI ruse.[84] The sad thing? We are just getting started with GenAI and this poor guy is not alone. This is just one example of deepfakes causing real headaches. So, maybe next time you're at work and your boss asks you to do something offbeat, double-check that their voice isn't coming from a computer.

Almost 40 percent of AIAAIC-reported incidents involved some aspect of trust. In a nutshell, if you struggle to trust automation, you can be forgiven. Negative outcomes from bias, self-driving automation, or a faulty algorithm dominate the repository. They can make life unsteady and less predictable, leading to stress or insecurity about an automation's outcome. Going forward, trust is the biggest issue.

Invasive automation was number one and accounted for 50 percent of AIAAIC reports. Evidence of uncomfortable forms of monitoring and surveillance continue to advance. In a 2024 court ruling, Meta, Facebook's parent company, will pay Texas $1.4 billion for illegally collecting and using users' biometric data without consent. Automation overloads us with information or targets vulnerable workers with data breaches or scams. Incidents of copyright infringement, security breaches, and perpetrated frauds are also a form of invasion.

Lastly, automation can make us more isolated at work or at home. Reported incidents that lead to isolation are fewer than trust or invasion (less than 11 percent). They include algorithms that create excessive device time or GenAI that spawns conspiracy misinformation. Mental state effects are subtle, more psychological than physical, and less traceable. Yet their outcomes of depression and anxiety may be the hardest to reverse.

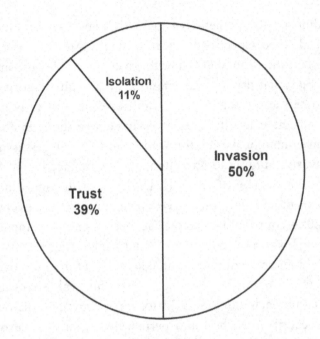

Figure 8-1: Random acts of automation will affect our mental state.

How technology affects our mental state is a daunting subject, and one beginning to get attention. Disciplines such as psychology, sociology, and neuroscience all must be considered. Leading books make a list of scary titles. *The Shallows: What the Internet Is Doing to Our Brains* by Nicholas Carr, for example, explores how the internet affects our ability to concentrate and think deeply and changes the way we read and process information. Or, *The Net Delusion: The Dark Side of Internet Freedom* by Evgeny Morozov examines the ways technology is used for good and evil by controlling and manipulating populations.

There is a constant theme in these books. For one, a complete view of technology's impact on our psychology and effective interventions will take time and more research. Secondly, humans and technology will work together in more sophisticated ways, and we need to design and deploy automations that respect their psychological and mental state. And third, mental state issues need more attention.

They are starting to do just that. The year 2021 will go on record as the year mental health issues came out of the closet. The world cheered the Olympic star Simone Biles when she shared her struggles with anxiety. Today, one in five kids have a debilitating mental issue before turning eighteen years old. One in ten are on antidepressants, and we are approaching forty-five thousand suicides a year. Project Healthy Minds, one of many organizations trying to help, reports that 615 million people live with mental health conditions, twice the population of the US. Depression and anxiety cost the global economy $1 trillion a year.[85] We need a greater focus on mental state issues in general and in the workplace.

CHAPTER 8

TRUST

FREQUENT FLYERS WILL CRINGE AT this incident. Turbulence caused a serving cart to bang into a passenger's knee during a routine flight. Due to our litigious tendencies and abundance of lawyers, the airline, of course, was sued. An attorney named Steven Schwartz was swamped but took the case. Fortunately, he had been playing with OpenAI's chatbot and found it useful to write the brief. In a few seconds, the bot returned six perfectly aligned and summarized legal cases. They were augmented with crisp "excerpts" from other rulings that even cited other precedents for support.

Unfortunately, it was all fabricated. Hardly a word was truthful. The judge's disposition was a few French fries short of a happy meal. He angrily pointed out that the briefs included six "bogus judicial decisions with fake quotes and internal citations." He sanctioned and fined the lawyer and sent him to ethics class.

Steven is not alone. We all risk being lulled into trusting technologies that we shouldn't. The lawyer, presumed to be licensed and to have passed the bar exam, defended himself, "Your honor, I was unaware of the possibility that ChatGPT's content could be false."[86] This example demonstrates a growing problem with automation: we risk trusting it prematurely.

Automation and Trust: The Twenty-First Century Labyrinth

As Joe Biden might say, here's the deal: we just don't know what to believe anymore. We cannot differentiate between a blog post crafted by a human and some fraudster bot. A heavily edited video showed Nancy Pelosi, the former Speaker of the US House of Representatives, slurring her words, appearing to have a drinking problem. Fake pornographic videos are also popular, unfortunately. Congresswoman Alexandra Ocasio-Cortez (AOC), the youngest woman to ever serve in Congress, was the subject of hundreds of deepfake videos and images. The 2024 World Economic Forum's Global Risks report paints a chilling picture: AI-powered disinformation, like a digital wildfire, has become the world's number one immediate threat, ranking ahead of climate change and economic turmoil.

GenAI Adds to Our Misinformation Woes

Misleading information has expanded with GenAI usage. Since the initiation of the AIAAIC repository index, GenAI comprised only 23 percent of reported incidents. This figure skyrocketed to 63% in 2023. This alarming trend indicates that GenAI is poised to become a primary source of misinformation.

Google, Microsoft, and hundreds of other companies have now invested billions of dollars in GenAI solutions. The excitement is unlike anything we've seen in years. ChatGPT was released to the public in November 2022 and by January 2023, it reached one hundred million monthly users, setting various records. With its uncanny ability to mimic human dialogue, ChatGPT sparked another "aha" moment reminiscent of finding answers at your fingertips with Google or navigating the world with ease on your iPhone or Google Maps that ended arguments about directions with your driving partner.

OpenAI created a simple prompt that lets mere mortals interact with AI for the first time. This innovative UI puts the user at the center of AI's power, tailoring interactions to individual needs and preferences. Previous innovations in how we interact with technology also created breakthroughs as well. Netscape's browser and crawling capabilities gave birth to the web in the 1990s. Apple's 2008 iPhone interface allowed apps to be downloaded and launched the sharing economy.

Here we are again: humans, for the first time, can exchange and develop ideas with AI. It is a major first step into the HCA period described in Chapter 2. Trish Wethman, chief customer officer of Marlette Holdings, tweeted this while attending a Forrester conference:

> It's a game changer. You better get on the bus or the Bot operating it will run you over. It is the Czempic (long-term weight management program) of the workplace. Everyone will use it, but no one will admit it, because they want others to think they did it the hard way.

GenAI is the latest shiny object in the tech industry, and like Blockchain, the metaverse, or previous AI periods of excitement, it will tarnish. Businesses will struggle with the cost of each word entered into a model. In the absence of skilled resources, progress will be slower than expected.

Lawyers will find growth areas in copyright and intellectual property disputes. Fear of job loss will rattle through all workers.

And the trust issue will loom large. GenAI has a unique talent: they produce perfect-sounding answers that can be incorrect. Imagine Bernie Madoff, the infamous con artist, purring sweet nothings in your ear disguised as financial advice. Media attention to hallucinations will force companies to tap the brakes.

Due to factors like these, we often overhype the immediate impact of new technologies while underestimating their long-term potential, as evidenced by the internet and smartphones. GenAI will likely follow a similar trajectory. In the short term, it may struggle to find a definitive role, but its long-term implications are profound. By democratizing intelligence, it could reshape the workplace, and make workers less tolerant of inequities like job displacement, government inefficiencies, and wealth disparity

GenAI marks a significant leap towards artificial general intelligence (AGI). While the Turing Test, designed to assess machine intelligence, may not be the ultimate measure, the advancements in GenAI like ChatGPT and Gemini are impressive[87]. These AI systems can hold conversations that are indistinguishable from those of a teenager. In fact, their factual knowledge and processing power far surpasses a thirteen-year-old's. If Alan Turing were looking over our shoulder today, witnessing these advancements, he'd just smile and agree that we are inching closer to intelligent machines.

Let us try to better understand them. While humans use letters to describe words, LLMs prefer numbers called "word vectors." The use of numbers in this way is not new.

Hipparchus, a Greek astronomer (190–120 BC), used latitude and longitude as coordinates to provide a unique location. We can see, for example, that New York is closer to Chicago than to London.[88] LLMs use numbers in a similar manner to understand that the word "tires" is used more often (is more probable) after the word "car" than after the word "makeup."

How do they know how likely these word associations are? Algorithms are trained on a trillion words from the general internet, archived books, and Wikipedia (which also explains why these are called large language models). By leveraging the existing word relationships, they make statistically based guesses on how often one word is used after another.

It is worth noting that they are good at this. They write coherently, revise text, compile software, generate creative ideas, and casually explain complex scientific principles. Twitter became flooded with screenshots of complex scenarios that ChatGPT was requested to untangle. It took the system only a few seconds, for example, to advise how to extract a peanut butter sandwich from a VCR and provide elaborate instructions in the style of the King James Bible. But what does that mean for us? In short order, we will have meaningful conversations with machines.

Remember that GenAI platforms existed before the ChatGPT explosion, and we can learn from them. Stable Diffusion was a mid-2022 startup and popular for two reasons: in addition to offering its services for free, it had virtually no content filters. Underground artists and twisted minds became their sweet spot. Emad Mostaque is the brain behind Stability AI. In his pitch, he blends Mark Zuckerberg's reckless innovation swagger with Crypto's democratization rhetoric. Using the tagline "radical freedom," he argues the product will spark an explosion of creativity among the public.

What could go wrong? Anna Eshoo, a Democratic Representative out of California, would say, "a lot." In a letter to federal regulators, she cited graphic images of beaten Asian women generated by a fringe group by using Stable Diffusion's platform to urge a crackdown on open-source AI models.[89] Reddit shut down numerous forums infected with nonconsensual nude images created using Stable Diffusion and other GenAI software. Innovators and investors, their vision clouded by riches, spin positive narratives to skate around the apparent negatives of automation.

Social Media Platforms Mislead with a More Subtle Approach

You can't tell anymore whether a social media post is generated by a bot or a human. They can smear competitors' reputations or push a marginal product. "Influence bots" try to sway voters and threaten our political system. How big of a problem is it? Twitter executives testified before Congress that bots, not humans, operate 5 percent of Twitter accounts. Before pulling the trigger on the Twitter acquisition, Elon Musk questioned the 5 percent number, and he was right to do so. Cyber security experts at Forrester revealed that the number is even higher.

Before Musk acquired Twitter, the company suspended thousands of accounts for spreading misinformation. Musk then polled Twitter users to see if they thought the suspended accounts, including those that promoted conspiracy theories, should be reinstated. A total of 3,162,112 votes were cast, with 72.4 percent voting in favor. Musk tweeted the next day, "The people have spoken. Amnesty begins next week. Vox Populi, Vox Dei." Although the Latin ending was a nice touch, the following question does emerge: can you trust the results of this Twitter survey? It is safe to claim that the bots voted in favor of amnesty quickly and in large numbers.

Researchers have been documenting social platform accuracy and trust issues for some time. *The Filter Bubble: What the Internet Is Hiding from You*, written by Eli Pariser, makes the point emphatically. She explores how algorithms influence our worldview and limit exposure to diverse perspectives. But legacy media also faces bias and misinformation challenges, so why are we picking on social media?

The reason is simple—social media uses engagement algorithms while traditional media does not. Thus, the former spreads misinformation at a rate and intensity that traditional media can't. Alternate views on anti-vaxxing and climate change, as well as conspiracy theories, drive us down rabbit holes where we connect with like-minded peers. The more bizarre and outrageous the claim, the faster it spreads. A few researchers at the MIT Media Lab studied 126,000 rumors spread on Twitter by three million people from 2006 to 2017. False news reached more people than the truth: the top 1 percent of false news diffused to between one thousand and one hundred thousand people, whereas the truth rarely diffused to more than one thousand people.[90]

Legacy media also competes for attention by leveraging and emphasizing conflict and tension. Major storms, airplane disasters, and sex scandals are perennial bestsellers. While tension sells, here's the difference. Social media platforms employ AI and more facile digital channels. Their audience is not the two million viewers of the Fox network or 1.3 million people who view MSNBC. These are rounding errors for social media, which works to grab the attention of the five billion social media users around the world, which amounts to approximately 57 percent of the world's population. It is not a fair contest.

Before we launch into workplace implications, take this to heart. We do not possess the knowledge to know what to believe, what systems to trust, or how an algorithm is trying to alter our thoughts, feelings, and motivations. The worst and most dramatic examples from the Far Right or the Far Left will be used to spread their agendas. If social media taught us one thing, it's that half the people in the world need to be medicated.

Before diving into the workplace, consider this: the lines between truth, manipulation, and algorithmic influence are increasingly blurred. Discerning what to trust and how AI shapes our thoughts require a critical eye. The "Dead Internet" theory is the most extreme view along these lines. It argues that the vibrant human-generated content that defined the early web (think quirky blogs, heartfelt experiences, honest reviews, and bustling communities) has been replaced by an army of AI-powered bots churning out artificial content. Put simply, the internet is "dead" because the content we consume is no longer a product of human creativity.

While AI-powered bots have undeniably dampened the internet's value, GenAI's infusion threatens to diminish it further. Google will release its "AI Overview" box at the top of search results to billions in 2025, for example. It will direct you to a specific answer based on your search intent. The question is will we trust it?

The introduction of AI Summaries brings us closer to the Star Trek ideal that we have been projecting for some time. When Captain Kirk had engine trouble he might ask the computer, "where is the best planet to head for based on distance, friendliness of population, and climate", he got a direct answer. He was not given links to Kaminar, Vulcan, or Talos IV for further research. This is where we are headed.

Here's an example that may clarify: Google News today calls itself a news aggregator, simply displaying links to headlines from various media partners. In the future, Googles AI Overview may summarize the news for you, tailor it for your interest, and render traditional media sources less relevant, in part because you may never see them. Some Industry analysts predict online media traffic could decrease by up to 25%[91]. While Google assures respect for both content partners and its ad base, their recent tech event tagline, "Let Google do the Googling," says it all, and will lead to unintended consequences.

Sure, it sounds convenient—less clicking, fewer annoying ads. But convenience comes at a cost. Curated summaries, shaped by potentially biased AI algorithms with commercial interests prioritized, risks ceding control of our online experience to the Tech Titans. Independent and diverse perspectives, the lifeblood of a healthy internet, could be drowned out or hidden behind paywalls. Even worse, their streamlined search may disrupt the internet's core economic engine that drives revenue for small businesses and threatens Googles primary business model (sponsored ad revenue).

On the fringes of the web, conspiracy enthusiasts' are even more dystopian. They allege governments and corporations are actively using AI to manipulate our thinking, suggesting the shift toward AI-generated content isn't organic. While the idea of a coordinated effort to manipulate public opinion through AI might seem far-fetched due to its complexity and lack of concrete evidence, it's undeniable that AI presents new challenges. Groups with strong agendas, from political extremes to commercial interests and even foreign actors, will likely leverage AI to further their causes.

AI-Generated Content Lacks Human Connection

Going forward, we will struggle with how we feel about transferring creative tasks to machines. AI-generated art is the most extreme example and can provide interesting insights into this evolving debate. The merging of art and technology began in the 1960s.[92] Computer-aided graphic design began to make near-perfect output around that time. The first computer-generated art software, AARON, was introduced in 1973.[93] These early attempts at computer-generated art provided the artist with various options. Once selected, there were explicit rules that were meant to be followed. In AI lingo described earlier, these programs were deterministic: each step the software would take was clearly defined with no variability.

AI-generated art is different. It gives the computer full autonomy to produce images. Algorithms do not follow a predetermined set of rules, like the classical pianist of Chapter 1. Instead, they analyze thousands, if not millions, of images to absorb and synthesize their characteristics. New images emerge, adhering to the patterns prevalent in the art used for training. Artistic decisions, which humans formerly made, are now shaped by software.

Classic works of art have an honesty or truthfulness about them. Positive and virtuous feelings such as integrity and passion emanate from that harshly realistic New York City street scene or the agony of Edgar Munch's *The Scream* or the loneliness of Edward Hopper's *Nighthawks*. AI-generated art can have none of this. The direct connection between a human and the work of art is severed.

Although it's a new ballgame, art collectors seem okay with it. In 2018, Christie's auctioned off *Portrait de Edmond Belamy*, the first AI-generated work, for $432,500. To some, AI-generated art is just the next movement. It is undeniable that the artist's contribution has changed: they will select the set of images for the algorithm to learn from and what results to throw away. The proponents of AI argue that this new form of art brings something new into the world, like all past artistic movements.

Others counter that it's not real art and is untrustworthy. Embracing it, we lose art as an innovative form of direct human communication.[94] I'd be shocked if the artist understood what the AI algorithm is doing. In fact, even the programmers who built the model may not be aware. The AI techniques are famous for their unexplainable inner workings.

Here's the takeaway. History has repeatedly shown that innovation, whether in art or technology, often catches us off guard. Despite our tendency to resist change, new ideas inevitably prevail. Automation is no exception. While we may initially resist the displacement of human roles by AI, recognize that innovation will progress regardless of our immediate rejection. Just as the art world has continuously evolved, so too will the automation landscape. There is little question that human writers, producers, and creators will be displaced by GenAI at some rate, but as legendary baseball figure Yogi Berra said, "It is difficult to make predictions, especially about the future."

Here's What We Can Do

We depend on automation constantly. It finds us partners, governs our relationships, tells us where to eat, and how to get there. These are positive. But we need to draw the line regarding automation in many areas. We should not let it manipulate us at work, create anxiety, and dictate what content we should absorb and enjoy.

Throughout this book, we argue workers must fight automation's advancement when it is no longer beneficial. Battle lines regarding trust in the workplace will need you to take action: don't blindly trust automation; become a trust watchdog at work; use AI to build trust in the workplace. Down the road, you may also need to fight technology-driven behavioral modification used to improve your productivity.

Rethink Your Trust in AI: It's an Ally, Not a God

We started the chapter with the lawyer Steven Schwartz, who admitted he used OpenAI's ChatGPT to help with his brief, which cited six non-existent court decisions. He told the judge he "never" could have imagined ChatGPT could make up cases. Random acts are inevitable consequences of unhealthy trust in automation, as demonstrated by this example. Previously, we assigned only low-level functions to automation, like dispensing money at an ATM. Now we expect automation to drive our cars, diagnose an ailment, write a resume, and sentence criminals. In contrast to the "intelligent automation" period of skepticism, overpromises, and under-delivery of AI, we now risk a period of blind faith, optimism, and acceptance.

Trust in automation is not a big issue yet. Our "intelligent automation" goals are modest, to mimic less important, lower value, and repetitive tasks at work. Advances in cognitive automation like GenAI and physical robotics, such as an android guarding a workplace, will change this. It moves us firmly into the "human-capable" period, where machines take on higher-level human traits and trust becomes critical. This means we will have to make difficult decisions about whether to trust specific automations at work and in many other areas.

For example, consider today's average chatbot. They are not good enough to engage in an actual conversation. They are boring, lose context, repeat themselves, or respond to keywords only. They miss obvious connections. We don't trust them for something important, and neither do their owners. Despite the enticing names, banks don't assign them crucial tasks like moving money. The bank will transfer you to a human, secure website, or portal. Chatbots of dubious quality have proliferated in recent years. A Forrester analyst put it this way: "During the pandemic any idiot thought they could build a chatbot, and unfortunately, they did." They are so bad that we don't trust them and don't give them important things to do.

That's all about to change. GenAI, and various other areas of AI, will take on more important tasks. This means trust in these systems will become a critical issue. To illustrate this point, let's have a thought experiment.

If your car is in a collision, how might you handle this repair scenario? An Advanced Driver-Assist System (ADAS) is installed in your late-model car, meaning it can drive itself.[95] Your accident requires precise adjustments to the ADAS system, but most body-shop workers lack the expertise to do so. Former territories of the British Empire accurately called them "panel beaters." They are good with a hammer and a torch but lack the training of more advanced auto technicians.

The question is, would you be comfortable with an AI bot guiding these panel beaters through the adjustments? According to Jim Fish, the vice president of Opus IVS, you will have little choice. His cognitive assistant GenAI bots are currently being tested by twenty-one thousand field mechanics. In short order, GenAI will turn Jeff Daniels's character from *Dumb and Dumber* into a repair rock star.

The bottom line is that automation will continue to amaze us. The desire to augment or replace human judgment will intensify, as seen in refined courtrooms and rough-and-tumble body shops. We need to be skeptical. Irrational trust and acceptance are how random acts start.

Cultivating Trust: Become the Workplace Watchdog

Sure, let algorithms find us partners and tell us where to eat or how to reach a destination, but the line in the sand is forming. We should not let automation tell us what art is and what content we should absorb and enjoy. And we certainly should not let it do things at work that make us nervous.

To deal with trust issues, authentic human intelligence will be at a premium. That's good news for you. GenAI and social media platforms will misinform at a scale never seen, as argued at the beginning of this chapter. These trends directly affect the workplace. It's inevitable. Automation will do more of the work that you currently do. As in the modern warehouse described earlier, humans will try to stay out of the robot's way. Automation will generate a customer letter; an AI Agent will update a website or tailor advice for an investor.

Your opportunity is to become a trust watchdog. Make a point to understand automation's strengths and limitations. This will raise your value at work. Know which tasks are safe for machines to do and what decisions are safe for them to make. This will require an attitude adjustment and a more data-driven approach than you probably have today. You will use your judgment but also need to develop the ability to collect, analyze, and interpret data effectively. This will allow you to make informed decisions about what you can trust machines to do. Job titles such as digital trust officers are popping up and will offer job enhancement, but all workers will benefit from this focus.

And here's why this is an important workplace perspective going forward. Machines will become more adept at making decisions but still lack the emotional intelligence and empathy essential for complete trust in resolving issues. Your CT and emotional intelligence can analyze situations that advancing automation will create and miss.

But becoming a trust expert alone will not save you. You must make yourself more productive with automation. If you are in a creative position like marketing, AI will generate ideas and written output faster and more efficiently. GenAI, for example, can wrap a million convincing personal parameters around a customer message or encounter, which is impossible for a human to do. Novice technicians, like the car mechanics referred to earlier, will benefit from the model's embedded wisdom and completing repairs faster. In a nutshell, you must employ algorithms while maintaining a competitive advantage over them.

Creativity was thought to be a uniquely human quality, but GenAI will now compete to undertake creative work. It will find new ideas, insights, and content as it becomes more human-capable. This is an issue for you in the workplace so you must raise the bar. Automation will surpass your human efficiency, but you can't let it surpass your creativity and innovation. Focus on fostering creative thinking abilities, exploring new ideas, and generating innovative solutions. This human ingenuity will be given a premium.

Fight Behavioral Modification Techniques in the Workplace

Behavioral modification (BM) is the process of influencing and transforming human behavior using various motivational techniques. Blast a rat with an electric shock for doing one thing and reward it with a piece of cheese for another, and soon it is trained. Ivan Pavlov, an animal lover, trained dogs to salivate at the sound of a metronome or buzzer. B.F. Skinner was a Harvard University psychology professor whose early research approach seemed harsh. To test his BM theories, he kept his daughter Debra in a specially designed cage for two and a half years. Bells and food trays delivered rewards and punishments. Sensational headlines portrayed the "Skinner's Box" approach as overly harsh, but contrary to some reports, the daughter neither sued her father nor died by suicide.

Now, you might wonder why this dark history matters, and the answer is worrying. As a worker you might be on the cusp of entering a digital Skinner's Box. Techniques honed by social media platforms, echoing early behaviorism research, could soon shape your work lives in unseen ways. Concrete evidence is still limited, but the trends discussed in this chapter suggest a future where work becomes a carefully crafted online environment designed to influence your behavior to maximize output, potentially at the expense of your mental well-being.

In the digital world, no electric shocks are used. Small doses of social pain and pleasure are the primary tool. Digital isolation results if you cross their algorithm's desire for engagement or a high rating or a "like" is awarded that soothe one's ego. You track the number of people following you, wanting to touch your flowing robe as you virtually pass by.

Algorithms are designed to control our highs and lows when online. Research has shown they manipulate our dopamine levels, a self-generated drug.[96] If you spend hours on social media or video games waiting for that next digital delight to explode on the screen, your dopamine hormone may be altered and damaged. One predictable outcome is that other aspects of our lives become staid and boring and hold less interest. This notion was emphasized by rodents in a study conducted in 2022. A special button, when pressed, delivered dopamine to the rodents' brains. In no time, the mice forgot about everything. They stopped eating and running around and even gave up sex.

Here's the fear: It is inevitable that techniques, such as social pain and pleasure and manipulation of dopamine levels, as facilitated by social media, will leak into the workplace. This may seem like a good plot for a sci-fi flick, but automation has a history of invading an environment with unpredictable outcomes, as argued throughout.

Here's the problem: as described in previous chapters, all three worker types are destined to stare at screens for hours a day. The future workday for many will be interacting with screens. The new security officer will monitor androids patrolling the workplace. Janitors will coordinate three or four robot janitors with a tablet, and office workers will collaborate with AI Agents.

Algorithms incapable of empathy will replace human bosses, particularly in middle manager positions. These automations are bound to monitor and learn from the workers' behavior. Metrics will be presented to workers to compare their output to that of coworkers. Dopamine levels will rise if they outperform their peers and fall if they don't. Gaming scenarios will integrate with output goals in clever ways. Inevitably, these digital BM techniques will be used to motivate the employee to serve enterprise goals.

Here's what you can do. You must guard against BM techniques in the workplace. Mistrust the intentions of your algo overlords. Be sure your employer has safeguards, transparency measures, or humans that remain in the loop so automation is applied with reason and management.

Tame the Information Torrent: Conquer Information Overload

At some point, we have all stared at a device, unable to change the simplest things, like a.m. to p.m. on a car clock. The clock on my now-retired VCR displayed 12:00 a.m. for most of its life. For many people, the digital experience has gone too far. For example, Tesla designs its own primary computer chips to create an integrated digital experience that surpasses its rivals. They are the only car company to do so. Yet they have turned simple functions into a digital adventure. Want to open a Tesla glove box? Simply press "Home," then "Controls," followed by "Glove Box" on the flat screen. This is a good security measure. The parking valet will struggle to find that well-deserved tip, but honestly, is this better than reaching over to push button?

Automation drives us crazy with too many options. Streaming media is a decent example. Doesn't it seem like everyone is creating content for our viewing pleasure? Traditional content creators like Disney and Time Warner have become digital platform companies. Amazon and Netflix are creating content like there's no tomorrow. In 2023, 2,900 scripted originals were released globally, of which one thousand were produced in the US, according to Parrot Analytics, a data science company focused on the entertainment industry. The result is a confusing array of options, too much content to sort through, and too many platforms competing for monthly recurring revenue. Even the silly cartoon *Scooby-Doo Returns to Transylvania* required a subscription. The only "monster" in this mystery is the recurring assault on our bank accounts.

In simple terms, this has turned into a streaming mess.

Our relationship with technology is getting more complex and challenging, piling up our anxieties. The 737 Max pilots, referred to in Chapter 1, were overloaded with sometimes conflicting information at critical moments, like altitude readings and warning signals from various systems. Making sense of all the readings proved challenging, especially due to the mounting pressure with only seconds to act.

Indeed, we often feel overwhelmed by the relatively simple screens in our cars or the intrusive pop-ups during online shopping. The SCO systems introduced in Chapter 3 frustrate us. Imagine a senior citizen squinting at a six-digit, four-point font code on an avocado, to enter it on a small keypad, while impatient youths behind her impatiently watch.

Here's where we are headed. Humans will struggle with conflicting digital signals and directions and will not know which ones to trust. Their skills will be challenged as technology races ahead and demands we change our behavior.

Stress, decreased productivity, and even burnout, are all possible, but there are things you can do. For example, prioritize and set boundaries such as designating times for checking email or social media. Identify the most relevant and reliable sources of information for your work and limit your exposure to distracting sources. Use task management apps and email filters to organize and prioritize your information intake. Become a digital minimalist: minimize the number of open tabs, windows, and applications on your computer to reduce visual clutter, promote concentration, and regularly disconnect from digital devices to allow your mind to rest.

Lessons from Psychology Can Help Reduce Anxiety

We have shown that automation can lead to anxiety and threaten people's sense of identity. Enzo's machine upgrade in Chapter 4 exposed his outdated mechanical skills. No longer a machinist and now driving a taxi, he lost status and part of his identity. Like Enzo, many wonder if they can keep pace with changing technology. They worry their job will require skills they do not have or even vanish.

Fortunately, researchers have studied anxiety for decades, honing insights from its psychological origins. "Reframing" is one technique that potentially reduces workplace stress.[97] Here's an example: many workers are overwhelmed by the technology they see coming. As automation looms, many have developed a black-or-white or all-or-nothing perspective. For example, they fear they must become an AI whiz or a master of the latest data visualization app like Tableau after spending years honing their Microsoft Excel skills. This broad ambition and reach often triggers negative thoughts such as, "I may not be smart enough to learn this new tool, or I'm too lazy and poorly motivated to put in the effort."

Experts in treating anxiety advise workers to reframe the technology challenge so they can succeed. Reduce the challenge to a manageable set of needed new skills. "I don't have to become an AI expert but only have to get better in one or two areas." By reducing the challenge to attainable goals, negative self-talk and anxiety will be reduced. Put simply: when facing automation, actively shift your perspective on challenges. Instead of fearing them, turn them into achievable goals.

Reframing automation challenges as opportunities for learning and growth can decrease anxiety and frustration. I've spoken to workers with the mindset, "Sure, I may lose my job, but I'm in a great spot. This company will let me learn all this new stuff on their dime. They're increasing my market value and giving me more job options and flexibility."

Imagine a World Where AI Builds Trust

It may help to move in a more positive direction and ask if GenAI can build trust. I think it can. They can explain insurance policies, contracts, investments, or warranty agreements at the required educational or knowledge level. Today, few people read these opaque materials because, to the average person, they are incomprehensible. The legal jargon fosters a lack of trust. People fear various ways they could be taken advantage of are hidden within it.

An investment prospectus for a mutual fund is a good example. As part of the Securities and Exchange Commission's efforts to regulate the investment industry, financial advisors must provide one to investors after a mutual fund is sold. Yet the information as presented is useless. Despite an abundance of good data, most people cannot make any sense of it. It's as clear as concrete, smothered in legalese, and written by lawyers for lawyers to read and argue about in court.

Wouldn't it be great for a potential investor to have a conversation with that prospectus, "How much is this mutual fund costing me a year? How does the management expense compare with others? How many companies in the portfolio have low ESG ratings?" In other words, GenAI can turn that pile of confusion into a meaningful, more transparent, and honest exchange. By patronizing businesses that use AI in this way, consumers can actively support its adoption. At work, request that standardized operating procedures and other documentation use GenAI to keep you efficient, safe, and compliant.

The unchecked advancement of automation threatens our ability to trust information and decisions made by machines. We must actively resist automation when it ceases to serve our best interests, especially when building trust. Unfortunately, there's no easy solution for the trust issue. As automation produces more content trained on our data—a running sewer of human emotion, love, hate, and confusion—it risks becoming a breeding ground for misdirection.

This chapter outlined a few actions to help with the growing trust issue. If we take this advice, authentic human interaction and content will be at a premium and humans will maintain a competitive advantage over the models. It will be a fight but here is a summary of the practical advice for workers and individuals (see Figure 8-1).

What We Can Do	Why It Matters
Don't expect GenAI to offload the things you need to learn.	Too much dependence on AI will leave you more vulnerable to replacement.
Become a trust watchdog at work. Use a data-driven approach.	Your work will pass to machines. Those who understand when to trust them will be valued.
Get grounded in basic art history to gain insight into GenAI art creation.	A better world will direct AI toward menial tasks and leave art to humans.
Beware of "influence fraud bots." They hamper the spread of freedom worldwide.	Social media has not propagated democracy. Authoritarianism has increased.[98]
Tame the information torrent: Use filtering to reduce information overload.	Information overload can lead to anxiety.
At work, demand verifiable sources. Support labeled source material.	Unreliable information will increase at work.
Recognize that social media techniques used to manipulate behavior will reach the workplace.	Our minds risk being shaped by increasingly powerful technology. Don't let it.

Don't let LLM excitement seduce you into placing premature trust in critical systems.	A false sense of trust is dangerous.
Creative workers: organize digital content to augment LLMs and protect your IP.	GenAI will be part of your work life going forward.
If you are a creative worker, learn to speak to AI. Treat "prompt engineering" as a skill.	Creative workers: need to prepare for disruption. Expect your LLM future to be volatile.
Recognize that LLMs will generate misinformation and occasionally "hallucinate.	Human trust in AI is accelerating faster than the accuracy and reliability guardrails.
Math and science will not help with the trust issue. Lean on liberal arts to help.	Philosophy and ethics are critical to assessing truth and fairness.

Figure 8-2 Trust—a crisis of authentication.

CHAPTER 9

INVASION

MANY HOMELESS PEOPLE SUFFER FROM mental or physical health problems or abuse drugs or alcohol. Often, it's a complex mix of these factors, on top of difficult family backgrounds. Hawaii has over six thousand homeless people. Picture this: You're a homeless person walking down the street when a three-foot-tall robot dog approaches you. It scans your body temperature, a new reality for residents of Honolulu during the pandemic, where the police department deployed these robotic canines to combat COVID-19.[99]

At $150,000, Spot was pricier than your average golden retriever but was paid for through the $2.2 trillion CARES economic stimulus bill passed by US Congress in 2020.[100] In short, your tax dollars at work. It seemed like a win-win for the police. First, the project was paid for outside the current budget, and second, robot dogs might be useful for other police missions.

But Spot was not met with the love and affection that a dog expects. The people of Hawaii hated Spot. Critics actively denounced the indignity of subjecting people, already facing a multitude of challenges, to robotic surveillance. Some have called it dystopian before insisting on a ban on their use.

Tracking the virus in the homeless population was a valid goal, but needed checks and balances were set aside. Input from the homeless community was not taken. There was a lack of testing to determine if the technology was appropriate for humans and pushed on the homeless without the extra human review that advancing technology requires. As we saw in earlier chapters, this type of physical automation is far from the "human adoption window."

Invasion to most people means some form of physical incursion. It could be a military force crossing a border for conquest or plunder, or a burglar breaking into your home. By contrast, the invasion discussed in this chapter is subtle, largely invisible, and more varied. It sheds light on several issues: escalating concerns about personal surveillance, the rise of innovative digital scams and cybercrime, evolving challenges with data privacy, the potential displacement of offshore workers by onshore automation, and the growing sophistication of bots that not only go after concert tickets but also threaten jobs in various sectors.

This chapter argues that these new forms of invasion, unlike more physical forms, will be slow, subtle, powerful, and loaded with unintended consequences. To make the case, we examine invasive trends that affect everyone today and are headed for the workplace. The second part of the chapter provides specific advice for digital elite, middle, and human-touch workers to manage invasive trends at work.

Surveillance Has Crossed the Line

The role of sensors in invasive trends cannot be overstated. They are everywhere. They help trucks optimize their routes, tell workers when to empty a trash can on a German train, alert you when your car's tire pressure is low, help detect pollution when placed on a robotic fish, and even monitor the behavior of bees.[101]

All good, but we risk going too far. We need to be more careful about the signals we gather on humans. Eat at a restaurant, ride an elevator, work in an office, fill the car's gas tank, and someone will be watching. Cameras combine with AI and tighten the screws on any desired autonomous behavior. Corporate and governmental monitoring will be deeper, better, and more pervasive.

That ship has sailed in China and Russia. China has invested heavily in CCTV cameras with automated facial recognition programs. Monitoring also includes obligatory DNA sampling used for ethnic profiling.[102] Many cities in the US have adopted facial recognition as well. Bumper stickers and t-shirts are showing up with the quip, "Let's make Orwell fiction again."

Surveillance has crossed the line, and here's an example. MSG Entertainment doesn't like lawyers. They are not alone in this view; many don't, until they need one desperately. Any lawyer that has sued MSG, or works for a firm that has, is banned from their entertainment venues, including Radio City Music Hall and Madison Square Garden. Facial biometrics pulls the lawyer out of line. They are embarrassed and punished. A mom, who had never sued MSG but worked for a law firm that had, was rudely banned (along with her daughter) from seeing the Rockettes in the 2022 holiday season.

Of course, it's not just MSG Entertainment that uses facial recognition. AmazonGo stores use it to track shoppers, airports use it for global entry, retail stores use it to identify shoplifters, and casinos use it to keep an eye on questionable gamblers. But where do we draw the line? Should movie theaters ban critics who give negative reviews? Should employees of competitor companies be banned from certain events?

MSG's use of facial recognition technology is a new form of invasion to punish people it just doesn't like. It takes a routine business relationship, albeit an adversarial one, and makes it personal. MSG should take advice from Sonny Corleone in *The Godfather*, "Tom, this is business, and this man is taking it very, very personal." It's a slippery slope, and it's clear we have entered a new phase of privatized surveillance. Courts are challenging MSG's approach.[103]

Scams Target Middle and Service Workers

Watson Bricius came to the US from Haiti at the age of eight. With sad eyes he spoke of his home country, "In Haiti the gangs are stronger than the police and have better guns. When that happens, you have no country." He was thrilled to be in the US with a steady job at Whole Foods, even though the hours were long and tedious.

One day, during his regular deli counter shift, he started a conversation with Sam, a chain restaurant cook and a passionate crypto investor. Sam's account had just reached $80,000 before the recent market downturn. Watson ignored the customers waving their numbered tickets at him and listened carefully. After several conversations with Sam, he bought into XRP, a top ten coin by market capitalization, and less than a dollar a coin. Sam convinced him that XRP was different, not just another coin, and less about speculation than the other crypto options, and a payment network like a SWIFT. Watson described his transformation:

I have no idea what a SWIFT is, but I'll bet XRP can do it a lot cheaper. Sure, there are a few lawsuits going on which I don't get, about whether the coin is a security or something else but that should be no big deal. That's just the government trying to figure out and slow down crypto. They are just scared of it and don't understand how it works. They are old timers stuck in the past. And here's the best part: you can get it a coin for less than a dollar now. I don't see any other way for a guy like me to get ahead.

Limited in his knowledge of finance and technology, Bricius ventured into the crypto economy, a world brimming with risk. He was vulnerable and easy prey. The digital landscape is rife with new threats: crypto scams, data breaches, and ransomware attacks are commonplace, posing a significant mental challenge, especially for middle and human-touch workers.

Bernie Madoff pulled off one of the most brazen scams of all time. He betrayed thousands of investors and bankrupted his favorite charities. His scheme cost his victims billions. Madoff would have loved the commercials at the 2022 Super Bowl, the primary symbol of American consumerism. There were four crypto ads that year: FTX, eToro, Crypto.com, and Coinbase.

My favorite was the FTX commercial with Larry David. The commercial's goal was simple: create a crypto fear of missing out (FOMO) for the masses. David dismisses indoor plumbing, electricity, and even the wheel as technologies that will never work. The commercial begs you, "Don't be like Larry. Don't miss out on the next big thing," with crypto being that thing.

I've always loved David's work, but you must question whether these celebrities think about what they are endorsing. In this case, pumping crypto to the unwitting masses, where the mean retirement savings is $40,000, may not be right. He was paid $10 million to create the sixty-second ad, but better for his legacy to have brought *Curb Your Enthusiasm* to the picture.

These commercials had two goals: provide legitimacy for the crypto-economy and get risk-oriented males like Bricius to buy coins. To do so, the crypto industry spent lavishly on promotions, and even compromised major league baseball, our national pastime. In a brazen move to build trust, FTX put their logo on major league umpire uniforms, but unfortunately the company embraced few of baseball's core values. In 2022, FTX evaporated overnight, stiffing more than one million creditors. Deposits in the FTX exchange were illegally moved to Almeda Research, the co-owned hedge fund. The management team is headed for long jail terms. Yet despite all the crypto turmoil, celebrities supporting questionable crypto schemes continue. Soccer legend Cristiano Ronaldo is the latest mega sports star to be sued.

Today, our scams and frauds are more complex, varied, and frequent. Preying on desperation is nothing new. America has a long history of exploiting the desperate. America's airwaves and inboxes still overflow with get-rich-quick schemes: debt consolidation, gold scams, lottery fantasies, and reverse mortgage nightmares. The seemingly friendly emails from strangers promising hidden wealth, a hallmark of the Nigerian gold scam, have plagued inboxes for years.

Here's what's changed: the playbook has evolved for a digital age. AI allows bad actors to use digital scale to be more invasive and effective, and these thieves don't get caught often. They are fluent in the latest digital technologies and innovative in ways to use them. Automation like ChatGPT will help them analyze code, detect vulnerabilities, and write software to hack into enterprise systems and create persuasive pitches for the masses. Forrester analysts expect the cybersecurity industry to triple in a few years.

Let's Bring Back Good Old Bank Robberies

For hackers, locking up businesses and demanding hefty ransoms has proved more profitable than robbing banks. Digital extortion via ransomware is a modern-day kidnapping scheme for your data. A cryptoworm bends and twists its way into a computer system to encrypt or threaten to destroy sensitive data. The cybercrook sits back and collects a ransom—a low-risk, high-reward bonanza. In 2022, 456 million in ransoms were paid. The US is the big target and healthcare is the big industry.

In 2022, a Russian cyber gang threatened to overthrow Puerto Rico. The word "Russian" is almost not needed. Most elite ransomware cyber gangs are based there.[104] It is a little like saying a Kenyan won the Boston Marathon. They almost always do.

The cybercrooks' message did not mince words: "We have our insiders in your government. We are gaining access to other systems as well; you have no option but to pay the

20 million dollars." The Puerto Rican government quickly declared a state of emergency.

These are organized gangs but without identifiable tattoos or street presence. They don't operate in the internet shadows and back alleys but are more likely from seaside condominiums. The top Russian hackers are now global enterprises that have launched franchise opportunities. So why open a fast-food joint when a small McRansom franchise might tie you down less?

Let's bring back the good old bank robberies. There are still about three to four thousand a year, a mere 2 percent of all robberies, according to the FBI. But they are starkly different from today's surging cyber crimes: the perps are stupid; they mostly get caught and don't get much even if they don't. Each bank robbery only nets $4,000 to $5,000, on average. Banks lost a mere $482 million in 2019, while crypto crimes, by contrast, saw $3.2 billion stolen in 2021.

Legacy bank robbers get caught about 80 percent of the time. Most crimes are committed during the day, when banks are open, with tons of witnesses and security footage. I don't mean to offend all bank robbers, but they don't seem like Mensa candidates. Angel Luis Masdeu will serve about six years in prison and is an example. On February 25, 2021, he hailed a cab in Hartsville, South Carolina, and asked to be driven to a nearby bank. He then asked the driver to pull up to the drive-through window and pass an envelope to the teller. The scribbled note demanded money and threatened to blow up the bank if not delivered immediately. The teller calmly activated an alarm. The police arrived ten minutes later and found Angel still in the taxi's back seat and made an easy arrest.

The Bot Wars Have Started

The online assault on privacy has been described, but how about robots that want the same things we do but are better at getting them, mimicking our desires and competing directly with our actions? Consider this: Dianne was sixteen years old and dying to see Taylor Swift in concert. She wasn't the only one. Swift was America's most beloved artist, and she hadn't performed live in years. So, Dianne logged onto Ticketmaster with stars in her eyes and a hopeful heart. She saw a glitzy picture of Taylor ready to rock, but the link to buy tickets was not. She found herself stuck in a "waiting room" for hours. In the end, she couldn't snag a ticket. But hey, the music while on hold was great.

The GrinchBots got there first and crowded out legitimate fans like Dianne. These bots monitor the internet to scoop up any hot product. They go after hard-to-get graphic cards, toilet paper in Germany, NFTs, baby formula, or cool sneakers, which was their starting point. Try to get a reservation at a hot New York City restaurant, and chances are the Resy booking bot will beat you.

So, what are these bots? Much like the invisible RPA bots invading us at work, they are tiny automations that behave like humans. They invade our lives, annoy us, disrupt business, steal from us, and lie to us. They are pervasive. By some accounts, 25 percent of all internet traffic is created by these software robots.[105] Others put this higher; startling when you think about it.

Like the cookies described above, they are not all bad. It's like the *Wizard of Oz* story with the scary, bad witch of the East and the pleasant Glinda, the good witch. The bad bots use their powers for selfish and nefarious purposes, while the good bots use their powers to benefit others. Google search crawlers get us better search results. Travel aggregator bots personalize options for us, and yes, RPA bots relieve humans of boring work. Glinda helps Dorothy find the wizard, just like our good bots guide us on our journey through the digital world.

But sadly, the bad bots, like the GrinchBots above, outnumber the good ones and are growing. Credential stuffing bots gather usernames and passwords sourced from data breaches and "stuff" them into online login pages. Ad fraud bots copy legitimate product images to a fake website and then ship you a counterfeit item in their place at a great price. Web reconnaissance bots stalk a target online to gather data for a specific attack. You get the picture. These are a few of about a dozen categories. Bot "most wanted" posters would fill a post office wall.

In the Taylor Swift example, the GrinchBots bought tickets the second they were available and flipped them on StubHub or eBay for multiples of the list price. Ticketmaster had known about the automated scalping for a long time. Bots bought thirty thousand Hamilton tickets in 2017.[106] But they acted like Captain Louis Renault in *Casablanca* as he was taking his winnings from the croupier: "I'm shocked, shocked to find that gambling is going on here!" The CEO of Liberty Media responded to the media outcry, "We had fourteen million people hit the site, including bots, which are not supposed to be there."

Got it. The bots should not be there but who is responsible for keeping them out? Indications are that Ticketmaster has under-invested in its technology. A quick scan of reviews will reveal a litany of frustrating and confusing digital experiences; it can't handle high demand and has minimal filters to control the bots. It's possible bots were not a priority: a ticket sold is a commission made, whether a bot buys it or a human. But customer experience should be.

And Ticketmaster hasn't changed. In 2024 a hacker group called ShinyHunters waltzed right in and snatched the personal details of a cool 560 million customers. The hackers demanded a $500,000 ransom to prevent the data from being sold via the dark web. So, here's to you, Ticketmaster, for proving once again that you're about as secure as a toddler with a box of matches.

Invasion Is an Everywhere Issue

Most of us don't want to be spied on. We don't want the neighbor to know when that special friend left in the morning. It's no one's business how much we earn, whether we buy hair replacement treatments, or what medicine we use to deal with a recurring rash. Yet we seem willing to keep giving up our data. Pew Research found that 60 percent think they can't go through a day without tossing some personal data up for grabs. Yet, we remain puzzled when we are targeted by a creepily specific ad.

Invasion is a workplace issue, but when we close that laptop or jump in the car for the commute home, it doesn't stop. Online behavior is getting monitored, a shock to almost no one these days. Cookies started it all. Such an innocent name. Who would not want to allow cookies to join them? And in the beginning, we did. They verified whether you had visited the website before and helped websites remember your preferences and login credentials. In the beginning, the so-called first-party cookies were benign and positive, but over time, like the kid crashing a party with his rowdy friend, uninvited "third-party" cookies joined the stalking party.

They might pick up your IP address, device type in use, screen size, location, items viewed, and links to other sites visited. Cruise to a brand's website and fifteen cookies might be dropped into your browsing session. What happens next? The squadron of private investigators follows you, but unlike humans, they are tireless with terrific memories. They know where you bank and shop, what you're interested in, and how much you spend. Firms like Equifax, Epsilon, Experian, or Pipl purchase and sell the data. Companies will buy it and place us in a commercial segment, like a thirty-five-year-old, outdoorsy vegan, and sell us things. This is the dark data economy that operates in the shadows of our digital lives.

HIPAA may protect health data stored in a hospital EMR system, but cookies are free to exploit any medical-related search pattern. Expectant moms, adults fighting depression, or worried youth looking up HIV symptoms are fair game and sold to the highest bidder. The Department of Justice fined Epsilon, one of the largest data brokers, $150 million in 2022. Data was sold to sketchy operators who targeted senior citizens with fraud schemes. In a 2019 book, Shoshana Zuboff introduced the term "surveillance capitalism" to describe the risks associated with this growing industry.

Our data privacy is being compromised. Violators include Amazon, Google, WhatsApp, and Facebook, but also airlines, clothing retailers, and telecom companies. Violations include misuse of data captured by cookies, forcing people to accept cookies, inadequate communication of privacy policy, illegal monitoring of employees, and aggressive marketing tactics. The amounts these companies were fined under the EU's General Data Protection Regulation (GDPR) laws can create an "invasion" scorecard. Amazon inched out Google and now leads with $877 million. The top ten GDPR fines in 2020, 2021, and 2022 total over $1.5 billion.[107]

That's an invasion of our online lives, but how do we feel about unsolicited calls and texts on our mobile devices? First, let's all agree we hate robocalls and the soulless companies that use them. They get us at work, home, and everywhere in between, at any time. They try to scam us into extending our auto maintenance warranty coverage, the top 2021 call complaint, according to the Federal Communications Commission. In the first half of 2022, the US received twenty-four billion robocalls.[108] People in Atlanta received an average of 141 in the first half of 2022. GenAI will allow robocalls to learn and adapt to a conversation in real time and make them hard to distinguish from a human. The point is that automation is a great enabler of personal invasion. Tech companies and businesses will find innovative ways to invade personal and work lives.

Here's What You Can Do

We explored invasive automation trends in the previous section and how they impact everyone. More than half of all AIAAIC incidents involved invasive practices, with workers reporting many of these incidents. It's another example of how automation presents a double-edged sword for workers. It has the potential to provide greater flexibility and less tedious work, but it also raises troubling questions about privacy and control. Heightened scrutiny, the potential for intrusion, and AI's growing presence will undoubtedly heighten worker anxiety. As Forrester CEO George Colony chillingly stated at a recent event keynote: "You may not be interested in AI, but AI is interested in you."

Middle Workers: Assert Your Digital Rights

For some, getting out of back-office cubicle jobs can't come soon enough. Julie's job is to solve customer issues in a contact center and she wants to leave. She wants to get off the treadmill and do a different kind of work where she will not feel pressured all the time.

> I've spent more years than I want to admit in a cubicle, and over those years I've learned that it is a terrible thing to wish on a person. We weren't meant to be in cubes. They keep the reception area pretty spiffy but back here with the grunts, efficiency rules, and it's just not for me. Management tells you to think outside the box to solve customer problems, but how can you, when you're in one all day?

> It's all about dashboards, dashboards, dashboards, that reduce us to rows and columns. You're supposed to keep calls short, but the stupid bots grab the easy ones. What's left for me gets harder all the time. The apps I need to know get harder, and now they want "me" to figure out more work to give to the robot. Now I must train the thing to do all my account updates. You don't have to be a genius to see where this is going.

Julie is telling us first, she needs a new job. She feels cubicle workers like her are under pressure from automation. Sure, her job before the robot had tedious elements. Mindless data entry, sending messages, cutting and pasting data, and simple questions filled much of the day, but they allowed her to "zone out" and disengage, reducing stress. These are all tasks the new robots do, leaving her only rapid-fire challenging activities. She has deep animus toward the bots replacing her work. And she should.

Julie and other employees whose repetitive tasks are susceptible to automation should be wary of invasive technologies like task mining. This is a subset of the expanding process intelligence software market. Your employer will use it to identify hours out of your workday that can be given to an AI bot.

Here's how it works. A "listening agent" is put on your desktop. Every click of the mouse or keystroke is recorded. The time spent on every application is captured. Data on an individual worker is valuable, but when combined with recordings from other workers with a dash of machine learning to identify repeated tasks, it becomes pure gold.

Machine learning will find patterns that seem unnecessary or can be automated. It's a winner for process improvement. Yet, the same data can compare employees, and this is where ethical questions are raised. Why does Gene spend so long on those two screens? Why is Jill slipping off onto Instagram for an average of three minutes an hour? This is the invasion risk. Workers will be stressed by the hidden scrutiny.

Consider, Suzie Cheikho, a dedicated employee at Insurance Australia Group (IAG). For 18 years, she met deadlines, hit regulatory targets, and was an asset to the company. Working from home offered flexibility, but it also came with unexpected consequences.

One day, Suzie was fired. IAG claimed she missed deadlines, meetings, and was difficult to reach, citing data as proof. Their report stated she started late 47 out of 49 days, left early 29 times, and even had four days of complete inactivity, all based on keystroke monitoring software installed on her work computer without her knowledge. Suzie disputed this data, arguing it didn't reflect her actual work, and filed an unfair dismissal claim. However, the Fair Work Commission ultimately ruled in favor of IAG.

Many companies I talk to are investing in technology to monitor employees this way. Companies are implementing technology that translates to a more watchful eye, which could become intrusive. Remember Julie from the contact center. Imagine she contemplates a career change. Her online searches for new jobs, moving companies, or even a quick chat with a potential employer could all be monitored. Without proper internal governance, this information could jeopardize her job security.

You can fight this form of monitoring. While many countries lack specific laws addressing employee monitoring in the workplace, regulations are developing to protect you. Become familiar with techniques such as task mining and employee monitoring software and the emerging laws against them. You can alert employers to the ethical ramifications of their use. For example, Germany has several laws protecting workers' desktop activities from being recorded for review. The German Federal Data Protection Act, for example, states that employers must have a legitimate reason for monitoring and need to inform employees about the purpose and extent.

Human-Touch Workers: Fight Invasive Monitoring and Digital Scams

A quick peek into McDonald's can provide additional insight into where advancing scrutiny may take us. When it comes to fast food, it wrote the book. More than thirty-four thousand restaurants serve sixty-nine million people in 118 countries each day.[109] It sells seventy-five burgers every second. All this activity generates vast amounts of data. In the past, McDonald's produced summary metrics on a per-restaurant basis, which made it difficult to pinpoint problems at a specific store. But now, machine learning algorithms analyze in-store traffic, data from point-of-sale (POS) machines, and drive-through window activity. The restaurants still look the same, but data now makes each unique.

A director of technology at one of McDonald's oldest franchises (recruited by the founder, Ray Kroc) told us how these advances affect workers. He chuckled and said there is a metric for almost everything, but he admitted they are not perfect. You often lose the full story. Maybe the store had a string of bad customers or bad weather.

Some uses of the data he doesn't like. Headquarters calculates the number of sales per employee, not at the end of the month or week, but in real-time. They tell the franchise partner to reduce staff when sales drop below a certain level. A worker might be traveling to work on a bus, and sometimes they are told not to check in for an hour or so until more customers are predicted. They try to give them enough hours so they don't lose them. It's a balance they don't always get right.

But here's the thing. The metrics make the workers nervous. If someone underperforms, they will be very unhappy. And sometimes they shuffle the execs at corporate and a new guy will change the metrics. Store managers and employees scurry around and try to adjust. It is not a relaxing place.

The just-in-time worker scheduling is already a third rail for worker's rights, and it should be. The State of New York's Department of Labor now forces companies to pay a fee to workers for what's commonly identified as "just in time," "call in," or "on call" scheduling.[110]

That is just one example. As a human-touch worker you will have to fight many forms of invasive monitoring. Your best hope comes from emerging laws designed to protect you. The US National Labor Relations Act (NLRA) protects your right to discuss wages and working conditions, for example. Invasive monitoring can be considered a violation if it inhibits you from doing this.

Many of you work in the healthcare industry. Regulations govern employee monitoring practices due to the sensitivity of the work and information inspired by HIPAA. Check on and become familiar with laws that apply to your workplace. Employers will be sensitive to potential violations. Gaining a basic understanding of these laws can be effective, as simply mentioning them may deter invasive practices.

You must guard against digital scams directed at you. I'm not sure how Walter Bricius's investments are doing, but as of mid-2022, 73 to 81 percent of users had likely lost money on their crypto investments.[111] The sad reality is that if you are a male under 35, you will be a prime target.[112]

This form of invasion is brutal. The medium retirement savings in the US is only about $60,000. This means two things: first, the retirement plan for many of you is to win Powerball, and second, you can't afford to speculate or be lured into shaky propositions. The average crypto investor is a low wage–earning minority, who, in this writer's view, might be better off going with the Powerball option.

Digital Elite: Resist Monitoring That Doesn't Benefit Your Work

Both Julie in her cubicle and the McDonald's employee are measured by their output, such as tasks completed, or burgers sold. These are typical for human-touch and middle workers. The digital elite will not be monitored in the same way. Their objectives are strategic, less tangible, and hard to reduce to a number. For them, activity metrics are better. They don't always translate to progress, but at least show you are trying.

Here is my advice. First recognize that you as a digital elite have more leverage than middle or human-touch workers. You have a better chance to hold your employer accountable for violating your privacy rights. You can push them to be transparent about the data collected and how it is used. You should be able to access and correct data about you, for example.

Trust me. Work-from-home trends will make this important. Many of you now embrace some form of hybrid or remote work. Businesses and governments will rethink how you are managed. Early returns for your productivity were surprisingly positive, but firms are ready to question this early optimism, and they have some good arguments, as debated in Chapter 5.

Sure, a manager could jump on a Zoom call and speak to you, but once the session ends, they have no idea what you are doing. No more laps around the office to count heads on that Friday afternoon before a long weekend. The bottom line is that many managers want the same control they had before. And they want to keep their jobs. So how will managers know what's going on? If you come from the tech world, the answer is obvious: enhanced analytics.

Indications are that digital elite workers will be monitored with greater precision going forward. Already, Microsoft Viva keeps track of your email, calendar, and team chats and provides an activity report, complete with colorful charts and graphs, for example. The number of "quiet days," when you were not doing much, is shown. Today this activity data is sent to the employee but could easily be provided to your manager or robot coworker.

The following is not far-fetched. Your robot work companion, who you like for some tasks but don't trust, might send you this message: "John, you have spent 10 percent of your work time today searching for backyard irrigation systems. Please stop or I will need to report you to your supervisor." Remote employee monitoring is surging, with an over 50 percent increase in demand for surveillance software in 2021 alone.[113] This includes home cameras, keystroke tracking, and screen recording software that can be installed without employee knowledge.[114]

Take as much control of any automation monitoring your activity. The ability to configure and adjust and see data about you has been shown to reduce monitoring stress. In short, your mental state will improve when you know and can control an automation.[115] You will also become less fearful if learning automation can advance your skills and careers. Forrester's Psychology of Automation survey concluded that reduced anxiety and increased positivity were found with these conditions.[116]

It boils down to this: resist any data collection that doesn't directly benefit your work or home life. Data gathered on you can make you more productive, raise your self-esteem, and allow a more balanced work and home life. Melissa Cohen is a global process transformation lead at nVent, an electronics manufacturer, and said:

> If we start monitoring employees, we need to have something in it for them. They won't be comfortable participating just for the company's benefit. Monitoring needs to have a positive benefit for the employee, not just for the organization.

Well said, but don't assume a business will see it that way. Here's a third area where automation trends require you to take a stand. GenAI and low-code apps are a form of invasion as well that will add to your stress in the workplace. Suddenly, you are expected to develop software. How could this be? You probably studied finance or law but now to maintain value you must be an automation creator. You will be responsible for creating and managing automation going forward.

Enterprises have invested billions in "low-code" apps in the last five years and will expect many of you to write software without knowing how to program, using English-like language to build automations. As GenAI has shown, you can tell a machine what you want, and it will write a program. The next programming language is human, and being humans, we may not be ready.

We will give millions of you the ability to build automations without understanding the potential of unintended consequences. New forms of automation insecurity will unfold in the workplace at the management level and trickle down to you. You will be concerned about introducing new vulnerabilities to the company, such as data privacy, biased decisions, or security breaches. Cybersecurity experts say there are only two types of companies: those that have been hacked and those that will be. Even those companies charged with preventing attacks, like OKTA, Microsoft, and Samsung, find their systems getting breached. As a nation, we are not prepared, and as a digital elite, you are not either.[117]

Here's what you can do: take a balanced and careful approach to the pressure to create and maintain automations. Remember, these low-code platforms infused with GenAI are powerful tools but still require an understanding of basic programming concepts and the ability to think logically. Don't try to build a complex app from scratch right away. Start with small, manageable tasks you can gradually learn from and build upon. Use GenAI for tasks like generating text content, code snippets, basic research, and test cases.

Prepare for Your New Offshore Coworkers

I took a tour of the Infosys campus in Bengaluru, India, to see the effect of these invisible robots. As you recall, the invisible robots are software that usually runs in a public cloud or private data center and are becoming worker sidekicks. Forrester calls them AI Agents that can make decisions or perform a service based on environment, user input, and experiences.

They take many forms. An RPA bot may automate a simple data entry task, a virtual agent might take a customer service call, or a GenAI infused agent might summarize a police report for a news article or develop software for a US-based company. Much of this work today is done with low-cost offshore labor. Automation will bring much of it back. Once an invincible economic force, the worldwide scavenger hunt for low-cost labor and production may be ending.

Infosys is credited by some as starting the outsourcing business in India. They were founded by seven engineers in Pune, Maharashtra, India, with an initial capital of $250 in 1981, and have grown to over 250,000 employees around the globe. Not too shabby.

A golf cart took me around their campus, passing through a utopian workplace of fountains, open spaces, clean water, and smart young people on the move. I passed building after building, where thousands of workers answered calls, developed software for US companies, or entered transaction data for global banks. I escaped my host and wandered around on my own and spoke to several workers.

It does not take long to learn that things have changed. It was always growth, growth, growth, but now big new deals aren't there anymore. An industry used to double-digit growth is now lucky to show growth in low single digits.[118] Offshore rising costs don't help. Ocwen Financial Corporation is a mortgage company servicing over 1.3 million US customers. Their total staff is 5,400, with four thousand in India that handle document tasks, data entry, and loan review. I spoke with Rick Chin, Vice President of Lending Solutions. He believes globalization will die a slow death[119]:

> Wages keep going up in India. Back in the day, you could hire seven workers in India for the cost of one in the US. The ratio went to four-to-one and may reach two-to-one. Meanwhile, AI keeps advancing to make onshore processing viable once again. Globalization's value prop is being eroded by automation.

Offshore workers are worried and so is the Indian government. Inside the Infosys walls, they may feel secure, but they can't ignore the reality outside: 40 percent of India grinds it out in the informal economy. People huddle in tents, cook on makeshift stoves, and scramble. Workers count their blessings but realize that many good cubicle jobs that have lifted India's middle class will soon be gone.

The tasks outsourced to offshore locations are repetitive, structured, and well-documented. And, no surprise, perfect for robots. US companies will invest in automation and become less dependent on outsourced staff. Virtual agents or chatbots now take many contact center calls at lower costs.[120] GenAI will make virtual agents even better. Rather than fire Harry, who works down the hall and plays a good third base on the softball team, managers will look first to offshore contracts. They've never met those people.

Other forces push against globalization as well. The pandemic showed how vulnerable an integrated global economy was. Chip shortages, for example, exposed the risks associated with poor control of supply chain components. Going forward, automation will keep labor and production at home. Ironically, the automation that once promised the flattening of the world will evolve to make it hillier.

Here's advice for digital elite and middle workers. Be aware of these global tech industry and emerging immigration trends. The impact of AI and automation on offshore workers will be severe in countries like India, where many workers are employed in low-wage, labor-intensive jobs. This could lead to significant job losses and social unrest in these countries. And new coworkers for you.

Facing slow growth, offshore digital talent will flock to developed countries like the US, potentially competing for your job if it falls within a high-demand field. India had over 140,000 individuals receive green cards to gain legal US residence in 2022.[121] They will be upskilling, reskilling, and challenging immigration laws.

Globalization's decline paves the way for a more diverse workplace. Embrace this shift—actively develop the skills you'll need to succeed in this new environment. Your best bet is to embrace them as coworkers and help them navigate cultural differences and language gaps. Help with the higher cost of housing and be sensitive to many who have had to leave their families behind. You can easily make a long-term friend with simple kindness.

Here's what we can take from this chapter. Businesses will invest in automation that understands what a human is doing. This is ultimately an issue for all workers, the digital elite working at home, Julie in the uneasy middle, and the human-touch worker at McDonald's. In the future, they will be subject to more precise monitoring, and without proper controls, their mental health will be adversely affected. There are things we can do (see Figure 9-1).

What We Can Do	Why It Matters
Don't let monitoring be your boss. Check applicable laws designed to protect you.	Companies will monitor our internet, phone, and email, an inevitable trend.
Take as much control of an automation as practical, especially when monitoring you.	The ability to configure and adjust automation reduces anxiety.
Don't let technology, particularly LLMs, dumb you down. Keep current on knowledge for work.	Too much reliance on automation will make you lose knowledge, skills, and process expertise.
Ask your employer what analytics monitor you. Use them to enhance skills and non-work life.	Invasive analytics to monitor you will increase in the workplace.
Support relocation of digital talent from depressed economies. Sponsor someone if you can.	Automations advances will soften demand for traditional offshore outsourcing.

A human footprint will keep the robots at bay. Leave evidence of your personality everywhere.	You can't compete against the invisible robots. They will do the same task faster.
If you can't beat the bots, you may want to join them.	15 percent of US adults already use a shopping bot or bot service to find goods and services.*
Take time to manage your technology to limit exposure to "cookies" and invasive scenarios.	Data brokers will sell your browsing history for others to invade you.
Advocate for automation that is simple, adapts to you, and improves work life.	Workers have strong voices. Support positive automation progress.
Seek automation that reduces stress from overwork, even if it requires skills enhancement.	Overwork is a health issue and makes you vulnerable to depression and anxiety.
Hold celebrities and brands that pay them accountable for pushing unproven technology.	New digital environments have cash to burn and will always find celebrities to take it.

*Forrester May 2022 Consumer Energy Index and Retail Pulse Report.

Figure 9-1: Invasion: the bot wars have started.

CHAPTER 10

ISOLATION

IN 1903, TEDDY ROOSEVELT CAMPED for three nights in the Yosemite wilderness with John Muir, the famous environmentalist. They awoke among the sequoias, covered by a thin layer of snow, and visited El Capitan. They wandered among the cascading waterfalls, the amazing cliffs, and wildlife. The trip was considered the most significant in the history of conservation and influenced the president to support our national parks and protect the environment.

Today most people live in what I would call a mixed reality of blended digital and physical experience and hardly interact with the natural world. Unfortunately, this ignorance of nature may lead to indifference to its fate. The question is, will our future leaders even care about the planet if they spend most of their time in virtual environments?

Our digital immersion now takes many forms: social media, gaming, the metaverse, and online shopping. Cyberbullying, sexual harassment, hate, and digital addiction are well-covered issues, but less discussed is the harm from separation from the physical world that results from extended digital immersion and stimulation.

Children caught up in their digital world may stay in their basements or bedrooms for extended periods. Less sunlight, fewer outdoor nature excursions, or "Roosevelt" moments are inevitable. The digital world gets more interesting, and the physical world pales in comparison. This is already a concern to those worried about climate change, according to Zaurie Zimmerman, chair of the board of Citizens Climate Lobby, a non-partisan organization that promotes carbon tax legislation. Today's level of screen time and digital interaction is worrisome to her, and the metaverse is terrifying:

> Our youth are getting further pulled into the digital world. They have already lost many communication skills with their peers and parents, preferring text to conversation. But here's my worry. They will experience less and less of the physical world, and thus the enjoyment and appreciation of nature. How can we expect them to care about our planet when they have no experience with it?

The environmental science community cites positives and negatives. They worry that those with an agenda will use the metaverse to present nature in a biased way. An oil and gas interest might show pipelines harmlessly snaking through a national forest, for example. An environmental group might create an overly dramatic vision of pollution or climate risk. On the plus side, children could virtually visit environmentally sensitive sites as a teaching curriculum to connect youth with endangered species and landscapes.

Isolation Trends Are Worrisome

In this chapter, I argue that powerful mental state isolation risks are at work. To start with, WFH trends will further separate the digital elite from human-touch workers. Second,

rural areas that fall behind in automation will further separate from urban areas that don't. Finally, extreme digital
immersion, such as the metaverse, will erode human skills
and leave us vulnerable to AI in the workplace. The second
part of this chapter outlines the implications of these trends
for workers. I also argue that separation from the natural
world will inhibit problem-solving and other skills needed
in the future workplace. Recommendations are made that if
adopted by workers will mitigate these unintended acts of
automation.

WFH Drives Isolation

Many digital elite offices are in our major cities, now with
historically low office occupation rates. As workers have
stopped going in, the service jobs to support them have
declined. Workers in retail, janitorial services, restaurants,
hotels, nail salons, or bars are reduced.

WFH trends mean digital elites are less likely to meet
someone from a different work and lifestyle. They are more
likely to stay within their circle, which has gotten smaller.
Workers will become increasingly sectionalized by their job
and where they live. In short, the decline in daily commuters
will reduce interaction of formerly associated worker groups.

Multi-day or weeklong business road trips will be greatly
reduced as well. Having discovered that Zoom meetings are
productive, what company will fly a sales manager across the
country for a day's worth of meetings? A lasting reduction in
business travel is a near certainty. Some will miss the smell of
Cinnabon at the airport, but the majority will not miss the
drudgery of TSA security or the risk of being jammed into an

airplane shoulder to shoulder with a stranger. They will miss those accents to their work life that travel provides and the chance to get to know their colleagues.

Automation changes our use of physical surroundings. Retail and commercial buildings, the health club, and parks are where we socialize. The pandemic made their use nearly impossible, and automation helped us adjust. We built the home exercise room, tweaked our cooking skills, and learned how to manipulate online sites to meet our needs.

Meanwhile, independent shops, galleries, bookstores, antique shops, and lifestyle businesses that provide that vibrant neighborhood feel continued their downward spiral. Chains and big-box stores that use automation to scale now dominate. Dunkin' Donuts, Popeyes, Taco Bell, and box stores offer standard offerings and decor, a placid sameness. Every place is like no place, dead zones that do not encourage interaction as the individual shops they replaced. Our consumer behavior has become convenient, low-cost, and dull.

We are better at being alone. We stay home to work on our laptops and devices. We use dating site algorithms to find partners rather than going out. We binge-watch streaming content instead of hitting the movie theater. We forego that beer after work to socialize with coworkers. We don't seek out other humans for company. In her book *Alone Together: Why We Expect More from Technology and Less from Each Other*, Sherry Turkle puts this isolation trend front and center. She argues that technology erodes our ability to connect with others by interfering with our relationships. Most people are alone when on a platform and there is no substitute for being with someone in person. Millions who work from home will lose important human connections.

Lack of Automation Can Isolate Work Communities

My automation research has mostly involved interviews with industry and government workers, and primarily from urban settings. To get balance on automation's effect in rural areas, I spent several weeks in Eastern Kentucky and conducted worker interviews. They were not an optimistic bunch, and you can't blame them. West Virginia boasted 140,000 coal jobs in 1940. In 2017, there were 11,600.

The coal jobs aren't likely to come back, and there's little to replace them. Worker discontent is at an all-time high, particularly for white men lacking college degrees, which is almost everybody in Appalachia. It's hard to find a more challenging place for workers to adapt to the digital economy. Long-held stereotypes of Appalachia don't help: *Li'l Abner*, *The Dukes of Hazzard*, *Deliverance*, and *The Beverly Hillbillies* haven't put the region on the map of emerging talent pools. The 2019 Amazon team that searched for a new headquarters location never gave it a thought.

Nick Mullins is a ninth-generation Appalachian and the fifth generation to work in the coal mines. He's also the first in his family to go beyond high school. He worked in the mines for five years but left; he wouldn't subject his family to the dangerous water quality and mining practices. Nick tells us that Appalachia now is scarred mountain tops, toxic slurry ponds, contaminated water, and a population depleting as fast as the underground coal seams.

He likes that visitors enjoy the coal mine museums in Lynch and Benham, Kentucky. He points out that tourism only helps a few local businesses and doesn't provide the living-wage jobs we need. He adds that few tourists learn the dark history of Appalachia. They don't see places like the Hurricane Creek miners' memorial near Hyden, where thirty-eight miners lost their lives.

Mullins felt the gap between his people and modern digital jobs was too big. His part of Kentucky still struggles with basic internet access. He managed to get work in a call center that opened nearby, diagnosing computer and hardware problems. He didn't like it and neither did his miner friends. The call center had decent wages and job security but lacked the camaraderie of the mines.

> Most of the guys I worked with in the mine were damn good people, even some of the foremen. They worked hard, and most had families that loved them—families they'd do anything for. We called Johnny Vanover "Old Man" because he wouldn't let us call him anything else. He started in the mines at age eighteen. By the time he was seventy he'd spent over fifty years underground. He always showed up, often worked twelve hours a day. He lived in constant danger of roof falls, electrocution, injuries from equipment, suffocation from oxygen-deficient air, but developed a close bond with peers. Many of us would ask him why he didn't retire. He'd say, "I don't know what else I'd do with myself. I enjoy it," but that was only half the story. He had paid to send all his children to college and was now paying for his granddaughter.

Mullens concludes that the attitude of minors like Vanover more than gaps in skills divides the rural poor from urban dwellers. Meanwhile, high unemployment rates contribute to deep poverty in mountain communities, with all its many symptoms: substandard housing, depression, and substance abuse.

Digital Immersion Will Foster More Isolation

Bambi is the most-watched Disney movie of all time. Like most kids, I watched it many times. The first half of the movie was joyful. Bambi and Thumper, his pink-nosed rabbit friend, grew up having endless fun, but this would soon end. It was Bambi's first winter, and times were tough. He and his mom were hungry. One fateful day his mother took him to the meadow to find the first shoots of spring grass peeking up through the snow. All good, but then the scary background music started. "Man" is spotted in the forest. Not good.

Bambi doesn't notice the danger, but the mother does. As they run away, his mother is shot and killed by the hunters. Bambi goes from happiness, "We made it, Mother!" to a devastated little fawn, mournful and alone. The death of Bambi's mother shocked me as a small child. It was disturbing. The possibility of my parents dying had not yet registered in my evolving brain.

I've gotten over it, yet my dream would be to enter Disney's metaverse, when available, and purchase virtual firearms with their cryptocurrency, Dragonchain. I would wander into that dangerous meadow and keep those hunters from shooting Bambi's mom. Call it Bambi's revenge.

Disney, the world's foremost storyteller, is investing in the metaverse. In 2022, CEO Bob Chapek announced a new senior vice president position to take charge of "next-generation storytelling"[122] with the metaverse being front and center. An all-Disney digital playground is easy to imagine. Mickey, Goofy, Donald Duck, and Pluto could frolic with famous songs in the background. You could visit Snow White's castle or dive undersea and chase Ariel.

The initial excitement surrounding the metaverse quickly peaked, followed by a gradual decline as challenges and limitations became apparent. Yet the metaverse remains a golden opportunity for Disney and other brands. The term is far from new.[123] It now refers to a network of virtual spaces where your avatar lives and social and business connections can be made, often with the help of virtual reality headsets. Gaming enthusiasts are already there. Billions play games like *Fortnite* that operate in a metaverse. *Second Life*, created by Linden Labs in 2003, was an early version. It was not a game like today's *Fortnite* or *Roblox*. Users created a digital avatar in their likeness to explore, meet others, create digital content, and trade goods in Linden Dollars. *Second Life* is still holding steady with about sixty thousand concurrent users at peak times.

Many people are concerned about the metaverse, a complete and immersive digital experience. Callum Hood is the head of research at the Center for Countering Digital Hate, a title that gets right to the point. Hood recorded interactions in the VRChat environment, where people with VR headsets play cards and meet in a virtual club or park. In one eleven-hour period, he recorded more than one hundred problematic incidents, some with children under the age of thirteen. In several cases, avatars made sexual and violent threats against minors. Surprisingly, even the tech industry has concerns. Andrew Bosworth, CTO of Meta, was direct in a memo,[124] "Governing what people do in the metaverse at any meaningful scale is practically impossible."

The metaverse will need to transition like 42nd Street in Manhattan. From the Great Depression to the 1980s, it was known for seedy porn shops, peep shows, drugs, scammers, crime, X-rated movies, and a likely place to lose your wallet. It was not a place for kids or even adults. No more: it is now flashy, with blinding LED screens and Disney-fied wholesomeness, but perhaps lacking its former soul.

The takeaway is that automation is charging ahead without a full view of the consequences. Full digital immersion, in addition to the safety concerns described, will enhance our digital skills and reach but is unlikely to advance the human skills we need in the workplace. Now we turn to workplace implications and advise you to deal with these isolation trends.

What You Can Do

The metaverse, social media, and excessive screen time can all contribute to isolation and echo chambers and diminish human skills needed in the workplace. To combat these issues, we must actively seek balanced perspectives, reconnect with nature, and hold the tech industry accountable for its impact on society.

Pump the Brakes on the Metaverse, Social Platforms, and Screen Time

The pandemic pushed us hard down the digital path and some off a psychological cliff, according to David Sax, author of *The Future Is Analog*. If you were a digital or online neophyte in 2019, well, you had to become at least passable in 2021, and it was hard to fake it. You could not go to a bank or visit a store. If you wanted to see the grandkids, you had to get on Zoom. Yet, as argued by Sax, in short order we realized how awful physical isolation with reduced human interaction can be.

Extreme digital immersion, like the metaverse or gaming, blunts the human traits that have evolved over thousands of years. Back then, if you encountered someone in the woods and couldn't tell if they were your friend or foe, you may have been eliminated from the evolutionary process. You needed to read body language, interpret visual and verbal signals, and ask the right questions. Consistent human interaction keeps these human skills sharp. They become dulled if you are by yourself too much. Depression, attention deficit disorder, eating and body dysmorphia, and platform addiction have also been cited conditions.[125]

According to recent studies, working in isolation hinders the maintenance of needed workplace skills.[126] Effective communication, emotional intelligence, problem-solving, empathy, conflict resolution, collaboration, and adaptability, for example, are hard to develop in isolation—exactly the traits you need as automaton takes over many of your tasks. You can guess where this is going. These skills become essential for maintaining relevance as we enter the "human capable" automation period described in Chapter 2. How do you expect to keep pace with AI at work if you spend most of your time staring at screens and not engaging with people?

Escape the Echo Chambers: Bring Balance to Work

Technopoly: The Surrender of Culture to Technology by Neil Postman argues that our culture is now dominated by technology, which has profoundly influenced our values, beliefs, and behaviors. Netflix's 2020 documentary *The Social Dilemma* went even further. It illustrated how social and mobile platforms segment and isolate us unwittingly. They build motes around us. Their algorithms maximize our time on the platform and produce division as a byproduct.

The dangers created are well documented. Extreme left and right platforms, with values that should be disqualified from civilized society, are given life and oxygen. In the 2020 election, social media platforms such as Facebook, YouTube, and Twitter (X) spread untruths about politics. Could QAnon get a million members without the social media engine behind it? Unlikely.

Human interaction can temper the divisive effects of automation. They expose us to diverse perspectives, allowing us to appreciate individuals despite differences. Without digital distortions, real-life interactions make it easier to embrace diverse viewpoints, fostering better understanding and collaboration in the workplace. Conversely, isolation and digital immersion amplify division. Algorithms create echo chambers, reinforcing existing biases and hindering meaningful connections.

So, get off the screen and see people. Human interactions improve your adaptability and ability to express yourself clearly, listen to other opinions more attentively, and adapt your communication style to different situations. Human interaction will promote balance in your views that help you in the workplace.

Demote Your Devices and Spend More Time in Nature

Studies show spending time in nature directly boosts creativity and problem-solving skills. Conversely, limited exposure to nature can hinder our ability to think creatively and generate new ideas. You don't have to become a John Muir protégé or environmental activist, but you can do two simple things. First, demote your digital devices. Lower their priority. Set limits on digital use, the time you spend on your phone, computer, and other digital devices. Turn off notifications for social media, email, and other apps that you don't need to check constantly and take a hike in the woods.

Try to spend time in nature each day, even for a few minutes. This can help reduce stress, improve your mood, and boost your creativity, and more importantly, your problem-solving ability.[127] Biophilia, the innate human affinity for nature, can help us confront automation at work in several ways. It's why we feel peaceful or energized by a walk in the woods. Studies have shown that biophilic design can have a positive effect on human health, reduce stress, improve mood, and boost creativity.[128] It is being incorporated into design and architecture. For example, natural elements like plants and water features in the workplace create more human-centered and sustainable spaces.

That is just one example. Nature has a well-documented ability to reduce stress and anxiety, which can be prevalent in the face of automation and job insecurity. It can help us relax, clear our minds, and approach work with a calmer and more focused mindset. Nature can improve cognitive function, including memory, attention, and focus, all crucial for learning new skills, adapting to new technologies, and performing in an automated work environment. Trade some screen time for outdoor time and watch your productivity and mental and physical health improve.

Hold the Tech Industry Accountable

How did we get here? Where was the meeting that gave control of our digital lives to a small group of companies? Wall Street calls them the "Magnificent Seven": Apple, Amazon, Alphabet (Google), Meta (Facebook), Microsoft, Nvidia, and Tesla. Technology innovation has propelled these companies to become the world's most valuable. Their unelected leaders control nearly every aspect of our digital lives.

When discussing his limited fan base, Wilt Chamberlain, the first seven-foot basketball player, said years ago, "Everybody pulls for David, and nobody roots for Goliath."[129] He was right: except for investors, few of us root for the Goliath-tech companies, yet we're happy to keep feeding them. We give them our most sensitive personal data in exchange for a little convenience. Connections to friends, ride-sharing ease, or the fun of online shopping is all it takes. We pour in baby photos, vacation pictures, locations, and political opinions.

At first, the exchange was fair. The smartphones in our pockets became awesome tools. We loved the instant access to product reviews, comparison sites, and unprecedented automation. All good. But over time, the value equation shifted. AI algorithms have made the data we give up more valuable. Click on a "like" or provide a reference and bingo, you've created value. Digital profiles now emerge from our browsing histories, social media posts, and location tracking and are used to segment us.

It may seem like David has little chance against these Goliath-type companies, but we can all take responsibility and be activists. Simple microaggressions like not accepting cookies, for example, can help. We can support regulations that hold executives accountable for abuses in the metaverse, for example. Europe's automation directives increasingly hold tech industry executives directly accountable, with evidence suggesting this approach deters irresponsible behavior.

Some of you will argue we have seen this movie before and are overreacting. New technologies arrive and are met with initial concerns that do not materialize. So called "dime novels" in the early twentieth century were blamed for young people acting crazy. No one pointed out they almost always do. Twenty years later, radio dramas were thought to give young listeners anxiety and sleep loss. Comic books and television were next and blamed for antisocial behavior. Video games were linked to criminal behavior in 2002, but by 2020, it was largely dismissed.[130]

Don't dismiss these unintended consequences of automation! Our growing isolation might seem like a fad, but what if workgroups become fractured, the rural-urban divide widens, and human skills become obsolete? Should we ignore these unintended risks or take action to mitigate them? My position is simple: the potential consequences are too severe to ignore (see Figure 10-1).

What We Can Do	*Why It Matters*
Take your kid to the woods.	Build early appreciation of the physical world.
Limit your children's time on social media and the metaverse, an unregulated environment.	The US Surgeon General cited diminished self-esteem and depression in a 2023 children's warning.
Experiment with GenAI with your children. Don't forbid their use.	Biases, inaccuracies, and stereotypes are to be expected and cautioned against.
Don't let your online self overshadow your offline personality.	Advancing digital lifestyles further isolates us and discourages community participation.
Fine-tune your use of automation to the level of human engagement that suits you.	Commercial forces create a FOMA tension for their next fashionable digital innovation.
Reduce your time on social media and monitor your mental wellbeing.	If you're feeling depressed, look to your friends rather than social media.
Recognize and fight divisive fringe ideas. Listen to both sides with an open mind.	Media commercial interests divide and isolate communities. Don't let them put you in a box.

Pump brakes on the metaverse, social platforms, and screen time. Your people skills will suffer.	Advancing automation requires communication, patience, empathy, and conflict resolution.
Support regulation and white-collar laws that hold executives accountable for abuses.	Direct accountability for tech industry abuses is a strong deterrent to irresponsible behavior.

Figure 10-1: Don't let automation isolate you.

PART IV

Can We Save the Workplace?

The final chapters argue that an optimistic outcome for automation is possible: random acts can be controlled and automation can benefit all workers.

Chapter 11, "AI Leaves 'Learn To Code' Behind," asks that all worker groups—digital elite, middle, and human-touch workers—alter their approach to education and skills development. Human-touch workers especially need to build self-esteem and constructive ambition. Middle workers must embrace retraining for entirely new roles. Even the digital elite should challenge the education status quo and seek innovative learning methods. Successful employee training programs provide examples, while the chapter critiques exploitative online programs from elite institutions.

Metrics hold immense power to shape behavior. Chapter 12, "Sorry, You Have the Wrong Number," explains that our current performance measures are flawed, failing to capture the true human experience. Humorous and historical references are used to critique traditional economics and highlight the limitations of current metrics, including insights from Tom Seaver, the tragic fate of prisoners shipped to

Australia, and greenwashing by "ESG" investment funds. The chapter concludes with a call for a new metric: a "Misery, Anxiety, and Frustration Index" to capture the human cost of automation.

Chapter 13, "Human-Centered Automation," offers hope. The core idea of the book is reinforced, that individuals can push back against the tide of automation. Government-led policies are critiqued as too slow and ineffective, while proposals for AI governance from the European Commission and the White House are seen as having limitations. To bridge the gap, the concept of "Automated Centers of Excellence" is proposed to address the negative impacts of automation. Finally, the chapter concludes with five key questions businesses should ask to mitigate negative automation effects and emphasizes the importance of optimism.

CHAPTER 11

AI LEAVES "LEARN TO CODE" BEHIND

RESEARCH ON UPSKILLING AND RESKILLING draws from a rich tapestry of disciplines and perspectives. Future of work books such as "The Second Machine Age" by Erik Brynjolfsson and Andrew McAfee "highlighted the importance of upskilling as early as 2014, while books like Clayton Christensen, "Reinventing Professional Education" delve deeper into specific lifelong learning strategies, for worker adaptability. Economists like David Autor and Daron Acemoglu emphasize the need for policy interventions to support worker transitions. Education is undergoing a radical transformation as well, with diverse perspectives on reinvention such as works like Sylvia Martinez and Gary Stager's "Invent to Learn."

The advice here draws from interviews with workers across the four segments most likely to be disrupted, where automation has already transformed their work. Workers with calloused hands, furrowed brows, and anxious thoughts told how they are grappling with the challenges of automation.

Automation presents a unique landscape for each worker group. Digital elites, middle workers, and those in human-touch roles will all need to approach skill development and education from distinct angles. Self-esteem and respect are a more important challenge for human-touch workers, for example. Middle workers must target and retrain for the new positions that AI creates; the digital elite should look at traditional education differently. Critical thinking is high-lighted and applies to all workers, not just the digital elite.

Human-Touch Workers: Self-Esteem and CT Can Beat the Robots

Walmart is the third largest employer in the world, after the US Department of Defense and China's People's Liberation Army. It has invested $2.7 billion in training its employees.[131] Two hundred Walmart academies are up and running. Two-to-six-week training programs teach retail skills for entry-level positions or advancement. Oculus virtual reality head-sets help employees improve customer service skills. The immersive experience is state of the art, but the full-stage graduation ceremony grabbed me. Many are in old ware-house spaces, now empty due to supply-chain automation.

Graduation is a big deal for many employees. One woman completed the training and put on a blue cap and gown to receive her certificate. Afterward, she was greeted by hugs and congratulations from family and friends, where she almost came to tears and said, "You know, I never graduated from high school. This was my first opportunity to graduate from anything and for my children to see me be successful."[132] This worker built transferable skills to advance, but more importantly, improved her self-esteem. The training with certification made the worker a better Walmart employee and lifted her spirit.

But this is just the beginning. Technologies with names like extended reality, augmented reality, mixed reality, and virtual reality will require human-touch workers to be productive in new ways, and as described in Chapter 5, you get to use your device skills and have less physical toil and boredom. You can fill these positions but need hope, self-esteem, a critical eye, and constructive ambition.

Self-Esteem and Respect—A Solvable Issue

Rahmel Hunter had almost given up. In the cycle of poverty so many endure, he had no job and little education to get a decent one. But there were nonprofits that gave him hope, like Merit America, Year Up, Per Scholas, and NPower. These organizations provide technical training for those with limited education and from disadvantaged communities.

Rahmel found NPower, which helps military veterans and disadvantaged young adults start tech-industry careers. They trained him in fundamentals such as cloud administrative support, networking, and cyber security. They also gave him social worker support and job connections, but most importantly, hope and ambition. Like many human-touch workers today, Hunter didn't just want to cover the rent.

According to NPower CEO Bertina Ceccarelli, the number one request for human-touch workers who go through their digital training is to show them a career path. When you speak to Ceccarelli, there is a healthy dose of enthusiasm:

> We have an EKG on the job market and can launch a new course in less than six months. Donations and grants allow us to not charge a student. And here's

what's important: we have corporate sponsors, and connections to them. They want to hire a more diverse workforce and they need digital skills of all kinds. Our sponsors, like many others, are softening traditional requirements for four-year degrees. It is a golden time for us right now.

NPower's sweet spot is mid-range technical jobs. They don't train students to be professional software developers. Ceccarelli estimates well over 50 percent of all jobs require some degree of digital skills. Work-training programs that promise skill development, hope, and a career path will be needed.

What I like the best about NPower's mission is the unwavering focus on self-esteem and respect for workers. Here's what we all can do better. Bottle some of the empathy and respect from the early pandemic period and use a little each day to treat all workers with respect. It's the right thing to do and there is an economic argument. According to Gallup, employees who are not engaged in their work due to a bad attitude cost the world $7.8 trillion in lost productivity. That's equal to 11 percent of global GDP.[133]

Lessons from a Warehouse Worker's Journey

Whether working in a car wash, an assisted living center, retail food, or warehouse, CT skills can help you advance to the middle, make informed decisions, and adapt to changing circumstances. Human-touch workers armed with CT can analyze situations, identify potential issues, and find creative solutions, even for seemingly routine tasks that you now perform.

At its core, CT is the ability to question, test assumptions, examine, interpret, evaluate, and reason. Historically, CT dates to ancient Greece and Socrates. He developed a questioning method to expose inconsistencies in an argument and encourage rational discourse. In the nineteenth and twentieth centuries, formal studies in logic and scientific methods laid the groundwork for modern CT frameworks. Influential thinkers like John Dewey and Charles Peirce emphasized active reasoning and problem-solving in education.

To deal with AI in the workplace, upskilling for soft skills like task delegation, strategic planning, and communication are correctly emphasized, but CT stands out as an essential skill across all work segments. A large-scale employer survey revealed a growing critical skills focus: 81% of companies strongly emphasize their employees' ability to think critically[134]

Let's get one misconception out of the way. CT is not about being cynical or negative. It's not about how you might scan your daughter's attire before she goes on a date, or your son's table manners. CT trains you to ask questions, challenge assumptions, seek diverse perspectives, examine information objectively, identify key points and biases, assess evidence carefully, and build well-reasoned arguments.

There's also a misconception that CT is solely for the "digital elite," implying that other workers somehow achieve success without using their brains. This is not only condescending but also inaccurate. Here is how a warehouse worker might use CT. Melissa is a warehouse veteran but currently at odds with the new robots. Like many, her company introduced them to optimize picking and packing, and they looked good at first. But after the first week, packages were being mislabeled, fragile items were damaged, and efficiency had stalled. The robots were programmed for specific tasks and struggled to adapt to the normal warehouse chaos. They seemed to struggle with oddly shaped items, delicate glassware, and packages with unclear labeling.

She could have blamed the machines, made the usual robot jokes, or rejoiced in how superior humans are, but she didn't take that route. She had been honing her CT skills through a diet of podcasts and free online courses, which she used to dissect the problem. She also had access to the newly deployed GenAI tool, which allowed her to ask questions via a simple "prompt" interface. She asked about some unusual patterns she observed when things went wrong. The model helped her pinpoint the types of packages causing issues. She suggested tweaks to the robot's algorithms to better identify fragile or odd-shaped items.

CT gave her a positive and proactive attitude, perhaps the most important thing. She realized the robots weren't the enemy. By suggesting additional sensors and improved data capture, she proposed ways for humans and robots to work together more effectively. Management was impressed. Melissa transformed from a potentially displaced worker to a valuable collaborator, leveraging her human skills to optimize automation.

Advances in physical automation will make examples like Melissa more common. Robots will give the human-touch worker the needed energy to apply CT. Warehouse robots will reduce the drudgery of endless walking and heavy lifting, for example. Kait Peterson of Locus Robotics, a company that builds robots for warehouses, reported that many workers have boosted their productivity by rearranging the robots' movement patterns. In some of her customer environments, employees listen to music and brainstorm ways to improve efficiency. They not only increased their Units Picked Per Hour (UPH) metric for more pay, but also showed management an ability to contribute. Put simply, CT will make a job better, and make sure you will keep it. According to Forrester data, business has its hands full retaining permanent staff anyway, and this will continue.

Domain-Specific CT Is Needed

This story shows how CT could translate to a workplace, but today it falls short. It does not translate easily to specific jobs. Frameworks prioritize logic and formal arguments and are too academic for most workers. CT needs to be directed at the specific automation context, to provide an appropriate lens.

For human-touch workers, risks and benefits from physical automation are highlighted, as Melissa has demonstrated. Middle positions will need specific CT skills to evaluate the feasibility of machine-guided decisions and support. To ensure cost-effectiveness and maintain necessary human oversight, the digital elite must carefully evaluate which tasks can be automated through a critical lens for responsible deployment.

Here's the good news: the application of CT to specific workplaces is gaining traction. For example, there are now CT books written for addiction professionals, kindergarten teachers, and even for all of us, such as *Critical Thinking for Dummies*. Nonprofit groups are doing excellent work.[135] For human touch workers like Melissa, I recommend *A Practical Guide to Critical Thinking* by Linda Elder and Richard Pau. Yes, it's a textbook with academic content but with a clear and engaging framework.

Melissa's story showcases the power of CT in the face of AI and automation. It's not about humans versus machines but a "trust but verify" collaboration. In addition to securing her job, Melissa became a catalyst for positive change by analyzing problems and proposing solutions.

Middle Workers: Use Automation to Your Advantage

As a reminder, we have argued that the middle will be the most threatened by automation and lose the most jobs. Middle workers will need the most help going forward. Pressure to retrain and figure out what to do will be intense. Common advice for struggling middle workers in years past has been, "Learn to code," but this has lost favor. Daniel Greene's *The Promise of Access: Technology, Inequality, and the Political Economy of Hope* takes this view, for example. He asks, "Why do we think everyone needs to 'learn to code'—or else?"[136]

The "learn to code" view is shortsighted as well. GenAI like the Turing bot described previously will make coding skills less important. GenAI models like ChatGPT are trained on AI chips like those made by Nvidia, a company now close to a $2 trillion valuation. Its founder and CEO Jensen Huang commented on careers going forward:[137]

> The mantra of learning to code or teaching your kids how to program or even pursue a career in computer

science, which was so dominant over the past ten to fifteen years, has now been thrown out of the window. You're already a programmer.

A lot of you today are intermediaries serving as brokers, emissaries, go-betweens, or agents between great piles of company data and the firm's customers, partners, or other employees. To be effective, you compile reports, or respond to customers, and must understand procedures, search through old knowledge management systems, work with legacy systems, and navigate poorly designed websites and applications. It's not easy to make sense of what is mostly poorly organized and opaque information at the insurance company or bank, but that's mostly why your job exists. Over time, AI interfaces will dissolve this friction and put your job at risk.

To succeed you must become an AI operator, as described in Chapter 4. Leverage AI guidance to give more valuable advice and support. Your job will require you to converse directly with a GenAI infused agent trained on company procedures with access to necessary systems. It will not be the android or physical robot that pushes you out of that cubicle. It will be a human equipped with an Iron Man–like, GenAI suit of armor that will do the work of several employees.

Working with Your Hands Deserves More Respect

First, appreciate the special combination of dexterity and problem-solving prowess that many of you possess. A digital elite with exceptional education may struggle with assembling the outside grill, putting a swing set together, and couldn't operate a nail gun, yet are quick to dismiss your work as repetitive, low-skilled, and the obvious target for automation.

Labor economists and academics still refer to those who work with their hands as "low-skilled," a term that should be discarded. Many of your jobs, like the floor-covering mechanic Bob Jacobsen told us in the introduction, require judgment, physical agility, experience, emotional fortitude, and attention to detail and won't be automated for some time.

To get a fairer balance you also need to stop looking up to the digital elite who work in areas like law and finance. In many of these roles you must search hard to find tangible value to society. Often, they gather a fee for sitting between routine financial transactions or recklessly pursuing personal injury claims. Does this add more value to society than building a custom birdhouse for a nature lover?

Today, as a society, we discourage our young from going into the trades. Why do guidance counselors and parents disparage working with your hands? We need electricians and plumbers, and lots of them. A robot to diagnose and repair a plumbing problem in a home will be far too expensive to build any time soon. Machines can beat a grand champion at chess (cognitive skill), but walking five feet (physical skill) is a challenge for them. Clean-energy jobs like solar panel installers now number more than 350,000 and will grow at double digits.[138] We do not have enough people to do these jobs, even before the $1.2 trillion infrastructure spending gets underway.

Take a drive through any suburb and stop at a strip mall. You'll see signs for plumbers, HVAC contractors, an electrician, a small bakery, and a dry cleaner. These commercial spots employ millions of middle workers. Fred Goff would say these are his people. He is the CEO of Jobcase, a social platform for over one hundred million service and middle workers. It's like LinkedIn for the working class, although Goff does not like that comparison.

He has an energetic personality. I worried he might jump through the phone when I suggested many see no hope for the middle class, robots will take their jobs, and high-school graduates won't move to the digital economy anytime soon. He calls that view condescending and snobbish and makes a strong case:

> Our people can be a Salesforce administrator and make $75K a year. Longer term, it's all about solving problems, fixing things and that's what our people can do.

He points to the encouragement his parents gave him growing up:

> Self-esteem and positive attitude are Jobcase's most important goals. Look, I had two hard-working parents. They told me over and over I could do anything or be anybody I wanted to be. This is not the case for most. They need empathy, and a simple message from another human—you can do it.

Automation will require millions of jobs for people to use their hands to fix things. Each of the eleven categories of physical automation referred to earlier needs your help. Android security officers, janitorial robots, robotic waiters, and chefs share one important attribute: they will all break. Watch a security robot, its gears sputtering and sparks flying, take an ungraceful tumble into the office park fountain, sending a flock of pigeons skyward in protest (on YouTube, of course).

We need a new generation of skilled human-touch workers to keep automation running. Companies are planning "robot management services" to augment their traditional server, desktop, and printer maintenance offerings. Millions of new jobs will be created by tomorrow's physical automation economy. The clean energy economy will create millions more.

Critical Thinking Will Keep Your Middle Job

While soft skills like relationship building, mindfulness, and adaptability are often touted as the panacea for job transitions like these, this view falls short. Our biggest challenge isn't simply being a more engaged and agile human; it's navigating a world saturated with misinformation, bias, manipulative systems, and automation. In this landscape, we need CT. We need to question everything. Even this paragraph.

And here is why: AI software is poised for explosive growth. Tools like OpenAI's ChatGPT, Google's Gemini, and Microsoft's Copilot will see a 36% annual surge from 2023 to 2030. Business will use these tools to build AI Agents that get work done at lower costs. To keep your position, you will have to work with them, but what skills will you need?

To find out, Microsoft surveyed 31,000 people in 31 countries[139]. LinkedIn data was also used. The results were published in their Annual 2023 Work Trend Index. The skills workers will need in this AI-powered future were ranked. The top skill on the list? Critical and analytic thinking. 'Flexibility,' and 'emotional intelligence' were second and third. "Bias detection" and "AI Delegation" meaning creating AI prompts, were also important.

Thousands of middle jobs will require CT. They include content curators ensuring the machines receive the correct data and librarians who skeptically review machine learning training data. Machines will make more decisions, and as they do, CT is needed to flag mistakes. Hundreds of HITL positions will develop.

Consider this scenario. You are a manufacturing worker concerned about the constant metallic clang of robots echoing through the factory. The steady invasion creates uncertainty and anxiety that gnaws at you. You scan the job postings in the breakroom and see words like "design," "maintenance," and "quality control." These positions require you to analyze production data, identify inefficiencies, and optimize workflows that collaborate with robots.

Skilled airline maintenance technicians are in the same boat. They must learn to use automated tools for aircraft inspections. They will need CT to analyze data, interpret sensor readings, and make repair decisions. This requires evaluating the information provided by automation to identify potential issues that the machines will miss.

Even truck drivers will see similar job transitions. There is a shortage of them today, and it's a big one. The American Trucking Association estimated a shortage of seventy-eight thousand drivers in 2022, but in five years, drivers will start to be augmented by self-driving vehicle technology.

Here's a near-term vision: a former truck driver, now titled a "vehicle systems manager," comes into an office and goes to his cubicle, but it's a fancy one. He sits in what looks like a truck driver's seat and starts driving using a VR headset. He's not dealing with a single windshield view with an occasional glance at the speedometer, but over twenty screens filled with diagnostics and route analytics now demand his attention. He will analyze route data, identify operational inefficiencies, adjusting his roles accordingly. He coordinates the arrival of a human driver for the final ten miles to navigate the aging loading dock.

Middle jobs need CT skills tailored to their roles, and GenAI can help. Why not give these middle workers access to a tailored model that uses CT principles to question, test, examine, interpret, evaluate, reason, and make informed decisions like the body shop technicians highlighted in Chapter 4?

Yes, the Robots Will Train You

Think of AI tools as a personal assistant to help you, whether you work for someone else or run your own business. Use it to build your skills. For example, AI can explain the basics of coding so you can understand what's happening behind the screen, or better yet write the code for you. If you struggle with effective communication, use it to structure emails, help you with persuasive writing, summarize a lengthy piece of content, or write ads or marketing copy. Within three to five years, an upskilling robot with AI-infused capabilities will be there to find you a new job.

Here is how it might work. George is an experienced accounts payable clerk, happily working in the back office of a major firm. He doesn't love his job but appreciates the steady $65,000-a-year salary. Not bad for a high-school graduate. But dark clouds are on the horizon.

Software robotics were installed that strip the important fields from incoming invoices and emails. That clean, organized data set is all the bot needs to make decisions George used to make, such as whether the invoice was legitimate and should be paid. He knows that most of his job will be automated, and he needs to find a new career. But where does he start?

Fortunately, his company was forced to escrow funds from a recently passed robot tax. With them, they developed a "reskilling robot." George allows this bot access to his LinkedIn, resume files, Facebook, Instagram, performance reviews, and emails that provide context on his current skills. With that access, the upskilling bot can get a better idea of his current skill set and what George might like to do. The embedded LLM also has access to the National Bureau of Labor job trends.

The skills robot takes a few seconds and suggests that data governance positions are the best match. George isn't so sure. For one, he has only a vague idea of what governance means. He also worries that collaboration, persuasion, and presenting skills are needed. In his current role, he rarely had to explain anything or even talk with anybody. He enjoyed his back-office solitude.

The skills robot says not to worry and suggests George put his virtual reality headset on. With that he enters simulated data governance meetings. Specific tasks, deliverables, and interactions with superiors are part of the immersive experience that seems like a metaverse demo he has seen before. The skills robot was trained on emails, instant messages, documents, and summarized meeting transcripts for governance positions. The simulated environment provides training, and a prompt interface for George to fill gaps in compliance laws and best practices. Links are provided to fine-tune his presentation skills with virtual speech coaches. After reflection George decides to pursue a career in data governance. The point is that automation began as George's enemy and now is his best friend.

GenAI will make the above scenario a reality for millions soon. Like the robot helping George above, GenAI can analyze employee work history and performance reviews to identify skill gaps and recommend personalized learning paths. Bite-sized, engaging training modules will cater to shorter attention spans and fit busy schedules. Language barriers are removed, and tech vendors are wasting no time. Udemy, a leader in online courses, is using AI to personalize learning recommendations based on learner progress. PricewaterhouseCoopers, a multinational professional services firm, is piloting an AI-powered coaching platform. Duolingo, a popular language learning app, uses AI to personalize language learning.

Kate Lepore is Senior Director of Learning Strategy and Solutions at the automation vendor Pegasystems. She spearheaded their customer training app, naming it Socrates after the famous philosopher whose method it uses—a series of questions to challenge assumptions and guide students. Your experience is questioned to tailor the interaction. To Kate, GenAI is the future of workplace skills development,

> "Our goal is to train regular businesspeople to build automations, that previously might require a professional developer. Previous training was step by step, complete this section and go to the next, with no real assessment of progress. Socrates is dialog based; driven by knowledge you prove. With the Socratic method, questions and answers lead the student to competence. Guidance is incremental and tailored to the proven knowledge of the individual."

These employers supplied skills robots sound great, but what if you are out of work? Sign up for a free GenAI model like ChatGPT. Just tell the model your story, your work history, ambitions and importantly what you value in life and what the character of your ideal employer would be. Give the model your resume and history but no personal data, like your mobile phone or home address. These AI tools analyze your career story, ambitions, values, and ideal work environment. It will identify weaknesses in your resume or job pitch related to your goals and offer strategies for improvement.

Digital Elites Have Tough Choices to Make

The traditional college degree isn't the only passport to success for the digital elite anymore. Today, learning options exist, from online degrees and internships to company training programs, free courses, and even AI-assisted CT. All have strengths and weaknesses and must be considered to chart your ideal career path. Keep in mind, this exploration doesn't cover every avenue—consider it a launching pad to craft your personalized learning journey.

College Makes Less Sense in the Future of Work

Elite institutions offer prestige and network value that can boost career prospects. Great value remains for those fortunate enough to attend them. The value proposition for all but the top college brands has been in decline for years. Non-elite institutions must redefine their worth through affordability, innovation, and skill development that target where automation will take us.

The guaranteed good job is not there anymore. A 2019 study by the Pew Research Center found that 44 percent of college graduates were underemployed, meaning they were in jobs that did not require a college degree. This is a staggering figure. Meanwhile, tuition at universities and colleges keeps rising with questionable investments in facilities and administrative positions.[140] People with college degrees struggle to find jobs that pay well enough to justify the costs. A 2023 report shows the median lifetime earnings of college graduates still exceed those of high school graduates but have shrunk dramatically,[141] for example. Majors like education and humanities face significant wage stagnation, while others like tech and healthcare offer higher returns.

It's tricky. The value of a college education is not just economics. Traditional education helps you think more efficiently and communicate more effectively. These soft skills are required to succeed in the human-capable period we are entering. The need for improved communication skills, critical thinking, and problem-solving skills has been highlighted in earlier chapters.

There is a status issue as well. Many parents feel they have failed if their children do not get that degree. But here's the most important part and most difficult to quantify: college broadens your perspective, enriches your life, and fosters engaged citizenship. For many, these are priceless rewards.

The equation for college's value is evolving. Going forward, many will realize not everyone needs to, or should, go into six-figure debt for an education that machines over time will marginalize. Parents and their offspring may decide college is not a practical route anymore. The college decision will be a tossup for many, dictated by individual circumstances, but if you have the resources and ambition to go, you probably should. If you don't, explore the alternative education and skills development options that follow.

Online Degree Programs Also Have Issues

Online degree programs service students at lower costs but have poor reputations. Commercial ventures like Trump University and the University of Phoenix have been described as boiler-room operations with predatory recruitment practices. Students pile up debt for near-worthless degrees.[142] Parents and students often feel ripped off.

Al Arsenault paid for his daughter to get an online master's degree at George Washington, one of the most expensive private universities. She had no shared projects with other students and no one-on-one time with teachers. There were videos to watch, papers and books to read, and assignments to do, but she never met anybody. Arsenault summed up what bothered him:

> She didn't see any point in attending graduation. She wouldn't have known anybody. Sure, she has her degree, but no network of colleagues and mentors. People her age need to build a personal brand. That's where work is going. And online education doesn't move that dial.

Here's one takeaway. Often, successful people talk about those who helped them along the way. Mentors who asked nothing in return, who sent the elevator back down to let a younger person on. They benefited from their college roommates or teachers who inspired them. Online education has a role in the future of work but falls short in human relationships.

Community Colleges Shine Bright

Community colleges offer affordable two-year degrees and vocational training programs. Early in my career, I was fortunate enough to teach at both Montgomery County Community College and George Washington University (GW), and the difference was like stepping from a bustling train station into a silent library.

At the community college, my data communications students were motivated. Many juggled two jobs and families but still attended night classes, eager to learn everything I could throw at them. Their enthusiasm was infectious, and I thrived on their energy.

GW, on the other hand, was a different story. Half the students seemed like they'd rather be anywhere else. The air crackled with apathy, and enthusiasm was a rare commodity. Oh, and did I mention the price tag? GW ranks among the most expensive private universities in the country, with tuition and fees exceeding a whopping $64,990 in 2023.

While this limited experience doesn't warrant generalization, community colleges are often overlooked and suffer from decades of undeserved condescension. They offer a quality education at a fraction of the cost. So, before jumping on the expensive university bandwagon, explore what community colleges offer.

Consider Josh Sinnott's story. He held a four-year degree from Arizona State University, but it wasn't working for him. He bounced between jobs at a bakery, Charles Schwab, and a local startup searching for a better fit. Then, at 26, he took a chance and enrolled in an Associate degree program in AI at Chandler-Gilbert Community College[143]. The program was a steal at $6,500 and packed a punch, offering advanced courses in statistics, and Python coding. The investment paid off. After graduation, he fielded offers from companies like Google and ultimately landed at a startup building an immigration research tool for attorneys. While his title is in sales, he also acts as a sort of AI consultant, leveraging his newfound expertise.

Josh's story supports what we see from the data: GenAI will be a disruptive force in the job market. Forrester estimates it will reshape over 11 million jobs by 2030. Forget the days when "AI" in a job title or description meant you needed a master's or PhD. Now AI is creating jobs that don't require years of higher education.

This disruption is forcing a hard look at traditional education. Enrollment at four-year schools is down, while community colleges are experiencing a surge. The message is clear: the future of work demands new skills, and higher education may be too slow to adapt. To shift careers, middle and human-touch workers should consider community colleges.

Here is the main point: Don't let a lack of formal education hold you back! A wealth of options exists to develop your skills, catering to various time constraints and budgets. Apprenticeships offer hands-on learning with earning potential, while intensive boot camps provide fast-track training in high-demand fields like technology and healthcare. Leading companies can equip you with industry knowledge through management training programs and internships. Finally, explore the vast library of free online courses—a perfect way to upskill or learn new things without a full-time commitment. These options empower you to chart your course toward a fulfilling career, regardless of your educational background.

Critical Thinking Will Be a Prerequisite

We have seen how CT benefits middle and human-touch workers, but the digital elite need it most. Let's start with keeping your job. Much of what you do today consists of searching for and interpreting pre-written text, existing data in corporate systems, operating procedures manuals, contracts, or technical documentation. Automation will take many of these tasks and along with them a solid chunk of your value. To maintain your position, you need to apply CT, question information you encounter, analyze arguments you hear, and make connections between new and old information, and increasingly new and old technology—all things AI can't do yet.

To be more effective at work, CT will also help you design intuitive interfaces and feedback mechanisms that help humans understand and trust automation, leading to smoother collaboration and efficient workflows. This will help you tell if a physical automation is ready for adoption by humans, for example. It can make you a better consultant and thought leader for your company or outside clients. You can identify areas for optimization, refine algorithms, and ensure automation meets its intended goals.

Imagine you're a journalist or market researcher. The rise of misinformation and deepfakes demands a combined approach: careful human judgment working alongside AI algorithms for fact-checking and information analysis. CT will help you challenge and verify information sources, assess the credibility of AI-generated content, and analyze data outputs with a skeptical eye. Upholding integrity in an age of technological manipulation will be a main function.

Here is a current example. Radiologist already use CT to verify AI results. Early research suggests AI excels at augmenting their work. Surveys indicate radiologists believe AI could reduce errors and detect subtle abnormalities in medical images.[144] They might use AI tools to prioritize cases and flag suspicious findings, for example However, there is no shortage of concerned radiologists who believe AI tools require extra vigilance to analyze complex findings, question automated alerts, and make the final diagnoses.

For most digital elites, a one-hour podcast, two-day seminar, or continuing education course is not enough. The CT gap for you is bigger than your human-touch and middle counterparts. They can benefit from direct tailoring to their workplace augmented by a trained AI bot, as described for Melissa in the warehouse. Your skills development needs to be embedded throughout your education and will require new ways to teach and learn. Students and teachers may co-create a curriculum to emphasize innovation and idea generation, for example.

The Digital Elite Can Reduce the Random Acts

In your leadership role, you have the greatest influence and responsibility for deploying automation wisely. By leveraging CT for complex situations, you can identify tasks ripe for automation while balancing cost efficiency and essential human oversight. This critical process requires analyzing workflow dependencies, understanding the capabilities of automation tools, and pinpointing tasks where human-in-the-loop (HITL) involvement remains crucial.

Put simply, preventing random acts will fall on you. You will become the de facto trust officer. You can analyze systems for potential bias, advocate for transparency and explainability, and raise concerns about potential job displacement.

All of Us Need to Do Better, but Especially Business

I've reviewed hundreds of automation projects at enterprises. Cost reduction is the focus for most. Change management, a discipline to treat skill gaps and job transition, is rarely implemented well. In many cases, the remaining workers struggle with more advanced tasks after the automation project is complete. Business can do better. They have the best shot at helping workers with tomorrow's skills challenge.

Government policy is not the answer. History is clear on this point. Incredible as it may seem, President John F. Kennedy pushed through The Manpower Development and Training Act of 1962 to answer the threat of automation. Over the years, scholars of large-scale retraining efforts have discredited this and similar programs. Automation's trajectory will outpace and diminish the value of most programs. Government training programs often conclude with no specific job, leaving more skilled but unemployed people in their wake.

Automation requires rapid and continual skills development, and much of this must come from the private sector and the job itself. Today's rapid pace of automation and innovation, with its ever-shortening refresh cycles, will outpace the ability of education and government to adapt. Private sector certification and upskilling programs must augment traditional forms of education. The Walmart and NPowers examples are winners because there is a job at the end, and a focus on self-esteem and improvement.

Here's another winner: the consulting giant Accenture has taken a positive step to address the skills gap left in automations wake, and they should. Implementing technology for clients helped generate most of its $64 billion in 2023 revenue. They have invested $1 billion in the LearnVantage platform to deliver personalized, training for both technical and business workers.[145] They are not starting from scratch.

They acquired Udacity, a training platform with a network of over 1,400 industry experts, 21 million registered learners and a library of co-created content with leading businesses.

Today's conversation around automation often focuses on potential threats to jobs. Instead of dwelling on job losses, we should focus on building a future-ready workforce. Intensive research and collaboration are essential to develop the skills needed to thrive in an automated world. By prioritizing human needs and technological advancements, we can create a better work future for all (see Figure 11-1).

What We Can Do	*Why It Matters*
Look for jobs and training that enhance CT skills, a prime future asset for all workers.	You will need CT skills to maintain your value at work. Reduction in random acts requires them.
Look for new careers that AI will open that previously required advanced credentials.	GenAI will allow millions of service and middle workers to move up.
Give those who work with their hands the respect they deserve.	Trade careers will advance in importance, aided by physical automation advances.
Look for companies that tout training and certification programs.	The best shot for skills development is in the workplace.

Evaluate education options in the context of automation trends.	Rapid technology change will challenge traditional education.
A human footprint will keep the robots out of your cubicle.	The only way to compete with invisible robots is to leave evidence of your humanity everywhere.
Explore innovations in learning that leverage new approaches and technology.	Innovation to close skill gaps will offer new learning opportunities. Robots can help.

Figure 11-1: Our approach to the skills gap must broaden.

CHAPTER 12

SORRY, BUT YOU HAVE THE WRONG NUMBER

I GOT TO SPEND TWENTY minutes with the great baseball hurler Tom Seaver in 2010[146] at a tech industry analyst conference at Citi Field in New York. Analyst events are where a tech company invites industry analysts in for a couple of days to get them up to speed on their latest offering. I had not been to the brand-new Mets stadium and heard Tom Seaver, one of my baseball idols growing up, would be there. Thankfully, the Mets were not playing.

I felt sorry to see the Hall of Famer reduced to signing baseballs probably for a few thousand dollars, but I stood in line like a dozen others shuffling my feet, trying to think what I could ask him. The hot topic at the time was Roger Clemens and steroids, but unlike Tom in his days on the mound, I choked. I could not get the words out to ask him those controversial questions. After an awkward pause, the best I could come up with was to ask how fast he threw the ball in his prime. Tom signed my baseball, scowled, and addressed me like a five-year-old, "There are three important things about pitching—and yes, velocity is one, but location is just as important, and the ball's movement as it crosses the plate, is the third. Speed is the least important."

So, I thought about this, went back to my hotel, and wrote a blog, "Tom Seaver on Performance Management," which got almost two thousand views. It occurred to me that we focus on the velocity of a baseball only because we have radar guns that can measure it. Movement and location are more difficult, so we ignore them.

Our understanding of how we are doing as a country suffers from a similar issue. Human metrics are difficult to grasp, controversial, and have few historic benchmarks, so we don't focus on them. We trumpet the ones we can conveniently measure, and this shortcoming translates to work as well. In running a customer service center, we measure the time an agent is on a call with a customer and try to reduce it instead of counting the number of happy customer encounters they had. We measure employment levels and economic growth but not how happy citizens are. So, thanks, Tom, for this insight, and you have earned a long and peaceful rest.

Here's the point of this chapter: what you measure influences behavior. And today we measure the wrong things. We need to capture data on how people are doing. While this is more difficult and has been tried in the past, automation now gives us hope, as there are now no excuses.

Automation's potential to measure things in new ways is exciting. It gives us a wider range of data to model and analyze. But this power doesn't matter unless we change our approach. Charts and tables of unemployment filings, layoffs, retail sales, and income levels, for example, reduce people to rows and columns and don't tell their stories. They do not capture how humans are doing.

In this short tale, we are reminded of the importance of what we decide to measure. If you were a brave and competent sailor, you could make a good living taking prisoners from England to Australia a century ago, but it wasn't for the faint of heart. Storms, disease, malnutrition, and dehydration were everyday events. Human prisoners were not considered the most precious cargo, and about half would die at sea. England's bureaucrats were at a loss to fix the problem and turned to economists who came up with an elegant solution.

They changed the captain's incentive to what matters. Going forward, they would only pay for prisoners who arrived alive—that is, prisoners who walked off the boat. Before this revelation, they would pay for each prisoner who got on the boat in England. You can guess how this ended. Like magic, the problem was solved. Near 100 percent of the prisoners safely arrived. The point is simple: what you measure is critical. It changes behavior. And today we measure the wrong things.

The Best Economist Joke Ever Told

I'm going to take a shot at economists, always easy prey. A hundred years ago, overpopulation was a concern. Leading economists said not to worry, food production would not keep up with the number of mouths to feed. People would starve and keep population growth down. The media compared this to the theory of evolution, where nature allowed only the fittest and well-fed to survive. The economists became known as "Social Darwinists." As a result of theories like this that lacked a human perspective, the profession became known as "dismal science." At the time, many believed the results of a personality test would come back negative for most economists. Few professions have joke books dedicated to them, such as the classic *On the One Hand*.

Empathy is one problem, but a healthy dose of realism is another. An economist is stranded on a boat with physicist, and an engineer and...oh wait, you've heard this joke a dozen times? Well maybe not this exact version. They are hungry with only a single can of corn to split. They want to open it, but how? The physicist says: "Let's start a fire and place the can inside the flames. It will explode and then we will all be able to eat." "Are you crazy?" says the engineer. "All the corn will burn and scatter. We should use a metal wire, attach it to something solid, push it and crack the can open." "Both of you are wrong!" states the economist. "The solution is simple: ASSUME we have a can opener."

Harsh, perhaps. After all, the economist's bland and abstract statistics were developed to support business, not humanity. Microeconomics helped improve business operations. Macroeconomic theories have guided government policy since FDR's New Deal. And today, we have details on unemployment, labor force numbers, and the stock market in spades, and they are worshiped. Politicians use them to rail against incumbents or take victory laps. They make front-page headlines, win or lose elections, and create winners and losers in the stock market.

But they do not capture human progress or suffering. It is not that the numbers are inaccurate, but they do not directly target what humans need. They do not care if automation replaces a good-paying job that supports a family. They do not care whether a building is torn down or built. Metrics for food access, hunger, housing insecurity, health care access, homelessness, and long-term unemployment, to name a few, are not formally and rigorously reviewed and discussed.

This is far from a revelation. In 1968, Robert F. Kennedy argued that material poverty was matched by an even greater poverty of "satisfaction." He railed against a GDP that included cigarette advertising, construction of jails, orders for napalm, and destroying redwood forests. Kennedy thought a better measure would capture the beauty of our poetry, strength of our marriages, and integrity of our public officials. The difference now is that advances in automation and data science allow us to measure things in more progressive ways. Our economists have better tools to work with and an opportunity for redemption. We need their statistical discipline developed over hundreds of years of academic bickering.

As in many areas, Robert Kennedy was ahead of his time. GDP versus a general progress indicator (GPI) has been debated for over a decade. At least two states, Maryland and Vermont, use GDP and GPI to measure progress. GDP only shows economic activity and goods and services produced in each period, whether good or bad for society. GPI takes a more nuanced view. Inequality, environmental pollution, and the loss of farmland subtract from the GPI, while the value of volunteer work adds to it. A 2018 study calculated the GPI for all fifty states and suggests the US economy is experiencing a significant "progress recession."[147] Critics argue the GPI is too subjective because, for example, the value of leisure time is anyone's guess.

It's Time for a Misery, Anxiety, and Frustration Index

Surprisingly, for an economist of that period, John Maynard Keynes paid attention to the role of psychological or human factors. He wrote that swings in economic activity have an emotional element; hope, attitudes, and feelings influence purchases, investment in new businesses, and motivation to work, thereby influencing the economy.

Coming out of COVID, Keynes was spot on. Many people have stopped working or work less due to a mix of emotions. Numbers are always changing but consider these: in 2022, we had 10.9 million job openings and 6.5 million unemployed.[148] That's nearly two job openings for every single unemployed person who can work.

High levels of sadness, anxiety, and frustration have led to work dysfunction. The 2019 "yellow vest" movement in France was triggered by higher gas prices but underneath was a cry for help from a distressed, frustrated, and furious middle class.[149] The social unrest of 2020 and attraction to alternative politics is rooted in part on middle-class anxiety, and "white rage" that stems from the middle losing ground. Historically disadvantaged groups cannot see any progress.

Other metrics circle around the human condition but don't nail it. The US Census Bureau started the Household Pulse survey to track food and housing insecurity but lacked measures of material hardship: such as changes in rent levels; black unemployment; labor force participation; new businesses started and closed; or long-term unemployed, educational attainment, eviction, or any measure of anxiety.

In some cases, we are clear on what data we need but can't figure out how to get it. Here's one example: the UN has put a stake in the ground for sixteen Sustainable Development Goals (SDGs), an urgent call for global action. But there is not sufficient data to measure and track progress. Amazingly, eleven out of sixteen or 68 percent of critically important environment-related SDGs lack reliable data.[150]

Getting the right number is not a new ambition. There have been at least a dozen attempts to overcome the limitation of traditional economic measures.[151] The term "Gross National Happiness" was introduced by the compassionate Bodhisattva Druk Gyalpo, the fourth King of Bhutan, as early as 1972. The leader of the landlocked Buddhist country in the Eastern Himalayas declared, "Gross National Happiness is more important than Gross Domestic Product." A similar Gross National Happiness index was later published in 2005 by the International Institute of Management and often confused with Bhutan's GNH Index.

How About Some Real ESG Numbers?

Chapter 7 argued that work-life pioneers would want to work for companies that align with their moral center, but can we reliably tell what that is, or if one exists? Solid metrics that track a company's performance beyond revenue and profit would help. The environmental, social, and governance (ESG) framework was designed to do that, but if ESG criticism emitted carbon, the planet would be baking soon.

For one, ESG is too broad to be consistently measured. The term "governance" alone could cover a wide range: board diversity, corruption, business ethics, compensation policies, and risk management acumen. For example, Tesla has a bad ESG rating, and I bet most risk managers would consider Elon Musk a governance train wreck, but Tesla has done more to promote electric vehicles and reduce carbon emissions than all other CEOs combined. By any practical measure, Tesla's ESG rating should be outstanding.

ESG investing is another criticized area. Investors with a moral bend want ESG-filtered mutual funds or to own stock in a highly rated company. ESG ratings are now provided by Moody's and S&P Global, alongside their traditional financial metrics. Yet, confusion and loose language make it easy for companies to get away with "greenwashing" and for investment managers to market questionable green products. Investment managers love the ESG concept and why not? It's a new thing to sell, there is a growing demand, and they can charge more to manage them. High fees are justified for screening companies, but how extensive is their review? In 2022, the SEC fined BNY Mellon Corps $1.5 million for not disclosing that sixty-seven of 185 companies in one of their green funds had no ESG score at all.

ESG metrics also need political balance. Critics on the right paint ESG as a thinly veiled attack on capitalism, driven by liberal groups like the World Economic Forum. They argue the scoring is rigged to promote causes they favor. Companies that pay the most taxes, have the right ethnic ratios, hire union workers, and adopt a progressive view on climate get higher scores. They point to the role of ESG in trending progressive movements like "stakeholder capitalism," for example.[152]

Better balance and broader agreement on ESG will help adoption. To do so, we need to lighten up on polarizing issues and focus on the many areas of bipartisan agreement. We can probably all agree child labor in a supply chain is not a good thing. We can agree slashing energy use reduces costs and conserves precious resources. We can agree investing in workplace safety and employee wellness protects workers and boosts productivity. We can agree strong data privacy isn't just an ethical responsibility but builds trust with customers. We can agree corruption and bribery are bad and audit quality and transparency are good. In other words, there is plenty of middle ground to work with.

The chapter began by arguing that behavior is influenced by what you measure. Sea captains in nineteenth-century England took better care of passengers when they were paid only on the number that safely reached the shore. Similarly, if we want to improve the workplace and society, we must capture data that tells us how we are doing and how businesses are treating workers and the community. Automation has the potential to measure things in new and exciting ways, but we must work collaboratively and in a balanced way.

Simplification Will Reduce ESG Arguments

Simplification and clarity are also needed. The July 23, 2022, edition of *The Economist* had ESG on its cover. The title was direct: "ESG: Three Letters That Won't Save the Planet." It showed a pair of scissors ready to cut out the "S" and "G," leaving just the "E." Their argument made sense: "E" is a metric that, at least compared to the more subjective and controversial "G" and "S," has hope for reliable and quantifiable measurement. The field of carbon accounting is constantly evolving, with standards and methods improving. Tom Seaver would approve.

This point was not made in *The Economist* article but makes sense. "E" is not the full picture we would all like, but it's probable that how a company treats "E" correlates with how they also address "S" and "G." It is likely that they are responsible in other areas as well if they are concerned about their carbon emissions. A similar process has been used by archaeologists who find primitive tools or other artifacts to determine the progress of an ancient civilization. They don't need to see everything.

Our Data Scientists Can Do This

In this chapter, we argue that we are headed in the right direction, but there are important measurement gaps. The blind spot will get bigger as more workers are pushed to low-wage service jobs and as prospects to live in good homes, support a family, and retire comfortably decline. Automation can help close this gap.

Our data should track the forecasted restructuring of the workforce. Movements from the digital elite, uneasy middle, or service segment to the gig economy, for example, should be reported. Why not capture movements from one segment to another? If one hundred thousand workers move from the human-touch segment to the middle or from the middle to the elite, we should celebrate. If we lose fifty thousand in a single quarter to the human-touch segment, then we should review training and upskilling practices.

AI's ability to analyze and connect demographic, cultural, and geographic factors offers a new lens to understand how humans are doing. It excels at gauging sentiment, a skill traditionally used in marketing to identify customer dissatisfaction. Adapting this technology to measure citizen well-being could prove valuable. Arthur Okun's "misery index," based on traditional economic indicators could be enhanced for deeper insight, for example.

The Social Progress Index (SPI) takes this modern approach to automation and data analytics. Entrepreneurs started the nonprofit in 2009 after the financial collapse. Perhaps they had more time on their hands. Their view was that traditional economic indicators fail to understand social progress and prioritize short-term goals that deplete the environment and increase economic inequality. Over fifty indicators rank 168 countries on social progress and cover 99.97 percent of the world's population. According to the index, social progress is improving but at a slow and uneven pace. Unfortunately, 116 of the 168 countries have seen personal rights decline since 2011. Wealthy, smaller, cold-climate countries own the top of the leaderboard. Norway is first in the world, with South Sudan at the bottom.

The US ranks twenty-fourth but is on a short list of four countries with significant declines since 2011, sharing the honor with Brazil, Syria, and South Sudan. Declines in personal safety are alarming: we rank below Senegal and Sierra Leone due to gun violence and increased levels of political unrest. But like all such rankings, there are head-scratchers: the recently overthrown Sri Lanka was on the greatest improved SPI list, despite a corrupt government and social and economic disruptions.

SPI's data science approach is just what we need. Subjective attributes are wrestled with. A common language and data platform that supports benchmarking, collaboration, and change improves over time. In short, it uses automation to measure what matters.

Automation can help improve ESG reporting as well. The enterprise software market is bursting with new products to help. The SEC, the Carbon Disclosure Project (CDP), the Global Reporting Initiative (GRI), the Sustainability Accounting Standards Board (SASB), and the Task Force on Climate-Related Financial Disclosures (TCFD) are just a sample of frameworks that will benefit.

Our official numbers don't capture what we need, but the automation discussed here can give us hope. In fact, the focus on getting the right number will shift to getting the "model" right, and many of those will be digital twins.[153] In this context, a digital twin would be a virtual representation of a country. The European Union has already created a digital twin of the earth. An Accenture survey found that 44 percent of global CEOs believe that digital twin technology will make a significant impact on sustainability in their industry.[154]

Our universities turn out thousands of aspiring data scientists each year. We have hundreds of tech companies with skills in analytics that produce valuable AI and machine-learning software platforms. Facebook, Google, and Amazon can encourage data partnerships, make data science expertise available, and provide cloud resources to help nonprofits work with large data sets. Google knows when I'm looking for furniture to buy, where I've been, and who I've been with. Why don't we use some of them to track human progress? Despite the highlighted challenges, we can do this.

CHAPTER 13

HUMAN-CENTERED AUTOMATION

THE NEXT DECADE PROMISES A tumultuous ride for workers. They'll be buffeted by automation's relentless march, sometimes landing in exciting new roles but often feeling like pawns on a shifting chessboard. This shared struggle will forge a common bond—factory workers in Detroit, service workers across the Midwest, software testers in Silicon Valley—all facing the same digital tide. Call center representatives will grapple with AI-powered chatbots while waitresses contend with increased workloads and automation-driven stress. The challenges and opportunities of automation will touch everyone.

We offer guidance to navigate this new landscape. But individual actions have limitations. For a better future, workers need help—a collaboration between businesses and governments. Businesses, after all, are the architects of this automated future, their investments driving both progress and disruption. They have a responsibility to shape a workforce that thrives alongside technology, not succumbs to it. This chapter explores how businesses and governments can work together to mitigate the negative impacts of automation.

But first, let me apologize if the initial focus on automation's challenges painted a bleak picture. It would take a longer book to cover how automation has improved our lives, but that chest pumping does not improve us, and we need help. The negative impacts on workers are undeniable, and it's easy to jump to conclusions about a future filled with inequality, isolation, and mental health struggles. We might even fear an emotionless digital world devoid of human connection. You may want to crawl under a bed and assume the fetal position, and few would blame you, but here's the good news: automation can help us forge a different path.

By focusing on human-centered automation, we can build a future filled with technological progress and human well-being. Consider this: before Johannes Gutenberg invented the printing press in the 15th century, a powerful few, like the Catholic Church, tightly controlled the flow of information. Society remained largely ignorant, impoverished, and complacent. Gutenberg's invention unleashed religious texts, scientific discoveries, and political ideas upon a wide audience. This revolution ignited the Protestant Reformation, challenging Church authority, and fueled revolutions in France and America. In essence, the printing press empowered a more inquisitive and assertive public.

GenAI represents a quantum leap beyond previous technological advancements. Unlike the printing press or the internet, which primarily facilitated information access, GenAI allows individuals to actively analyze and solve problems. This democratization of intelligence has the potential to reshape society.

By transcending barriers of socioeconomic status and education, GenAI can foster a more informed and engaged populace. This heightened collective intelligence can serve as a catalyst for progress, challenging the status quo on issues such as job displacement, government inefficiency, and economic inequality. Importantly, the capabilities of GenAI are not static; they are poised for continuous enhancement, promising an even brighter future.

Narrow and Target Investments Are Governments' Best Bet

This book is filled with individual directives to confront the consequences of automation. Our implication is that government policy is incapable of resolving these issues. Individuals must confront the repercussions of automation head-on. Regulation or policy will be excessively slow and ineffective and have unintended consequences of its own

To underscore this point, failed government job training programs were described. The tech industry emerges as an autonomous juggernaut, pursuing its interests with reckless abandon. Numerous examples of how the pace of innovation will outpace government oversight are provided. The takeaway is clear: we must stand as individuals against the tide of automation's relentless pace.

Robot Taxes and AI Governance Lack Teeth and Clarity

Examining the difficulties encountered with the robot tax initiative can show why policy creation remains complex. The roots of this concept can be traced to the genius of the early twentieth century British economist A. C. Pigou. He would have called our random acts "negative externalities." In layman's terms, it means, "bad stuff that happens."

In Pigou's time, trains were expanding rapidly. Sadly, they often emitted embers from their smokestacks and set farmers' fields and houses on fire. To solve the problem, he recommended that the railroads pay into an escrow fund to compensate the farmers for their damages. This way, the railroads were made aware of how their actions affected society tangibly. Economist Arthur Pigou, if alive today, would likely advocate for a robot tax. This tax would raise awareness among enterprises about the potential negative impacts of automation on workers.

A robot tax will require firms to contribute to an internal fund when they replace humans with automation, like railroads. The exact number would be based on the jobs they eliminated. The escrow supports and facilitates skill development and job transition. The private sector would retain the dollars internally. However, it must follow government guidelines regarding how it is spent.

Leaders like Bill Gates support the idea, but two problems emerge. First, automation is difficult to define. I spend time every day at Forrester explaining to clients what it is. I devote a full chapter here to define it. Any robot tax policy must first agree on what a robot is, and it will be difficult. Software that automates warehouse logistics will replace human workers, but is it a taxable robot? A self-driving forklift is a robot, yet, it may not have contributed to job loss. Robot taxes will penalize our most efficient and innovative companies and reward laggards who do not invest in automation. Is that what we want to do?

Drafting policies to address automation's negative effects is plagued by challenges like these. Competing agendas further complicate finding common ground on solutions. For instance, collaboration between top policy and tech minds from China and the US could be valuable, but political tensions make this cooperation unlikely. Nuclear treaties were easier. The threat was clear, certain, predictable, and frightening. By contrast, automation's effects are diverse, subtle, unpredictable, and hard to pin down—the key takeaway from this book.

AI governance proposals make this point even more clear. Those in search of a non-pharmaceutical equivalent of Ambien will find these tomes a useful substitute. The European Commission's Artificial Intelligence Act targets high-risk applications, such as those impacting critical infrastructure or generating biased credit scores. Unfortunately, this legislation was outdated upon its release. GenAI models have inspired hundreds of new use cases in the last year alone.

On the other hand, the US blueprint, outlined in the 2022 White House Blueprint "An AI Bill of Rights," suffers from being overly broad. While its five principles are sound with little to argue about, the lack of concrete legislative or regulatory mechanisms weakens its impact. In essence, effectively addressing the negative societal impacts of automation requires clarity, consensus, and political will—all currently in short supply.

Government Policy: The More Specific, the Better

Many thought leaders favor strictly regulating or even breaking up the big tech companies. But before we drag them into government-led lawsuits for five years or so, we must give them their due. We live in a better world now than even a few years ago. The car in the driveway is safer. And even though Enzo the machinist has dropped from a middle to a human-touch worker, he has access to better health care, water quality, and entertainment. Digitally scaled companies are essential for our global competitiveness going forward.

We need their innovation across industries such as health care, food, shelter, and education. And most of that will emerge from their freewheeling innovation approach.

Governments should wield policy as a scalpel, not a hammer, to address the challenges of automation. Large-scale, strategic investments, like those in the Inflation Reduction Act of 2022, can be unwieldy. While the act's goal of reviving the US chip industry is sound (we can't rely solely on Taiwan and Korea for advanced AI processors, especially considering China's ambitions), a more targeted approach reduces waste and drives accountability. Investing in solutions that address specific workplace disruptions caused by automation can increase the likelihood of success.

The more specific, the better. There are scores of good ideas, but here are examples of targeted investments that can work. Upgrade high-speed internet access in rural areas such as eastern Kentucky. Provide funding and resources to help small and medium-sized businesses adopt automation, so they can fight the large chains' digital scale. Invest in autonomous tractors, precision farming, and robotic harvesting for the agricultural sector. Allocate funding to enhance healthcare delivery, particularly for rural areas, by including telemedicine, robotic surgery, and AI-assisted diagnostics.

Business Needs Workplace-Focused Automation Governance

Businesses have a crucial role to play in shaping the future workforce. Since their investments in automation drive worker disruptions and challenges, they are uniquely positioned to envision and plan for this future. By proactively mitigating the potential negative effects, businesses can ensure a smoother transition and create a workforce that thrives alongside automation.

The business world is aware of the threats that automation poses. According to a survey among various CEOs in 2023, 43 percent believe AI will destroy humanity within five to ten years. The survey made the expected headlines, including a CNN segment, but these pessimistic views don't help.

The million-dollar question: will businesses prioritize broader workplace concerns over pure profit? Will they hit the brakes to establish responsible AI practices that address the issues we've raised? Based on the current AI gold rush mentality, the answer seems like a resounding no. Many companies I work with believe they'll fall behind competitors if they don't integrate AI into their offerings as soon as possible. In their minds, the early AI adopters will dominate the market. However, there are glimmers of hope amidst these commercial pressures. Many companies anticipating future metrics for responsible AI (as discussed in the previous chapter) are already taking steps to prepare.

Here's what any business aiming for the stars can do better. Just ask these five questions before any automation is considered. While this is not an exhaustive list, it is a good start. It will never hurt to ask them. Think of it this way: not all dates lead to marriage, but you might discover amazing new restaurants.

Have We Tested Well Enough for Random Acts?

Currently, excessive automation seems to stumble forward without required human and safety reviews. In the examples illustrated in Part 1, internal and external voices were not adequately consulted to measure confidence in a machine-based decision or account for all potential outcomes. New forms of testing are needed to determine if the automation is useful and reliable enough for humans. While we have mature software testing practices for normal enterprise software, accelerating automation raises the bar. Predictability, bias, reliability, and human-machine interaction are areas we don't adequately test for today. We also need what the industry calls "model ops," specialists and processes that manage AI models.

Is There Residual Value to the Automation?

Many automations have little residual value, particularly those affecting middle workers. Sure, they may replace tedious tasks and save money for a company, but beyond that, there are few redeeming aspects. New industries, jobs, or better employee experiences fall short. Thus, we may well argue that previous automations worked out better.

When the automobile replaced the horse, the result was a super new industry and an unprecedented explosion of jobs. But, in the IA period described in Chapter 2, we automate tasks already being performed by people. Virtual agents that support previous call center customers do not create industries. Similarly, any use of machine learning to help make a loan decision in a bank's back office only reduces headcount.

The point is simple. Automation that just mimics a human function traps us in the IA period. Erik Brynjolfsson, a professor at Stanford's Institute for Human-Centered Artificial Intelligence, calls this the "Turing trap" and argues that the "imitation game" will not create residual value. He argues that when automation augments rather than mimics human functions, we are paving the way for a more sustainable future. Businesses should ask a simple question before launching an automation program: what's the real value of this effort?

Are Power and Benefits of Automation Distributed Fairly?

Like the nuclear physicists in the 1950s, we risk abusing that new power and leave consequences to Adam Smith's "invisible hand" to sort it out. It need not and should not be this way. We can create a "power map" to show how automation's power will be distributed across customers, employees, or the institution spearheading it.

Businesses must emphatically ask where automation's value is directed. Will all benefits accrue to management and stockholders? If a new app is offered to consumers in exchange for their data, is that a fair deal? Will the worker share the productivity gains with higher wages or a more flexible schedule? Does automation help level the gender playing field, for example, by reducing the need for physical effort? Does it help parity between middle workers, human-touch workers, and the digital elite? Without conscious effort, automation's value and power will accrue more to the institutions that developed the automation and not the workers.

Is There a Workable Change Management Plan?

It's sometimes said that the only humans who like change are babies. Change at work is disruptive: new things must be taught and learned, and new roles will create winners and losers. Most of us hate it. That's why change management

(CM) evolved as a common business methodology. It is a catchall term encompassing approaches required to prepare, support, and help individuals, teams, and organizations handle change.

Like Alcoholics Anonymous, it has well-vetted steps one must take to recognize and accept the change. One-time events like a merger or acquisition were the basis for early CM methods and as such, they fall short of what is needed today. A more uncertain and rapidly changing world requires updated techniques to smooth the sharp edges of automation's relentless pace. Scenario planning, for example, focuses on multiple possible outcomes rather than on a single event, and CM needs to embrace it.

Is There an Automation Center of Excellence?

Good news is hidden amongst all this: for the past several years, enterprises (government and commercial) have funded automation centers of excellence (CoEs). Initially, their focus was tactical, to jump-start projects, evangelize the potential of automation, find new ideas, and govern vendor selection. But today, due to the issues discussed throughout, the focus is slowly shifting to strategy, training, and governance models.

I often start a client workshop with the ten most common mistakes automation projects make. These are broken into three areas: process, workplace, and customer experience (see Figure 13-1). Every random act described in this book can be traced to inattention in one of these areas. At Forrester, I've advised hundreds of enterprises on organizing these COEs, the problems to focus on, the skills needed, and the tasks to perform. COEs, although a good start, don't always ask the most important question: should we automate this process or work effort?

The Ten Oversights That Lead to Workplace Tension	
Process	Remove humans in the loop prematurely
	Fail to create transformative or residual value
	Cause exposure from faulty data or algorithms
	Keep the inner workings hidden
	Underestimate exposure to fines and reputation
Workplace	Fail to improve skills to advance careers
	Fail to improve physical safety or health
	Negatively affect an employee's mental state
Customer Experience	Create awkward and frustrating self-service
	Result in creepy experiences using robotics

Figure 13-1: Automation COEs can be a valuable checkpoint for potential automation problems.

Individuals Can Change How They Work for The Better

We make the case that attitudes about work are changing and highlight automation's role in that. Recent generations took wage-based work, or traditional employment as a given, and even considered them ethical and spiritual obligations. The Game of Life board game, created by Milton Bradley in 1860, gave you a lifetime job in the first few moves: doctors made $20,000 a year, lawyers made $15,000, and business-men made $10,000. There was no space to land on that said, "Gig worker with side hustles and a $500 a month UBI."

Work defined us. The farmer or ranch hand is outdoorsy, tough, and independent. The sommelier is sophisticated and well-traveled. The tech salesman is an agent of change and innovation; the auditor is good with numbers and plays by the rules. Your work was more than just a job; it identified you. This will be less true as we work less and in non-traditional ways.

The time has finally come. Almost a century ago, futurists predicted that most human labor would be replaced by automation, resulting in more personal time and a better life. In his 1930 essay, "Economic Possibilities for Our Grandchildren," the economist John Maynard Keynes predicted a fifteen-hour workweek in the twenty-first century, amounting to a five-day weekend. He said, "For the first time since his creation, man will be faced with a permanent problem—what to do with the endless hours?"

This has not happened yet, but automation and a revised attitude are helping us inch closer. In the industrial period described earlier, workers averaged a brutal seventy hours a week. In 2015, the US averaged just forty hours per week, and this seems to be declining by a few minutes each year. The French adopted the thirty-five-hour work week over twenty years ago and their fight for less time continues to mount.

In today's world, too many brilliant automation minds seem focused on marketing and business efficiency, which too often means labor reduction. Marketing applies automation to sell us more things which in the US we need, as much as Venus De Milo needed a manicure. These pursuits do not move us toward clean energy, lengthen our lifespan, address growing skills gaps, or garner the respect of those struggling to meet basic needs.

Here is an optimistic outcome. When we free ourselves from traditional employment constraints, productive hours can be applied to help others. Work-life pioneers can adopt altruistic pursuits. The big law firms can allow more hours for pro-bono cases or stints as public defenders. Tech companies can provide options for new engineering and computer science hires to apply technical support in health care, education, or clean energy, for example.

Embracing Radical Optimism

Throughout history, we've learned optimists make a difference. They are brave enough to work for the best possible outcome despite challenges. Colin Powell, the former four-star general and US Secretary of State, summed it up well in *My American Journey* when he wrote, "Perpetual optimism is a force multiplier."

Embracing optimism, let's acknowledge the immense potential of automation to improve our lives. Imagine longer lifespans, safer transportation, fewer hours dedicated to work, and the emergence of entirely new ways of living. I'll channel Buckminster Fuller, an American architect, futurist, and inventor. His last few lectures went along these lines. For thousands of years, we believed food, water, land, housing, and medicine were insufficient for all to share. Today, things are different. Humanity's accumulated knowledge can provide well for all life forms.

He argued that with technology, we could do more with less, live sustainably, and lift entire nations out of poverty. In the decades since his death, automation has made great strides, and Fuller would be amazed. He would argue that all of us can thrive on this "spaceship earth." So, let's embrace the radical optimism of Bucky and work for a better future for all of us.

ENDNOTES

1 Discussion with customer service agent named Tina at Waste Management, January 31, 2022.

2 Based on an interview with Olek via email between March and December 2018.

3 Here is an update on the Hertz fiasco: https://www.wsj.com/articles/hertz-customers-allege-false-arrest-problem-continues-after-bankruptcy-11663689278.

4 *Kaizen* is a compound of two Japanese words that together translate as "good change" or "improvement." It has come to mean "continuous improvement" that uses lean methodology and principles, with origins in post–World War II Japanese quality circles.

5 Interview with Donnie Williams on October 11, 2022. Sprinklr is a customer experience management software platform: https://www.sprinklr.com/.

6 This article shows the actual tweet along with the Uber response: https://mashable.com/article/uber-racist-tweet.

7 Julia Angwin, Jeff Larson, Surya Mattu and Lauren Kirchner, ProPublica, "Machine Bias," ProPublica, May 23, 2016, https://www.propublica.org/article/machine-bias-risk-assessments-in-criminal-sentencing. The vendor did not support these claims: https://www.equivant.com/.

8 Hannah Beech and Muktita Suhartono, "Confusion, Then Prayer, in Cockpit of Doomed Lion Air Jet," *New York Times*, March 20, 2019, https://www.nytimes.com/2019/03/20/world/asia/lion-air-crash-boeing.html.

9   Russell Lewis, "Ethiopian Flight Data Shows Similarities to Indonesian Crash of Same Boeing Model," National Public Radio, March 17, 2019, https://www.npr.org/2019/03/17/704313275/ethiopian-flight-data-shows-similarities-to-indonesian-crash-of-same-boeing-mode. Ethiopia's Transport Minister said a preliminary review of the flight data reveals "clear similarities" in that accident and the crash of a Lion Air Boeing 737 Ma.

10   Finally, the FAA fined Boeing $2.5 billion for fraudulent acts based on various news stories at the time and the 2022 Netflix documentary *Downfall: The Case Against Boeing*.

11   This joint blog by Forrester's top AI analysts makes the point that enterprises are at low maturity for responsible AI: https://www.forrester.com/blogs/navigating-the-business-roundtables-roadmap-for-responsible-ai/?ref_search=1216470_1675947253354.

12   Oliver Evans was an American inventor, engineer, businessman, and thought leader in the field of automation. He designed and built the first fully automated industrial process. For a description of Oliver Evans's automatic flour mill, see https://www.britannica.com/biography/Oliver-Evans.

13   Frey provides an excellent summary of automation's progress through the ages in *The Technology Trap: Capital, Labor, and Power in the Age of Automation*, released in 2019.

14   The Fourth Industrial Revolution was a German government project to study the computerization of manufacturing. IBM's article, "A framework for Industry 4.0: welcome to the next industrial revolution," provides

a well-structured overview of Industry 4.0 with clear delineation of the key elements and challenges.

15 Market size and growth estimates for tactical automation software that included RPA, BPM, and aspects of AI accelerated during the pandemic. This Gartner Group estimate is one example: https://www.gartner.com/en/ newsroom/press-releases/2021-04-28-gartner-forecasts-worldwide-hyperautomation-enabling-software-market-to-reach-nearly-600-billion-by-2022.

16 According to MIT professor Daron Acemoglu and Boston University's Pascual Restrepo, part of the problem is "so-so technologies." Unlike previous innovations in automation, few new jobs or business models emerge.

17 This is a quote by American speculative fiction author William Gibson. It means that the things that will constitute the normal, or every day, in the future already exist for some of us today and can be seen with keen observation.

18 Joshua Gans, Avi Goldfarb, and Ajay Agrawal. *Prediction Machines: The Simple Economics of Artificial Intelligence* (Harvard Business Review Press, 2018), https://www.predictionmachines.ai/.

19 Catherine Douglas Moran and Sam Silverstein., "As self-checkout expands in grocery, here are 4 ways the technology is leveling up," Grocery Dive, March 14, 2022, https://www.grocerydive.com/news/as-self-checkout-expands-in-grocery-here-are-4-ways-the-technology-is-leve/620122/.

20 This data was from a survey conducted by the tech company Shekel Brainweigh Ltd. Nearly 75 percent stated difficulty in entering goods and frequent overrides

were their biggest concerns. And 90 percent of consumers desire self-checkout machines that can automatically identify items. https://www.vendingtimes.com/blogs/shekel-brainweigh-survey-finds-90-of-shoppers-want-self-checkout-machines-to-automatically-identify-items/.

21   Edited from a post on the Reddit group "Tales from Retail," July 2022: https://www.reddit.com/r/TalesFromRetail/comments/w4rqgx/stupid_customers/?%24deep_link=true&correlation_id=5664b5a3-ac70-4fc8-81ef-413c14467407&post_.

22   ZDNet reported on resistance or consumer pushback on SCO in this article: https://www.zdnet.com/article/more-than-20-people-stood-in-line-at-the-supermarket-no-one-wanted-self-checkout/.

23   Spain has started to tip. The government is reviewing a customer service bill that would fine a company if a human does not answer the phone within a mandated timeframe. The bill would force companies to answer calls within three minutes. Fines would range from 150 euros to 100,000 euros.

24   Taken from this Amazon JWO website for retailers: https://justwalkout.com/?utm_source=newsletter&utm_medium=email&utm_campaign=newsletter_axios whatsnext&stream=science.

25   Heidi Shierholz, Margaret Poydock, and Celine McNicholas, "Unionization increased by 200,000 in 2022," Economic Policy Institute, January 19, 2023, https://www.epi.org/publication/unionization-2022/.

26   Lydia Saad, "More in U.S. See Unions Strengthening and Want It That Way," Gallup, August 30, 2023, https://news.gallup.com/poll/510281/unions-strengthening.aspx.

27 The "film fatigue" debate over whether superhero continues, but even about a third of self-identified Marvel fans say they're getting a little tired of them: https://morningconsult.com/2021/12/06/marvel-super hero-film-fatigue/.

28 Ellyn Shook and Mark Knickrehm, "Reworking the Revolution," *Accenture*, 2018, https://www.accenture. com/_acnmedia/PDF-69/Accenture-Reworking-the-Revolution-Jan-2018-POV.pdf#zoom=50. This Accenture strategy report, "Reworking the Revolution," is typical of the tech industry's exuberant and exaggerated self-serving posture toward AI.

29 Rory Cellan-Jones. "Stephen Hawking Warns Artificial Intelligence Could End Mankind." *BBC News*, December 2, 2014, https://www.bbc.com/news/technology-30290540.

30 Leading adherents of SCOT include Wiebe Bijker and Trevor Pinch. They argue that technological determinism is a myth that results when one looks backward and believes the path taken to the present was the only possible path. Lelia Green's perspective in *Technoculture: From Alphabet to Cybersex* is an example. Green demonstrates that the adoption of new technologies is never inevitable but coexists and interacts: industrial culture, media culture, and information culture. To Green, technology is embedded deeply in the social fabric and thus, society will determine how technology will affect it.

31 Middle workers fall between frontline human-touch workers and the digital elite. These jobs require a certain amount of education, several years of experience, and advanced skills. In the past, a middle worker with a high

school degree was akin to a kid experiencing the adult world for the first time, with a sense of endless potential.

32   Interview, January 2019. Enzo quit that machine shop and drove a cab for almost a year, then was hired by another machine shop.

33   Interview with HPA, a Cognizant company, regarding a mortgage implementation April 2019.

34   Indeed's September 21, 2023, AI at Work Report *How GenAI Will Impact Jobs and the Skills Needed to Perform Them* is a research report from Hiring Lab, Indeed's economic research arm.

35   According to Forrester's 2023 data, generative AI technology could replace 2.4 million jobs in the US by 2030, many of them white-collar and not affected by previous waves of automation. That's only between 2 and 3 percent of the eighty million professional or white-collar US jobs, so not much, unless you're one of them.

36   The term was coined as early as 1905 by jazz musicians. Today, gig work is any type of income-earning activity that exists outside of traditional employer-employee relationships. The government uses the more official term "contingent worker." Today 55 million toil away in the US according to government numbers. Ninety percent of employers use them in some form. And you can't blame them; they are a bargain, costing 25 percent to 40 percent less than the employee due to vacations, healthcare, and other benefits.

37   Noam Scheiber is a *New York Times* reporter covering work issues: https://www.nytimes.com/2023/07/20/briefing/piecemeal-work-hollywood-strikes.html

38 According to a 2019 study by the Center for American Progress, 11 percent of mass shooters in the United States between 2011 and 2019 had a history of working in the gig economy. The study analyzed data on 131 mass shooters responsible for at least four deaths in the United States between 2011 and 2019.

39 These estimates are from this article: https://www.inc.com/jessica-stillman/3-jobs-replaced-ai-fastest-analysis-5-million-job-postings.html.

40 GPT-4 took all sections of the July 2022 bar exam and earned a score that approached the 90th percentile of test-takers, according to researchers Daniel Martin Katz, a professor at the Illinois Institute of Technology's Chicago-Kent College of Law, and Michael James Bommarito, a professor at the Michigan State University College of Law.

41 US Bureau of Labor Statistics, Employment Projections Program. Projections are for 2016–2026: https://www.bls.gov/emp/.

42 This 2023 study fielded 195 randomly drawn patient questions from social media. A team of licensed healthcare professionals compared physicians' and chatbots' responses. See "Comparing Physician and Artificial Intelligence Chatbot Responses to Patient Questions Posted to a Public Social Media Forum," John Ayers, PhD, et al.

43 It is estimated that the worldwide market for low-code technologies will reach $26.9 billion in 2026.

44 Please see the Random Acts warnings that surround the use of low-code tools in earlier chapters. If everyone starts developing software applications, many believe it's

the equivalent of giving your teenager the keys to the car before his first driving test.

45 The full title is "How to Talk to Anyone: Nine Secrets for Success in Any Conversation."

46 "Labor Force Statistics from the Current Population Survey," US Bureau of Labor Statistics, January 18, 2019, http://www.bls.gov/cps/cpsaat11.htm.

47 Gritty individuals are willing to put in the hard work and effort required to achieve their goals are not easily discouraged and able to bounce back from failures. They don't dwell on their mistakes, but instead they learn from them and move on.

48 Forrester interview on June 27, 2022, with Ramone from the *Tastee Spoon*, both a Caribbean/Jamaican restaurant and food truck. Also a follow-up visit to the Tastee Spoon, October 2022.

49 Megan Pellegrini, "Robotics and Automation: Back to the future," The National Provisioner, August 2, 2020, https://www.provisioneronline.com/articles/109724-robotics-and-automation-back-to-the-future.

50 "Labor Force Statistics from the Current Population Survey," US Bureau of Labor Statistics, http://www.bls.gov/cps/cpsaat11.htm.

51 I had several email exchanges with Olek between March and December 2018.

52 These were two separate reported incidents regarding security robots. The vendors of these machines suggested they were overemphasized due to their sensational nature.

53 This article comments on the healthcare worker shortage in Japan. *Nikkei Asian Review*, November 19, 2016,

https://asia.nikkei.com/Politics-Economy/Policy-Politics/Japan-s-Diet-votes-yes-to-more-foreign-care-workers.

54 This article describes SoftBank Robotics' Pepper healthcare robot initiative in Japan. Malcolm Foster, "Aging Japan: Robots may have a role in future of elder care," *Reuters*, March 27, 2018, https://www.reuters.com/article/us-japan-ageing-robots-widerimage/aging-japan-robots-may-have-role-in-future-of-elder-care-idUSKBN1H33AB.

55 A study conducted by researchers at the University of Wisconsin–Madison found that individuals who played strategy-based video games showed better problem-solving skills in real-world situations. Dale, G., & Green, C. S. (2016). "Video games and cognitive performance." In R. Kowert & T. Quandt (Eds.), *The video game debate: Unravelling the physical, social, and psychological effects of digital games.*

56 Based on a Forrester interview for the "Future of Physical Robotics," February 2023.

57 Robot ethics, sometimes known as "roboethics," concerns ethical problems that occur with robots: https://www.researchgate.net/publication/325884319_Roboethics_Fundamental_Concepts_and_Future_Prospects.

58 For example, Catherine Liu in *Virtue Hoarders* (2021), characterized the PMC as white-collar left liberals afflicted with a superiority complex in relation to the working class.

59 Famous phrase uttered during confirmation hearing for Wilson to become Eisenhower Secretary of Defense in 1953. I cannot conceive of one (conflict) because for years I thought what was good for our country was

good for General Motors, and vice versa. https://www.
hemmings.com/stories/2019/09/05/fact-check-did-a-
gm-president-really-tell-congress-whats-good-for-gm-is-
good-for-america.

60   Anywhere work has become the norm for most
organizations, and hybrid is the most popular form. But
with speed bumps: doubtful leaders, dissatisfied managers,
frustrated employees, and a need for new processes,
technologies, and culture. This report interviewed forty-
six companies and 722 employees to understand the messy
and ever-changing world of hybrid work: https://www.
forrester.com/report/master-the-messy-middle-of-hybrid/
RES178135?scrollTo=CON49481.

61   Several studies support this view. A 2021 study by the
Stanford Graduate School of Business and a University
of Chicago study found that remote work can lead to
a decline in innovation. A 2020 study by the National
Bureau of Economic Research found that firms that
adopted remote work were less likely to introduce new
products or services.

62   Herein lies an optimistic view of the post-pandemic commercial real estate market: https://www.cushmanwake
field.com/en/news/2020/05/research-predicts-new-
normal-for-workplace.

63   This research documents the historic value of storytelling
to in building communities. https://onlinelibrary.wiley.
com/doi/10.1111/tops.12358

64   Will Markow, Soumya Braganza, Bledi Taska, Steven
M. Miller, and Debbie Hughes. "The Quant Crunch,"
Burning Glass Technologies, 2017, https://www.ibm.com/
downloads/cas/3RL3VXGA. Burning Glass Technologies

analyzed 26.9 million US job postings from 2015. Postings for analytics skills in 2015 were 2.3 million. The forecast for 2020 was 2.7 million.

65   Jenny Liu, Betsy Sparrow, Daniel M. Wegner. "Google Effects on Memory: Cognitive Consequences of Having Information at Our Fingertips." https://www.science.org/doi/10.1126/science.1207745

66   Forrester interview with Prasad Akella, founder and CEO of Drishti, August 2018. Drishti has a focus on human-driven processes—a unique application of computer vision and deep learning in manufacturing.

67   David Gelles, "C.E.O. Pay Remains Stratospheric, Even at Companies Battered by Pandemic," New York Times, April 24, 2021, https://www.nytimes.com/2021/04/24/business/ceos-pandemic-compensation.html.

68   Caleb Silver, "The Top 25 Economies in the World," Investopedia, July 3, 2024, https://www.investopedia.com/insights/worlds-top-economies/.

69   Vint Cerf, "A Brief History of the Internet & Related Networks," *Internet Society*, https://www.internetsociety.org/internet/history-internet/brief-history-internet-related-networks.

70   "On the Origins of Google," National Science Foundation, August 17, 2004, https://www.nsf.gov/discoveries/disc_summ.jsp?cntn_id=100660.

71   Pierre Bienaimé, "This Chart Shows How the US Military Is Responsible for Almost All the Technology in Your iPhone," *Business Insider*, October 29, 2014, https://www.businessinsider.com/the-us-military-is-responsible-for-almost-all-the-technology-in-your-iphone-2014-10.

72 A.J. Herrington, "Gallup Poll Finds More Americans Smoke Marijuana Than Cigarettes," *Forbes*, August 29, 2022, https://www.forbes.com/sites/ajherrington/2022/08/29/gallup-poll-finds-more-americans-smoke-marijuana-than-cigarettes/?sh=3c23dedcb7a1.

73 "Revenue of the yoga industry in the United States from 2012 to 2020 (in billion US dollars)," Statista, https://www.statista.com/statistics/605335/us-yoga-industry-revenue/.

74 You can find this information and more in the ESA's 2024 report titled "Essential Facts About the U.S. Video Game Industry." https://www.theesa.com/resources/essential-facts-about-the-us-video-game-industry/2024-data/

75 Judith Solomon, "Medicaid Work Requirements Can't Be Fixed," Center on Budget and Policy Priorities, January 10, 2019, https://www.cbpp.org/research/health/medicaid-work-requirements-cant-be-fixed.

76 The rise of the "herbivore" men is often attributed to the advancement of women in society in the 1980s and the downturn of the Japanese economy in the 1990s. Masahiro Morioka, "A Phenomenological Study of 'Herbivore Men," *The Review of Life Studies*, Vol. 4, September 2013, http://www.lifestudies.org/press/rls0401.pdf.

77 Matthew Frankel, "9 Baby-Boomer Statistics That Will Blow You Away," *The Motley Fool*, July 29, 2017, https://www.fool.com/retirement/2017/07/29/9-baby-boomer-statistics-that-will-blow-you-away.aspx.

78 According to the latest data from the Organisation for Economic Co-operation and Development (OECD), France ranks twenty-first out of thirty-seven OECD countries in terms of average annual hours worked per

person in employment. In 2021, the average French worker worked 1,565 hours per year, which is slightly below the OECD average of 1,656 hours per year.

79 The six are income, freedom, trust in government, health life expectancy, social support from family and friends, and generosity.

80 "Triple bottom line and B corporation certification are examples of attempts to measure the social value of companies and are gaining momentum. For more information on the B lab process, please see A Global Community of Leaders," B Lab, https://bcorporation.net/.

81 Jia Wertz, "Taking Risks Can Benefit Your Brand - Nike's Kaepernick Campaign Is a Perfect Example," *Forbes*, September 30, 2018, https://www.forbes.com/sites/jiawertz/2018/09/30/taking-risks-can-benefit-your-brand-nikes-kaepernick-campaign-is-a-perfect-example/#3dd5b33645aa.

82 AIAAIC is an independent, non-partisan, public interest initiative that examines and makes the case for real AI, algorithmic, and automation transparency and openness founded by Charlie Pownall.

83 Segmenting (AIAAIC) incidents into the three categories was not perfect. Incidents were tagged with multiple risk labels, with often a variety of negative outcomes. Importance was given to the first risk label listed. Incidents of racial bias, often unintentional, predictive analytics or self-driving errors were tagged as affecting trust. Security issues and scams were included in "vulnerability." Invasion often had the clearest mapping. For example, facial recognition abuse was put in the "invasion" category..

84 Reported by CNN based on reports from the Hong Kong police in February 2024. "Finance worker pays out $25 million after video call with deepfake 'chief financial officer,'" https://www.cnn.com/2024/02/04/asia/deepfake-cfo-scam-hong-kong-intl-hnk/index.html.

85 Project Healthy Minds is a millennial-driven nonprofit startup focused on the growing mental health crisis: https://www.projecthealthyminds.com/.

86 This was a 2023 incident reported by the AI, Algorithmic and Automation Incidents and Controversies (AIAAIC) Repository.

87 Noel Sharkey, "Alan Turing: The experiment that shaped artificial intelligence," *BBC News*, June 21, 2012, https://www.bbc.com/news/technology-18475646.

88 The longitude and latitude metaphor to explain LLM was explained in more depth in this article, "A jargon-free explanation of how AI large language models work." https://arstechnica.com/science/2023/07/a-jargon-free-explanation-of-how-ai-large-language-models-work/ /

89 The September 2022 letter was addressed to the National Security Council and the Office of Science and Technology. See www.9.20.22LettertoNSCandOST PonstabilityAI.pdf.

90 See the "The Spread of True and False News Online," published in *Science*, Vol 359, Issue 6380. To understand how false news spreads, used a data set of rumor cascades on Twitter from 2006 to 2017. False news reached more people than the truth; falsehood also diffused faster than the truth.

91   The 25% reduction in traffic to on-line publishers is cited in this report. https://www.cjr.org/the_media_today/google_ai_summaries_publishers_fears.php

92   This article from the Turing Institute puts art and technology in perspective: https://www.turing.ac.uk/research/interest-groups/ai-arts.

93   Chris Garcia, "Harold Cohen and Aaron—a 40-Year Collaboration," Computer History Museum, August 23, 2016, https://computerhistory.org/blog/harold-cohen-and-aaron-a-40-year-collaboration/.

94   Erik Hoel publishes "The Intrinsic Perspective" and argues that AI-generated artwork is an illusion of art, and if culture falls for that illusion, we will lose something irreplaceable. https://erikhoel.substack.com/p/ai-art-isnt-art.

95   ADAS adjustments will be a growing issue. According to Opus, 11 percent of all collisions already need an ADAS adjustment.

96   Dopamine is an important hormone secreted by the brain. https://mrvyilmaz.medium.com/dopamine-detox-it-will-change-your-life-d0bc733c1ddf.

97   A study in the *Journal of Applied Psychology* (2017) showed that framing organizational changes as beneficial rather than threatening led to improved employee engagement and reduced resistance. This principle could be applied to the introduction of new technologies in the workplace.

98   This article digs into the causes of democratic backsliding. The role of technology to spread of misinformation and hate is cited as a contributor but they point out that the

most developed nations and heavier users of these tools have experienced the least backsliding.

99 Lynn Kawano, "HPD defends use of pricey robot dog taking temperatures at homeless program," *Hawaii News Now*, August 27, 2021, https://www.hawaiinewsnow.com/2021/08/28/hpd-defends-use-pricey-robot-dog-taking-temperatures-homeless-program/.

100 The Coronavirus Aid, Relief, and Economic Security Act (the CARES Act), CARES stands for the Coronavirus Aid, Relief, and Economic Security Act (the CARES Act).

101 Caroline Kelly, "Reaping the benefits of big data with sensors in strange places," CPI, April 7, 2021, https://www.uk-cpi.com/blog/reaping-the-benefits-of-big-data-with-sensors-in-strange-places.

102 See this review of surveillance in China and Russia: https://link.springer.com/chapter/10.1007/978-3-030-97012-3_.

103 Julianne McShane, "Girl Scout mom kicked out of Radio City and barred from seeing Rockettes after facial recognition tech identified her," NBC News, December 21, 2022, https://www.nbcnews.com/news/us-news/girl-scout-mom-kicked-radio-city-barred-seeing-rockettes-facial-recogn-rcna62606.

104 Around 40 to 70 percent of ransomware is attributed to Russian-affiliated groups, commonly cited by sources like McAfee, Chainalysis, Flashpoint, and Recorded Future. See, for example, this report from Chainalysis: https://www.chainalysis.com/blog/2022-crypto-crime-report-preview-russia-ransomware-money-laundering.

105 Bots account for 28.2 percent of "user traffic" on the internet. Insight into the composition of traffic seen by

Cloudflare: https://radar.cloudflare.com/security-and-attacks.

106 Article describing how *Hamilton* tickets were purchased and flipped by bots as early as 2017: https://variety.com/2017/digital/news/ticketmaster-hamilton-prestige-entertainment-renaissance-ventures-1202578292/.

107 Total fines and a summary of the violations were drawn largely from this source: https://www.tessian.com/blog/biggest-gdpr-fines-2020/.

108 Statistics used in this session were drawn from this report: https://atlasvpn.com/blog/americans-received-more-than-24-billion-robocalls-in-h1-2022.

109 Dr. Mark van Rijmenam, "From Big Data to Big Mac; How McDonald's Leverages Big Data," Datafloq, https://datafloq.com/read/from-big-data-to-big-mac-how-mcdonalds-leverages-b/403.

110 "Employee Scheduling Regulations," New York State Department of Labor, https://labor.ny.gov/workerprotection/laborstandards/scheduling-regulations.shtm. This is a description of the hearings and regulations in New York.

111 This 2022 research was done by the Bank for International Settlements and is available on the BIS website (www.bis.org). They created a database of retail data from crypto exchange apps to understand the boom-bust cycles and various adoption trends.

112 Economists at the Bank for International Settlements studied crypto trading and Bitcoin prices and validated this marketing approach, that lower-income young men are an easy mark. Around 40 percent of crypto investors were male and under thirty-five.

113 Data from an Opinium survey on 2,424 remote employees in the UK. Thirty-two percent affirmed to being monitored by their employers in October 2021, up from 24 percent in April 2021. https://www.infosecurity-magazine.com/news/one-three-workers-monitored/.

114 Applications such as HubStaff, CleverControl, and Time Doctor can be installed without the employee knowing it. Features include screenshots of workers' devices at regular intervals, keystroke audit trails, screen sequences with time intervals, audio recordings, and websites and applications visited. Research by 2021 Top10VPN showed a 54 percent rise in the demand for employee surveillance software since the start of the Coronavirus pandemic. https://www.top10vpn.com/research/covid-employee-surveillance/.

115 Forrester conducted a 2020 survey of users experienced with mainstream (more common automations like Microsoft tools) and more advanced automations like intelligent agents or machine learning–based apps. The study differences in a mental state context. See https://www.forrester.com/report/design-automation-to-respect-employee-psychology/RES164679?ref_search=1216470_1663196883529.

116 I authored the following report: Design Automation to Respect Employee Psychology - Four Concepts Will Make Your Intelligent Automation Efforts Successful.

117 There are now thousands of cyber-security experts monitoring our digital pathways. The US government allocated over $720 billion in fiscal year 2020 to our national defense. By comparison, in Fiscal Year 2020 the DOD, the largest investor in cyber security, budgeted a

minuscule $9.6 billion in funding, not nearly enough for the future we face.

118 Ananya Bhattacharya, "56,000 layoffs and counting: India's IT bloodbath this year may just be the start," *Quartz India*, December 26, 2017, https://qz.com/india/1152683/indian-it-layoffs-in-2017-top-56000-led-by-tcs-infosys-cognizant/.

119 July 21, 2023, interview with Rick Chin, Vice President of Lending Solutions Ocwen Financial Corp.

120 Many "fingers on the keys" tasks, are well structured, repetitive, documented, and a noncritical business function. This profile makes those tasks easy to outsource but also easy for a software robot to do the task, and there is strong economics behind it. Growth in revenue at the beginning of this century was 60 to 70 percent a year for five leading Indian business process outsourcing (BPO) companies: Cognizant, HCL, Infosys, TCS, and Wipro.

121 From the US Department of State, Bureau of Consular Affairs: Visa Bulletin. You can find this information on page 8 of the document: https://travel.state.gov/content/travel/en/legal/visa-law0/visa-bulletin.html.

122 The appointment and Disney's strategy was covered in this article: https://www.fool.com/investing/2022/02/18/disneys-metaverse-strategy-is-beginning-to-take-sh/.

123 The science fiction writer Neal Stephenson coined it in his 1992 novel *Snow Crash*.

124 The memo was by the *Financial Times*.

125 Lin Sternlicht and Aaron Sternlicht, "A New Age of Digital Addiction - What The Metaverse Means for Mental Health and Digital Addiction," Family Addiction Specialist, 2024, https://www.familyaddictionspecialist.com/blog/a-new-

age-of-digital-addiction-what-the-metaverse-means-for-mental-health-and-digital-addiction#:~:text=The%20 Metaverse%20and%20Mental%20Health,%2C%20 and%20psychoses%2C%20among%20others.

126   See for example, "Loneliness and Social Isolation at Work: A Literature Review" by Jessica A. Gray and Julianne Holt-Lunstad (2020). This review of twenty-nine studies found that loneliness and social isolation were significantly associated with lower job satisfaction, lower perceived organizational support, and lower organizational commitment. Loneliness was also associated with higher levels of burnout, depression, and anxiety. Also see "The Impact of Social Isolation on Workplace Performance and Turnover" by Barsade and Colleagues (2020). This study of 672 employees and their 114 supervisors found that employees who reported feeling lonely were more likely to experience burnout, turnover, and lower performance ratings from their supervisors.

127   Valente et al., "The Effects of Social Isolation on Creative Problem-Solving and Innovation," 2016. This study found that social isolation can hinder creative problem-solving and innovation. Participants who were more socially isolated were less likely to generate new ideas and solutions to problems.

128   Edward O. Wilson, a biologist, popularized the concept of biophilia in his 1984 book of the same name. He believed that biophilia is rooted in our evolutionary past, when our survival depended on our understanding of the natural world.

129   Larry Schwartz, "Wilt Battled 'Loser' Label," ESPN, http://static.espn.go.com/sportscentury/features/00014133.

html. Chamberlain, one of the greatest basketball players of all time, was often criticized for not winning enough, despite an outstanding statistical career. He often said, "No one roots for Goliath."

130 Bushman & Anderson, 2002, is an example of research warning of the danger while Drummond et al., 2020; Ferguson et al., 2020 largely refuted the argument.

131 Based on comments from Becky Schmitt, Senior VP of Global People at Walmart, at the MIT Future of Work Conference, November 2018.

132 "Walmart Academy and Mobile Learning at BoxWorks 2017," Box video, https://www.box.com/blueprint/employee-training-walmart-academy. "There was one woman with a lot of family and friends who had joined the celebration. Per Candace Davis, director of content at Walmart Academy: 'She said, "I never graduated from high school. This is my first opportunity to graduate from anything, and for my children to see me be successful at anything."'"

133 According to Gallup's State of the Global Workplace: 2022 Report: https://www.gallup.com/workplace/349484/state-of-the-global-workplace.aspx.

134 Education researchers at Pearson teamed up with the Partnership for 21st Century Learning to assess critical thinking in K-12 and college classrooms. They found critical thinking is one of the most sought-after skills among new hires. https://www.pearson.com/content/dam/one-dot-com/one-dot-com/global/Files/efficacy-and-research/skills-for-today/Critical-Thinking-ExecSum-Employers.pdf

135   The Center for Critical Thinking and Moral Critique and the Foundation for Critical Thinking are two sister educational nonprofit organizations that promote educational reform through the cultivation of fair-minded critical thinking. https://www.criticalthinking.org/.

136   Furthermore, Greene believes that the advancing wealth and poverty divide can only be resolved politically as a policy issue.

137   Michael Petraeus, "Don't learn to code: Nvidia's founder Jensen Huang advises a different career path," Vulcan Post, February 23, 2024, https://vulcanpost.com/853029/dont-learn-to-code-jensen-huang-on-career/.

138   "Clean Jobs America 2019," E2, March 13, 2019, https://www.e2.org/reports/clean-jobs-america-2019/. This a review of job openings and levels in the clean-energy economy. Many job segments are growing at over 10 percent a year.

139   To ready leaders and businesses for the age of AI, Microsoft surveyed 31,000 people in 31 countries and analyzed trillions of Microsoft 365 productivity signals, along with labor trends from the LinkedIn Economic Graph. https://assets-c4akfrf5b4d3f4b7.z01.azurefd.net/assets/2023/09/e3227681-b882-4050-b201-a631431ad2a5-WTI_Will_AI_Fix_Work_060723.pdf

140   The *Wall Street Journal* reported on the irresponsible spending of best-known public US universities. https://www.wsj.com/articles/state-university-tuition-increase-spending-41a58100?mod=hp_featst_pos4.

141   A Georgetown University's Center on Education and the Workforce report shows the median lifetime earnings of college graduates still exceed those of high school

graduates but are still positive at 86 percent. However, the earnings premium has been shrinking, decreasing from 151 percent in 1996 to 86 percent in 2023.

142 The average student loan debt per borrower was $32,731 in 2022, according to the Federal Reserve Bank of New York.

143 This story was reported in this article. https://www. fastcompany.com/91118176/want-a-job-in-ai-start-at-your-local-community-college

144 See the "Impact of the rise of artificial intelligence in radiology: What do radiologists think?" https://pubmed. ncbi.nlm.nih.gov/31072803.

145 Accenture LearnVantage provides a technology learning and training service to identify gaps in skills created by advances in technologies. https://newsroom. accenture.com/news/2024/accenture-launches-accenture-learnvantage-to-help-clients-and-their-people-gain-essential-skills-and-achieve-greater-business-value-in-the-ai-economy

146 This blog contains the full interview with Tom Seaver: https://go.forrester.com/blogs/10-10-01-tom_seaver_on_performance_management/.

147 The Gund Institute for the Environment at the University of Vermont conducted the first fifty-state study to use the Genuine Progress Indicator, as an alternative to GDP. It found most US states face a "progress recession" due to unaccounted environmental and social costs. https://www.uvm.edu/news/gund/most-us-states-face-progress-recession.

148 Source: Bureau of Labor Statistics as of January 2022: https://protect-us.mimecast.com/s/gi07CYEq1Nt1ovpr U0FDP4?domain=bls.gov.

149 Protesters in France have adopted the yellow vest as the symbol of their movement. These are required in vehicles in France as a safety measure, but the color also speaks to the frustration of those who work in construction and related work categories.

150 According to the United Nations, there is insufficient data on all of the Sustainable Development Goals (SDG): https://un-spbf.org/guest-insights/jillian-campbell/ we-lack-data-for-68-of-sdg-indicators-closing-data-gaps- essential-to-achieving-sdgs/.

151 For example, Gallup published in their 2022 book, *The Global Rise of UNHAPPINESS and How Leaders Missed It*, a detailed breakdown of how to measure "non-traditional" indicators such as work, finances, physical health, communities, and relationships that lead to happiness, based on about five million surveys across 170 countries. The book concludes the world is suffering. Stress, sadness, and anger are rising and started well before the pandemic.

152 Stakeholder capitalism is an evolving approach to corporate governance that emphasizes the responsibility of businesses to consider the interests of multiple stakeholders, not just shareholders. This includes employees, customers, suppliers, local communities, and the environment. Proponents argue it leads to long- term sustainable growth and societal well-being, while critics question its feasibility and potential impact on shareholder returns.

153 A digital twin serves as a copy of a physical object or process, a simulation that allows you to test a change in a digital model without the expense of a test in the physical world. Like many technical innovations, it originated from public funding. NASA's 2010 research used a digital twin to simulate spacecraft operations.

154 Accenture survey in the 2022 book *Radically Human: How New Technology Is Transforming Business and Shaping Our Future.*

ABOUT THE AUTHOR

Craig Le Clair is a vice president and principal analyst at Forrester, where he has worked for over fifteen years. He is recognized worldwide as a leading industry analyst on AI and automation, and the future of work. He has authored hundreds of reports on the future of technology and authored two previous books on the subject. In 2017, he received a Forrester research award for first recognizing the RPA market.

Prior to joining Forrester, Craig held senior positions at ADP, MITRE, and BBN Technologies. A prolific writer and speaker, the author is frequently quoted in the *Wall Street Journal*, *USA Today*, *Forbes*, and many other publications and media outlets. Craig earned a BS in economics from Georgetown University and an MBA from George Washington University, where he taught economics and finance.

He has studied automation's effects on humans and their work and social life for two decades. This research led to a 2019 book titled *Invisible Robots in the Quiet of the Night*, a top five in Amazon's automation category. This book argued that it wasn't the hardware robots we needed to worry about but the ones you can't see that run on cloud-based servers and replace primarily lower-value cognitive jobs in call centers and back offices.